MARY ENGELBREIT

CROSS-STITCH

FOR ALL SEASONS

Meredith® Press

Des Moines, Iowa

Meredith® Press
An imprint of Meredith® Books

Mary Engelbreit Cross-Stitch for All Seasons
Editor: Carol Field Dahlstrom
Technical Editor: Susan Banker
Graphic Designer: Gayle Schadendorf
Copy Chief: Angela K. Renkoski
Copy Editor: Debbie Leece
Proofreader: Colleen Johnson
Editorial and Design Assistants: Judy Bailey, Jennifer Norris, Karen Schirm
Photographers: Hopkins Associates and Scott Little
Technical Illustrator: Chris Neubauer Graphics
Project Finishing: Margaret Sindelar
Electronic Production Coordinator: Paula Forest
Production Director: Douglas M. Johnston
Production Manager: Pam Kvitne
Assistant Prepress Manager: Marjorie J. Schenkelberg

Meredith® Books
Editor in Chief: James D. Blume
Design Director: Matt Strelecki
Managing Editor: Gregory H. Kayko

Director, Sales & Marketing, Retail: Michael A. Peterson
Director, Sales & Marketing, Special Markets: Rita McMullen
Director, Sales & Marketing, Home & Garden Center Channel: Ray Wolf
Director, Operations: Valerie Wiese

Vice President, General Manager: Jamie L. Martin

Meredith Publishing Group
President, Publishing Group: Christopher M. Little
Vice President and Publishing Director: John P. Loughlin

Meredith Corporation
Chairman of the Board: Jack D. Rehm
President and Chief Executive Officer: William T. Kerr

Chairman of the Executive Committee: E. T. Meredith III

Cover Illustration: Mary Engelbreit Studios
Cover Border Adaptation, page 185
Original Art translated into cross-stitch by Barbara Sestok

All of us at Meredith® Press are dedicated to providing you with the information and ideas you need to create beautiful and useful projects. We guarantee your satisfaction with this book for as long as you own it. We welcome your questions, comments, and suggestions. Please write to us at: Meredith® Press, Crafts, RW–240, 1716 Locust Street, Des Moines, IA 50309–3023.

Library of Congress Catalog Card Number: 97-71327
ISBN: 0-696-20707-9

Celebrate the Seasons!

Capture the beauty and excitement

of every glorious season with the warmth of Mary Engelbreit's

charming illustrations. Now, with floss and needle, you can

re-create the magic that Mary has shared with us all.

Choose your favorite season and favorite sentiment and start

stitching a glorious sampler or choose a smaller project to finish in

a weekend. Whatever you choose to stitch will

bring you pleasure, make you smile, and touch the hearts

of those around you for all seasons.

Table of Contents

Autumn

Winter

Spring

Summer

Each season had its

own wonderful charm for

me as a child—and still

does as an adult.

— *Mary Engelbreit*

Crisp fall evenings with the smell of burning leaves in the air, snowy days with hot cocoa and marshmallows, white gloves in springtime, summer tea parties with pink Kool-aid tea—the seasons came and went leaving me with fond memories that I'll always treasure.

We're all influenced by so many things in our lives: friends, family events, where we have lived, and circumstances that have made us who we are. I know that the almost perfect childhood that I experienced—all the fun and color

and family love—has certainly influenced my work. Each season had its own special charm for me as a child—and still does as an adult. Now with my own family, I try to make each season and each holiday a special time. In this book, I am delighted to see my work translated so beautifully into cross-stitches so you, too, can re-create the magic and splendor that each season brings. With your needlework skills, you can create heirloom-quality pieces for your family and friends that they will enjoy for a lifetime.

It seems like only yesterday that I was a child relishing each and every season and holiday event. In the fall, the trees in our neighborhood were beautiful. We had a big hill in our backyard, and my father would rake the leaves into a pile at the bottom for us. We'd take a running jump and land in the middle, scattering the leaves all over the yard and shrieking with laughter. The bonfire afterward was something to see! At Halloween I loved going to the dime store and picking out my

costume. My mother always wanted to make something, but I preferred the sequined, printed outfits that came in a package. I loved the plastic masks—the kind that made it hard to breath, as we walked all over town, the kind that made me have to look at my feet to know where I was going—the kind of mask that I knew must be scaring the heebie-jeebies out of my best friend! That's why I love to draw images of Halloween. It brings back the mystery of that autumn night. On page 25, you'll see my "Trick or Treat" illustration. I can't really say where that particular masked trick-or-treater came from, but I hope it gives you the same happy, mysterious Halloween feeling that I get.

Every winter we would hope for snow, and if our wish came true, Papa would pull us on the sled after dinner to the top of the hill in front of our house. It was a long, freezing, fun ride down, but by the time we hiked back home, we were ready to go again. The snowmen

I was posing with Santa at an early age!

I'm ready to play outside in my sweater and matching hat.

we built had raisins for mouths, charcoal eyes, and lots of personality. Many of my drawings show these jolly fellows that I used to build from snow. On page 73, I've created a "Let It Snow" snowman family that I hope you enjoy stitching.

At Christmastime, Santa always arrived right on schedule, and we left treats for him and carrots for his reindeer as well. My mother put a lot of thought into each gift she gave us. She taught us to put ourselves in the recipients' shoes when we chose presents. I thought I was doing that one Christmas when I painted a picture for my mother that matched our dining room wallpaper. She hung it up immediately, making me feel very proud indeed.

We all believe in Santa at our house. That's where my "Believe" Santa comes from. You can see the cross-stitched version on page 56.

Springtime was my very favorite time of year. As it got closer to Easter, my mother would take me and my sister to the department store downtown to pick out our new straw hats to wear

to church on Easter Sunday. My grandmother would send us each a pair of short, white gloves to complete our stunning ensembles. On Easter morning, we'd have a huge egg hunt with all my cousins. One year, my sister and I got tiny baby ducks in our baskets. They felt so soft and fragile, but soon they had befriended even the big dogs and other pets in the neighborhood. When they got really big, we took them to the zoo, where they lived happily for many years. I loved spring! Everything was so beautiful and new. One of my favorite springtime illustrations is my "Felicitations" drawing on page 100. What could be more springlike than the arrival of a baby?

Summer meant tea parties and playhouses. We would put together big boxes from the grocery store and make a rambling cardboard house in the backyard. That's where we would serve all our guests and their dolls pink Kool-aid tea in our tiny tea set. I still love tea parties! My "Time for Tea" drawing on page 146 reflects the bright colors and happy feelings of that time in the summer sunshine.

In the woods and creek near our house, we would explore nature of all kinds. During the day, we'd catch tadpoles, and at night we'd watch the fireflies. We'd stare at them in our jars and marvel at their magic before letting them go. I think that close

Here I am in my new straw hat and gloves.

look at nature has helped me draw all sweet creatures with more accuracy.

I hope you enjoy this seasonal collection of my illustrations translated into cross-stitch. As you stitch motifs from each charming, changing season, may you find pleasure in re-creating my drawings with floss and needle, and may each one of your creations become a very memorable part of your special year.

Perfect Stitches

We want each of your cross-stitch projects to reflect your

special needlework skills, and we hope that you have great success

with each piece that you stitch. In addition, we hope you use all of

your creative talents to make even more projects from the designs

in the book. That is why we have included charts with tints and

symbols and conversions for each design. We've also included

specialty-stitch diagrams when we think they will help, and at the

end of each chapter, we have given you some "Breit" Ideas for more

stitching fun. At the back of the book, we offer some cross-stitch

basics and a list of sources for special materials. We know that with

Mary's charming designs and your needlework talents,

all of your stitches will be perfect ones.

Autumn

Crisp, cool days of autumn,
a season brimming with color and
texture, inspire exciting stitching
possibilities. From samplers and
centerpieces to goody bags and
bookends, we've filled the chapter
with treats and treasures to
stitch and make.

Fall in love with

Autumn Stitching!

Everyone Needs Their Own Spot

Cuddle up in your favorite spot and start stitching one of Mary Engelbreit's most cherished illustrations. We've stitched our **Spot Sampler** and displayed it in a little boy's room with a favorite friend, but this simple yet provocative piece will be at home anywhere in the house. Turn the page for more charming renditions of this classic sentiment. Charts, instructions, and finishing ideas for all of the projects begin on *page 15*.

Make a fun **Puppy Pillowcase** for your own special resting spot by stitching a border of scampering pups. We've used waste canvas to stitch our playful trio. Our **Dalmatian Cap** is the one he'll reach for when he goes out to play. It's quick and easy to stitch and will make your puppy lover oh, so happy! And for that very special huggable pet in your house, create our **Doggy-Dish Place Mat** using washable vinyl weave.

Keeping all those special books in the right spot will be simple with our **Spot Bookends**. Worked in half cross-stitches, they stitch up quickly using bright-colored yarns on plastic canvas.

13

Three playful puppies adorn our **Puppy Trio Coatrack**. Stitched on white Jobelan fabric and trimmed with red braid, the threesome look cute as a button mounted across a polka–dot–painted coatrack. What a great way to show off a new spring jacket or state fair ribbons from the puppy show!

14

Spot Sampler

As shown on page 10, sampler measures 12⅛×8⅞ inches.

MATERIALS

FABRIC

17×13-inch piece of 32-count desert sand linen

FLOSS

Cotton embroidery floss in colors listed in key, below

SUPPLIES

Needle; embroidery hoop

Desired mat and frame

INSTRUCTIONS

Tape or zigzag edges of linen. Find the center of chart, *pages 16–17*, and of fabric; begin stitching there. Use two plies of floss to work cross-stitches over two threads of fabric. Work blended needle stitches as shown in key. Work straight stitches, lazy daisy stitches, and French knots using two plies and backstitches using one ply.

Press the finished piece from the back. Mat and frame as desired.

Dalmatian Cap

As shown on page 12, design measures 1⅞×2¼ inches.

MATERIALS

FABRIC

4×4-inch piece of 14-count waste canvas

FLOSS

Cotton embroidery floss in colors listed in key on page 18

SUPPLIES

Purchased cap

Six ⅜-inch-diameter black buttons

Two ½-inch-wide red pet collars, each 12 inches long

Tacky fabric glue; engraved dog tag

INSTRUCTIONS

Baste waste canvas to center of cap front. Find center of chart, *page 18,* and of canvas; begin stitching there. Use three plies of floss to work cross-stitches. Work the backstitches using two plies.

Stitch buttons, evenly spaced, around the top of cap using red floss.

Buckle collars together. Position buckle at center front; glue collars around base of crown, trimming ends to fit hat at back. Clip on dog tag.

SPOT SAMPLER

ANCHOR	DMC		
002	000	•	White
897	221	✱	Deep shell pink
352	300	◆	Deep mahogany
403	310	■	Black
218	319	★	Pistachio
9046	321	✕	Christmas red
150	336	☑	Navy
013	349	▦	Coral
351	400	▲	Dark mahogany
310	434	⊙	Chestnut
1045	436	▢	Dark tan
362	437	‖	Medium tan
683	500	⊞	Blue green
898	611	✚	Drab brown
8581	646	☆	Medium beaver gray
227	701	⊕	Christmas green
361	738	▷	Light tan
885	739	—	Pale tan
1022	760	◁	True salmon
176	793	◁	Cornflower blue
132	797	✛	Royal blue
359	801	◐	Medium coffee brown
043	815	◑	Garnet
360	839	◈	Dark beige brown
378	841	◇	True beige brown
850	926	●	Gray blue
381	938	▨	Deep coffee brown
1010	951	▯	Ivory
1001	976	◁	Medium golden brown
844	3012	⊛	Medium khaki
842	3013	◇	Light khaki
397	3024	◣	Brown gray
261	3053	◩	Light gray green
1024	3328	⊠	Dark salmon
382	3371	◀	Black brown
1020	3713	⊔	Pale salmon
169	3760	✳	Wedgwood blue
899	3782	▷	Light mocha
236	3799	◉	Charcoal
877	3815	◇	Celadon green
1048	3826	▶	Dark golden brown
373	3828	◿	Hazel
5975	3830	⊙	Terra-cotta

BLENDED NEEDLE

150	▨	336 Navy (2X) and
403	▤	310 Black (1X)
392	▥	642 Beige gray (2X) and
373		3828 Hazel (1X)
900	▨	648 Light beaver gray (2X) and
397		3024 Brown gray (1X)
023	◁	818 Pink (2X) and
1026		225 Pale shell pink (1X)
681	▼	3051 Dark gray green (2X) and
846		3011 Dark khaki (1X)
310	▲	3363 Loden (2X) and
1045		522 Olive drab (1X)
872	▷	3740 Antique violet (2X) and
360		839 Dark beige brown (1X)

BACKSTITCH

403	╱	310 Black – Spot's eye
150	╱	336 Navy – boy's pants
885	╱	739 Pale tan – windows, small stitches on sweater
043	╱	815 Garnet – shoelaces, sweater detail
380	╱	839 Dark beige brown – roof detail
360	╱	3031 Deep mocha – lettering
5975	╱	3830 Terra-cotta – sock and pants detail
382	╱	3371 Black brown – all remaining backstitches

STRAIGHT STITCH

403	╱	310 Black – small stitches on boy's sweater
898	╱	611 Drab brown – hair strands
900	╱	648 Light beaver gray – Scottie dog detail
360	╱	3031 Deep mocha – hair strands
236	╱	3799 Charcoal – sweater ribbing

LAZY DAISY

043	◗	815 Garnet – shoelaces

FRENCH KNOT

403	●	310 Black – shoe detail
900	●	648 Light beaver gray – Spot, sleeping dog, Dalmatian
360	●	3031 Deep mocha – lettering
382	●	3371 Black brown – dogs' eyes
899	●	3782 Light mocha – dog jumping up

Stitch count: 194 high x 143 wide
Finished design sizes:
28-count fabric – 13⅞ x 10¼ inches
22-count fabric – 17⅝ x 13 inches
36-count fabric – 10¾ x 8 inches

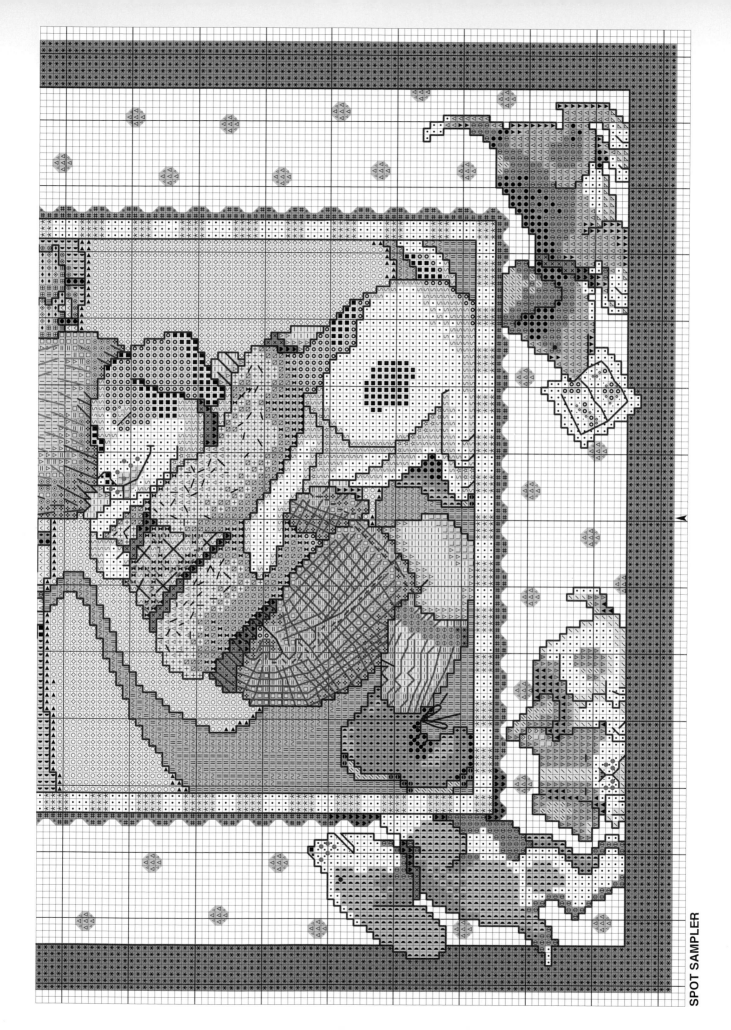

SPOT SAMPLER

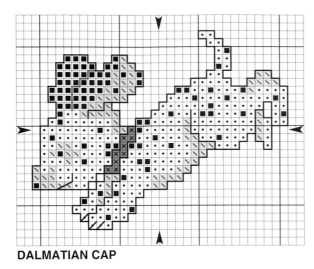

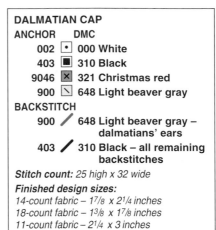

BACKSTITCH

900	╱	648	Light beaver gray – dalmatians' ears
403	╱	310	Black – all remaining backstitches

Stitch count: 25 high x 32 wide
Finished design sizes:
14-count fabric – 1⁷⁄₈ x 2¹⁄₄ inches
18-count fabric – 1³⁄₈ x 1⁷⁄₈ inches
11-count fabric – 2¹⁄₄ x 3 inches

DALMATIAN CAP

Puppy Pillowcase

As shown on page 12, design measures 2½×12¾ inches.

MATERIALS
FABRICS
5×14-inch piece of 16-count waste canvas; purchased pillowcase
⅓ yard of 45-inch-wide brown-and-white-checked fabric
5×45-inch strip of fabric to match pillowcase

FLOSS
Cotton embroidery floss in colors listed in key on page 19
SUPPLIES
Needle; 3 yards of red tiny rickrack

INSTRUCTIONS
Baste waste canvas to one side of the pillowcase, centering it slightly above open end of case. Find center of chart and of waste canvas; begin stitching there. Use two plies of floss to work all cross-stitches. Work blended needle stitches as shown in the key. Work backstitches using one ply.

Cut two 6×45-inch strips of checked fabric for ruffle. With right sides facing, sew short ends together to make one continuous strip. Press strip in half lengthwise with wrong side facing. Stitching ½ inch from raw edges, gather to fit pillowcase opening. Sew one long edge of 5-inch-wide fabric strip to gathered edge of ruffle; trim and turn under short ends of strip to finish. Press lining away from ruffle. Pin ruffle along pillowcase opening with lining to inside and ruffle extending 2½ inches below opening edge. Sew rickrack around

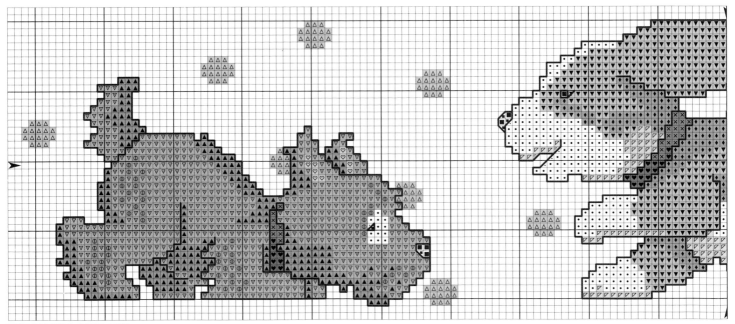

PUPPY PILLOWCASE

the outside edge of the pillowcase, securing ruffle. Turn under ½ inch along lining raw edge and pin to inside hem of pillowcase. Sew rickrack along the top edge of pillowcase hem, securing top edge of lining.

Spot Bookends

As shown on page 13, finished bookends each measure 6¼×6 inches.

MATERIALS

FABRICS

Two 7×7-inch pieces of 10-count plastic canvas

Two 7×7-inch pieces of red imitation suede fabric

THREAD

Tapestry wool in colors listed in key on page 20

SUPPLIES

Needle; two 3×6-inch pieces of tempered hardboard

Two 1×6×6⅛-inch pieces of poplar, each planed to ½-inch-thick

Jigsaw; extra fine grit sandpaper

Ten 1-inch-long No. 18 wire brads

Acrylic spray sealer

Red and medium blue acrylic paints

Paintbrushes; acrylic spray varnish

Crafts glue; pinking shears

INSTRUCTIONS

Find the center of one piece of plastic and the center of the chart on *page 20*; begin stitching there. Use one ply of tapestry wool to work the design using half cross-stitches. Work the backstitches using one ply. Stitch remaining piece of plastic in the same manner.

Using a jigsaw, round the corners on one long side of each tempered hardboard base piece.

Sand all wood pieces lightly. Using brads, affix each hardboard base piece to one 6-inch edge of poplar piece using the photograph, *page 13*, as a guide. Sink brads. Sand all edges.

Paint both sides of poplar board and bottom of base blue. Paint base top surface and all edges red. Use two coats of paint if necessary, sanding lightly between coats. When paint is dry, spray with acrylic varnish.

Trim stitched plastic one square beyond the stitching. Glue each stitched piece to a square of imitation suede; cut out ¼ inch beyond stitched piece using pinking shears. Glue each stitched piece to face of a bookend.

PUPPY PILLOWCASE		
ANCHOR		DMC
002	•	000 White
352	◆	300 Deep mahogany
403	■	310 Black
9046	✕	321 Christmas red
1022	♡	760 True salmon
359	◑	801 Medium coffee brown
043	♥	815 Garnet
378	◹	841 True beige brown
1001	△	976 Medium golden brown
397	◿	3024 Brown gray
382	▲	3371 Black brown
899	▽	3782 Light mocha
1048	▼	3826 Dark golden brown
BLENDED NEEDLE		
872	▽	3740 Antique violet (1X) and
360		839 Dark beige brown (1X)
BACKSTITCH		
382	╱	3371 Black brown – all backstitches

Stitch count: 41 high x 204 wide

Finished design sizes:
16-count fabric – 2½ x 12¾ inches
14-count fabric – 3 x 14½ inches
18-count fabric – 2¼ x 11⅜ inches

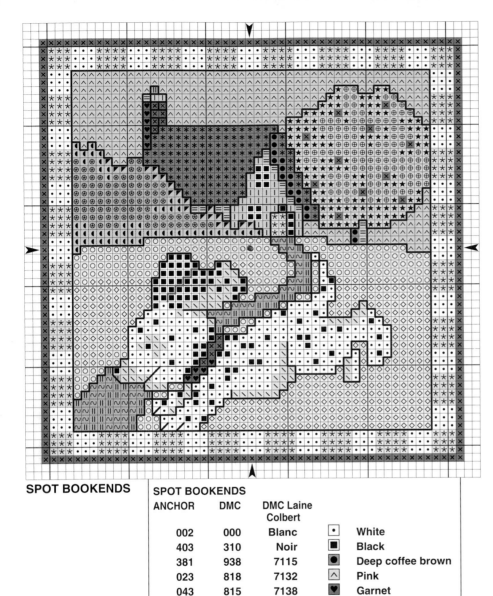

SPOT BOOKENDS

Doggy-Dish Place Mat

As shown on page 12, place mat measures 11⅝×17¼ inches.

MATERIALS

FABRIC

11⅝×17¼-inch piece of 14-count vinyl weave

FLOSS

Cotton embroidery floss in colors listed in key on page 23

One additional skein of red (DMC 321) floss

SUPPLIES

Graph paper; needle

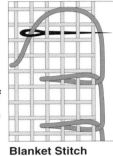

Blanket Stitch

INSTRUCTIONS

Using alphabet, page 21, chart name on graph paper. Find center of name and of mat; begin stitching there. Use three plies of floss to work cross-stitches. Work backstitches using two plies. Stitch chart, *pages 22–23,* around the name.

When stitching is complete, use one strand of DMC 321 Christmas red to blanket stitch around entire edge, referring to the diagram, *above.*

Puppy Trio Coatrack

As shown on page 14, finished coatrack measures 7⅛×18 inches.

MATERIALS

FABRIC

7×20-inch piece of 28-count white Jobelan fabric

FLOSS

Cotton embroidery floss in colors listed in key on page 23

SPOT BOOKENDS

ANCHOR	DMC	DMC Laine Colbert		
002	000	Blanc	•	White
403	310	Noir	■	Black
381	938	7115	●	Deep coffee brown
023	818	7132	∧	Pink
043	815	7138	♥	Garnet
681	3051	7359	◢	Dark gray green
844	3012	7364	⊛	Medium khaki
261	3053	7384	○	Light gray green
392	642	7423	‖	Beige gray
846	3011	7427	◖	Dark khaki
373	3828	7473	∼	Hazel
362	437	7503	=	Medium tan
842	3013	7549	◇	Light khaki
900	648	7618	◣	Light beaver gray
885	739	7746			Pale tan
897	221	7758	✳	Deep shell pink
169	3760	7813	★	Wedgwood blue
9046	321	7849	✕	Christmas red
218	319	7909	★	Pistachio
227	701	7911	⊕	Christmas green

BACKSTITCH

900	╱	648 Light beaver gray – dog's ears
382	╱	3371 Black brown – all remaining backstitches

Stitch count: 53 high x 53 wide

Finished design sizes:
10-count plastic – 5⅜ x 5⅜ inches
7-count plastic – 7½ x 7½ inches
14-count plastic – 3⅞ x 3⅞ inches

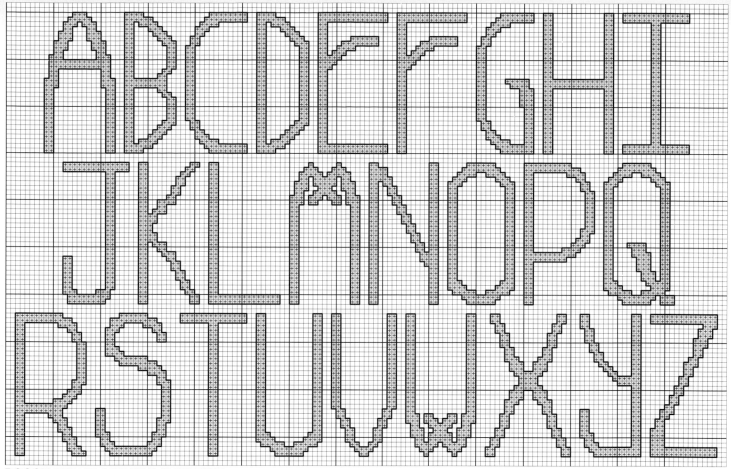

DOGGY-DISH PLACE MAT ALPHABET

SUPPLIES

Needle; embroidery hoop

Tracing paper

1×7¼×18-inch poplar board; bandsaw

Router; drill with ⅜-inch drill bit

Four wood shaker pegs; wood glue

Medium and fine grit sandpaper

Acrylic spray sealer; acrylic spray varnish

Yellow and barn red acrylic paints

Paintbrushes

5×16-inch piece of self-stick mounting board with foam

Erasable fabric-marking pen

1½ yards of ¼-inch-wide dark red flat braid

Crafts glue; mounting hook for hanging

INSTRUCTIONS

Tape or zigzag edges of the fabric to prevent fraying. Find the center of the design and of the fabric; begin stitching there. Use two plies of floss to work cross-stitches over two threads of fabric. Work the blended needle stitches using one ply of each floss color listed in key. Work the backstitches using one ply.

Enlarge and trace coatrack outline and cross-stitch mounting board, *below right*, separately onto tracing paper; cut out. Trace coatrack shape onto poplar; cut out using bandsaw. Sand or rout front face edges to slight bevel. Mark peg hole placement and drill ⅜-inch holes deep enough to accommodate peg to shoulder. Glue pegs into holes.

Sand the wood pieces first with medium grit and then with fine grit sandpaper. Spray with acrylic sealer. When the sealer is dry, paint the rack yellow with barn red edges and pegs. Sand lightly; apply a second coat of paint. Using the pointed end of paintbrush handle, dot outer 1-inch border of yellow painted front with barn red dots. Spray on a coat of acrylic varnish.

Trace the mounting board outline onto the mounting board and cut out. Center the mounting board right side up atop the cross-stitch and use an erasable marker to draw around the mounting board shape. Cut out the fabric ½ inch beyond the marked outline.

Peel protective paper from the mounting board. Center foam side of mounting board on back of stitched design and press to stick. Fold raw edges of fabric to back and glue.

Beginning at the bottom of the design, glue the braid around the perimeter. Glue the mounted cross-stitch piece in place on coatrack. Affix the hanging hook to the back.

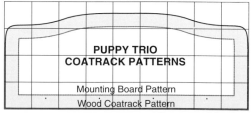

PUPPY TRIO COATRACK PATTERNS

Mounting Board Pattern

Wood Coatrack Pattern

1 Square = 2 Inches

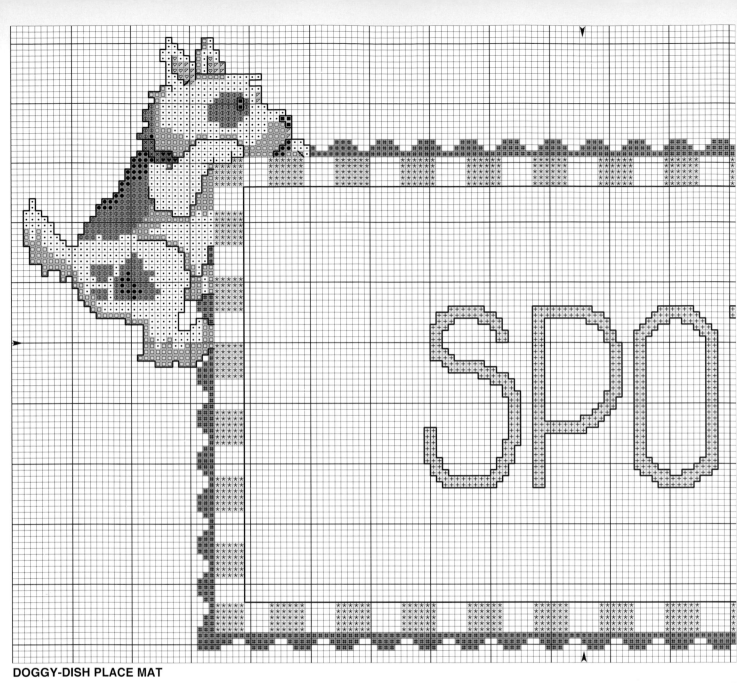

DOGGY-DISH PLACE MAT

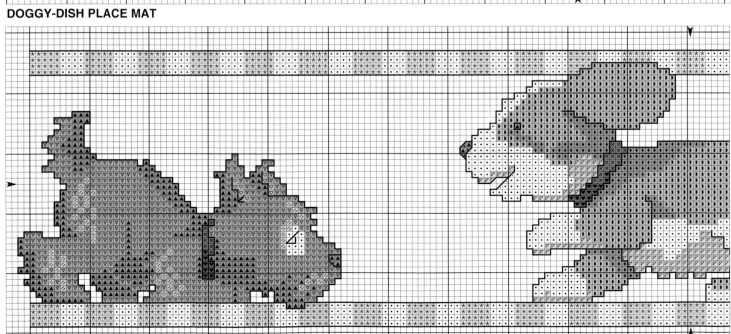

PUPPY TRIO COATRACK

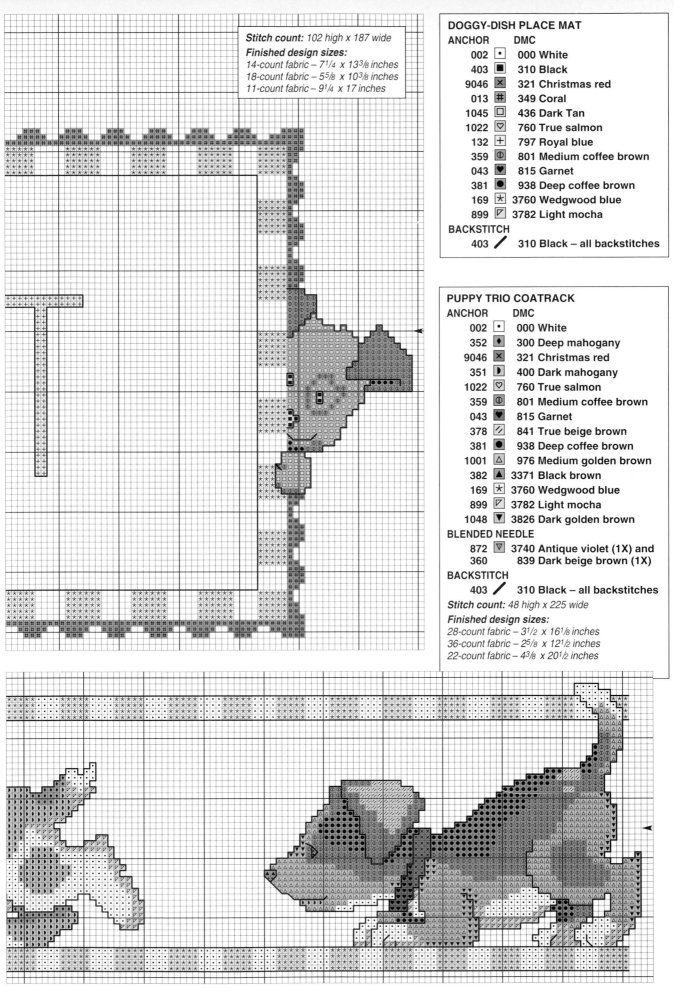

Stitch count: 102 high x 187 wide

Finished design sizes:
14-count fabric – 7¼ x 13⅜ inches
18-count fabric – 5⅝ x 10⅜ inches
11-count fabric – 9¼ x 17 inches

DOGGY-DISH PLACE MAT

ANCHOR		DMC
002	·	000 White
403	■	310 Black
9046	✕	321 Christmas red
013	⌗	349 Coral
1045	▢	436 Dark Tan
1022	♡	760 True salmon
132	+	797 Royal blue
359	①	801 Medium coffee brown
043	♥	815 Garnet
381	●	938 Deep coffee brown
169	✦	3760 Wedgwood blue
899	▽	3782 Light mocha

BACKSTITCH

403	╱	310 Black – all backstitches

PUPPY TRIO COATRACK

ANCHOR		DMC
002	·	000 White
352	◆	300 Deep mahogany
9046	✕	321 Christmas red
351	▶	400 Dark mahogany
1022	♡	760 True salmon
359	①	801 Medium coffee brown
043	♥	815 Garnet
378	╱	841 True beige brown
381	●	938 Deep coffee brown
1001	△	976 Medium golden brown
382	▲	3371 Black brown
169	✦	3760 Wedgwood blue
899	▽	3782 Light mocha
1048	▼	3826 Dark golden brown

BLENDED NEEDLE

872	▽	3740 Antique violet (1X) and
360		839 Dark beige brown (1X)

BACKSTITCH

403	╱	310 Black – all backstitches

Stitch count: 48 high x 225 wide

Finished design sizes:
28-count fabric – 3½ x 16⅛ inches
36-count fabric – 2⅝ x 12½ inches
22-count fabric – 4⅜ x 20½ inches

23

Trick Or Treat

Ghouls and goblins of all ages love Halloween, and what fun to decorate your happily haunted house with fun-to-stitch Halloween designs. We've stitched our **Trick-or-Treat Sampler** in two layers "one on black Aida and one on blue" to create a three-dimensional effect. Turn the page for more "spooktacular" stitching fun. Instructions, charts, and finishing tips for all projects start on *page 30.*

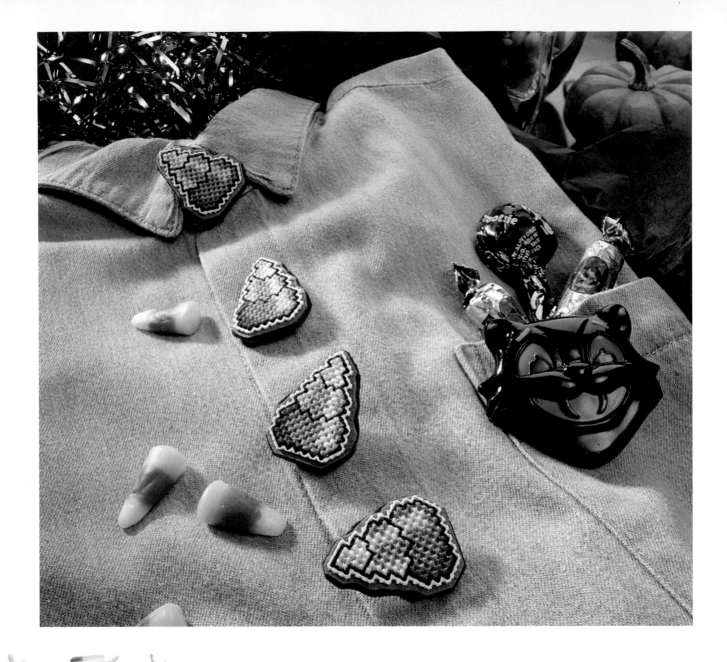

It's no trick to wear something sweet for your Halloween party. Stitch our **Candy-Corn Button Covers** in no time and dress up for Halloween. They work up so quickly, you can stitch an extra set and give these treats to special friends.

Scare the heebie-jeebies out of your party guests with our masked trick-or-treater disguised as a **Spooky Centerpiece**. We've stitched our friend on plastic canvas and displayed her in a real pumpkin. Dry ice in a cauldron, gourds, and miniature pumpkins complete this fun-and-scary table decoration.

Welcome all the little goblins at your door with sweet treats from a basket decorated with our **Goody Basket Trim**. Stitched on black Lugana fabric, the trim can be adjusted to fit a container of any size.

Send your little ghosts and witches out on Halloween night to gather treats with our **Jack-o'-Lantern Treat Bag**. Designed to hold lots of goodies, it is quick to stitch using 14-count Aida cloth.

Trick-or-Treat Sampler

As shown on page 25, sampler interior measures 11½×7½ inches; exterior measures 14⅞×10½ inches.

MATERIALS

FABRICS
20×16-inch piece of 14-count black Aida cloth; 16×12-inch piece of 14-count dark blue Aida cloth

FLOSS
Cotton embroidery floss in colors listed in key on page 32

SUPPLIES
Needle; embroidery hoop; desired frame

INSTRUCTIONS

Tape or zigzag edges of fabric. Find center of Interior Chart and of dark blue Aida; begin stitching there. Use three plies of floss to work cross-stitches. Work blended needle stitches as indicated on key. Work French knots and backstitches using one ply.

Find center of Exterior Chart, *pages 32–33*, and of black Aida; begin stitching there.

Press stitchery from back. Have a professional framer attach border stitchery to a mat; frame as desired.

Candy-Corn Button Covers

As shown on page 26, each button cover measures 1×1 inch.

MATERIALS

FABRICS
4×4-inch piece of 14-count perforated plastic

6×2-inch strip *each* of tan and red imitation suede fabric

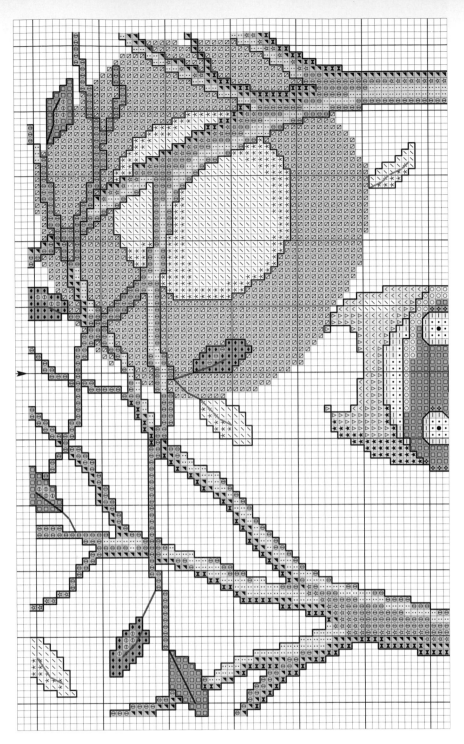

FLOSS
Cotton embroidery floss in colors listed in key on page 31

SUPPLIES
Needle

Tacky fabric glue

Five button-cover findings

INSTRUCTIONS

Divide the piece of perforated plastic into four 2×2-inch pieces using a basting stitch. Find the center of the button-cover chart, *page 31*, and the center of one 2×2-inch section of perforated plastic; begin stitching there.

Use two plies of floss to work cross-stitches. Work the blended needle stitches using one ply of each color listed in the key. Work the backstitches using one ply of floss. Stitch three more candy-corn motifs

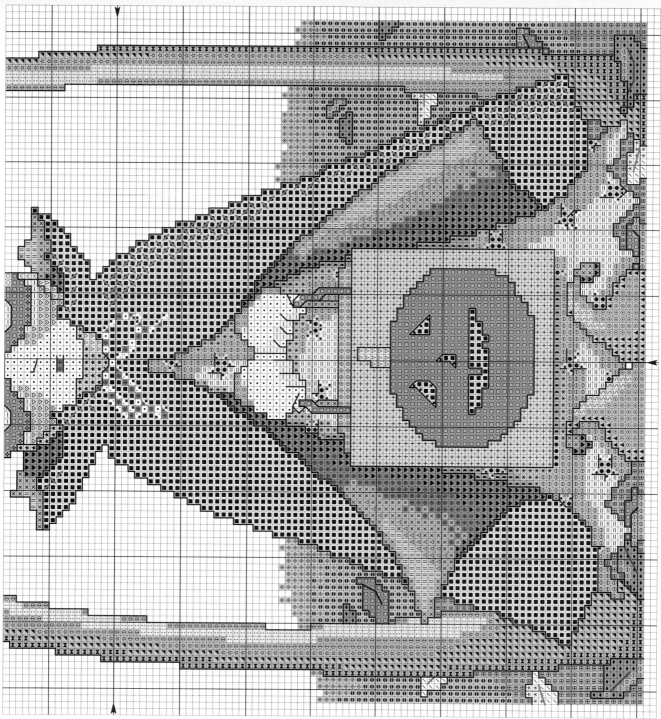

in the remaining sections of the perforated plastic.

For each candy-corn motif, trim the plastic one square beyond the stitching.

Glue each stitched piece onto tan suede; cut out slightly beyond the plastic. Next, glue each piece onto red suede; cut out slightly beyond tan fabric. Glue button-cover finding to back of each candy-corn piece.

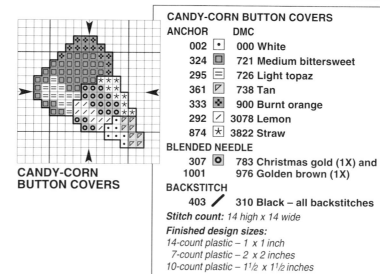

**CANDY-CORN
BUTTON COVERS**

CANDY-CORN BUTTON COVERS

ANCHOR		DMC	
002	·	000	White
324	⬚	721	Medium bittersweet
295	=	726	Light topaz
361	◿	738	Tan
333	✸	900	Burnt orange
292	╱	3078	Lemon
874	✳	3822	Straw

BLENDED NEEDLE

307	◉	783	Christmas gold (1X) and
1001		976	Golden brown (1X)

BACKSTITCH

403	╱	310	Black – all backstitches

Stitch count: 14 high x 14 wide

Finished design sizes:
14-count plastic – 1 x 1 inch
 7-count plastic – 2 x 2 inches
10-count plastic – 1½ x 1½ inches

31

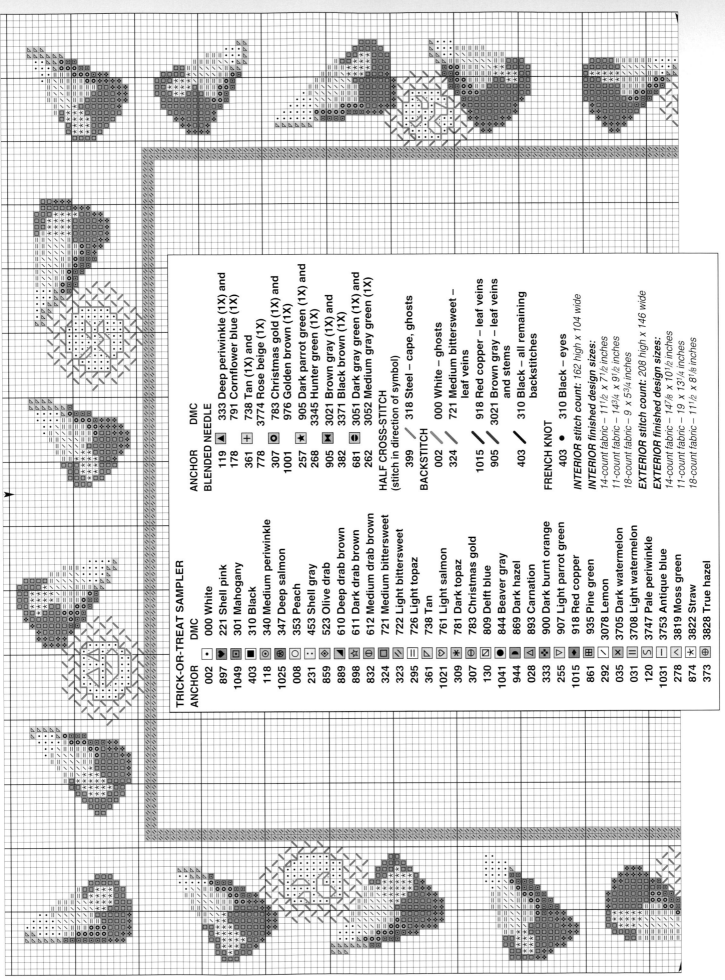

TRICK-OR-TREAT SAMPLER

ANCHOR	DMC		
002	000	•	White
897	221		Shell pink
1049	301		Mahogany
403	310		Black
118	340		Medium periwinkle
1025	347		Deep salmon
008	353		Peach
231	453		Shell gray
859	523		Olive drab
889	610		Deep drab brown
898	611		Dark drab brown
832	612		Medium drab brown
324	721		Medium bittersweet
323	722		Light bittersweet
295	726		Light topaz
361	738		Tan
1021	761		Light salmon
309	781		Dark topaz
307	783		Christmas gold
130	809		Delft blue
1041	844		Beaver gray
944	869		Dark hazel
028	893		Carnation
333	900		Dark burnt orange
255	907		Light parrot green
1015	918		Red copper
861	935		Pine green
292	3078		Lemon
035	3705		Dark watermelon
031	3708		Light watermelon
120	3747		Pale periwinkle
1031	3753		Antique blue
278	3819		Moss green
874	3822		Straw
373	3828		True hazel

BLENDED NEEDLE

ANCHOR	DMC		
119	333		Deep periwinkle (1X) and
178	791		Cornflower blue (1X)
361	738		Tan (1X) and
778	3774		Rose beige (1X)
307	783		Christmas gold (1X) and
1001	976		Golden brown (1X)
257	905		Dark parrot green (1X) and
268	3345		Hunter green (1X)
905	3021		Brown gray (1X) and
382	3371		Black brown (1X)
681	3051		Dark gray green (1X) and
262	3052		Medium gray green (1X)

HALF CROSS-STITCH
(stitch in direction of symbol)

399	318	Steel – cape, ghosts

BACKSTITCH

002	000	White – ghosts
324	721	Medium bittersweet – leaf veins
1015	918	Red copper – leaf veins
905	3021	Brown gray – leaf veins and stems
403	310	Black – all remaining backstitches

FRENCH KNOT

403	•	310	Black – eyes

INTERIOR stitch count: 162 high x 104 wide

INTERIOR finished design sizes:
14-count fabric – 11½ x 7½ inches
11-count fabric – 14¾ x 9½ inches
18-count fabric – 9 x 5¾ inches

EXTERIOR stitch count: 208 high x 146 wide

EXTERIOR finished design sizes:
14-count fabric – 14⅞ x 10½ inches
11-count fabric – 19 x 13¼ inches
18-count fabric – 11½ x 8⅛ inches

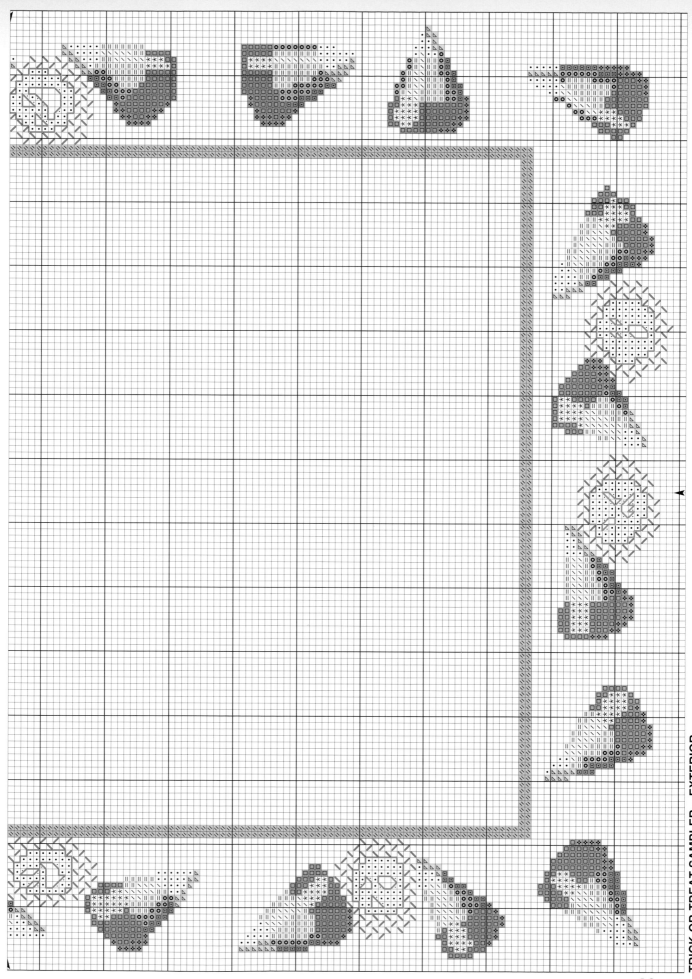

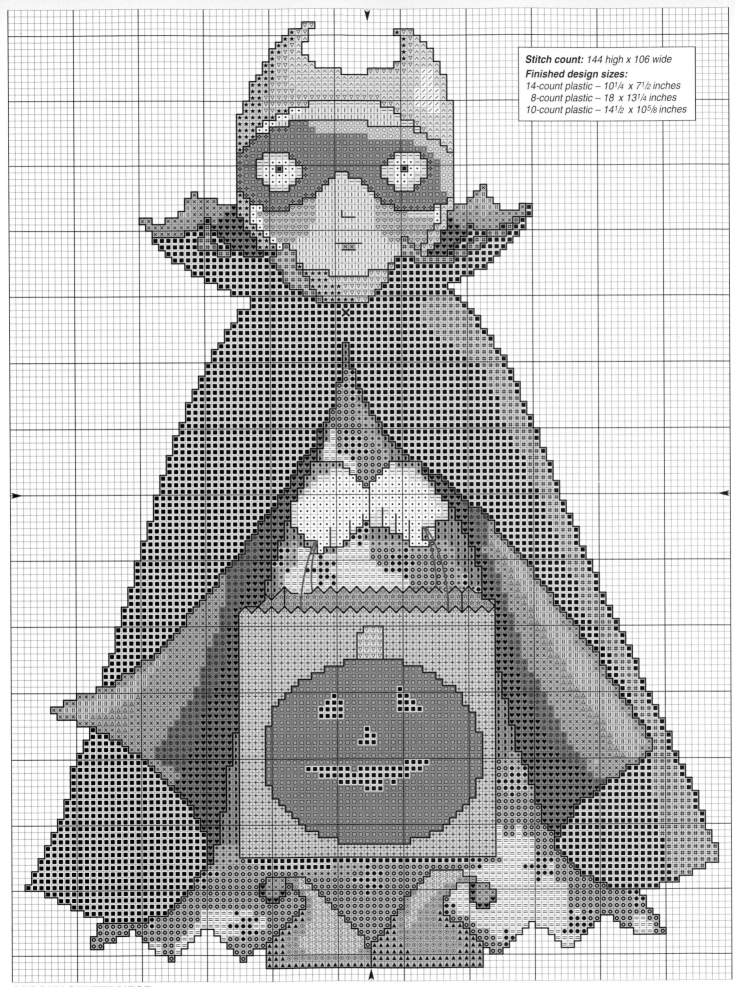

Stitch count: 144 high x 106 wide
Finished design sizes:
14-count plastic – 10¼ x 7½ inches
8-count plastic – 18 x 13¼ inches
10-count plastic – 14½ x 10⅝ inches

SPOOKY CENTERPIECE

FLOSS

Cotton embroidery floss in colors listed in key on page 36

SUPPLIES

Needle; embroidery hoop

Round basket with handles, and approximately a 32-inch circumference

Tracing paper

1¼ yards of extra-jumbo black rickrack

2 yards of 1-inch-wide orange ribbon

2 yards of 1½-inch-wide black wire-edged ribbon

3 pumpkin or cat novelty jingle bells

Covered floral wire

Spooky Centerpiece

As shown on page 27, centerpiece stitchery measures 10¼×7½ inches.

MATERIALS

FABRICS

11×8-inch piece of 14-count perforated plastic

9×11-inch piece of purple felt

9×11-inch piece of yellow felt

FLOSS

Cotton embroidery floss in colors listed in key, above

SUPPLIES

Needle; white fabric-marking pencil

Pinking shears; paint-stirring stick, with one end cut into a point

Yellow acrylic paint; paintbrush; crafts glue

INSTRUCTIONS

Find the enter of chart, *page 34,* and of plastic; begin stitching there. Use three plies of floss to work all cross-stitches. Work the blended needle stitches as shown on key. Work the backstitches using two plies of floss.

Trim stitched plastic one square beyond stitching.

Trace stitched piece onto purple felt; cut out using pinking shears. Cut yellow felt piece in same manner, making it ¼ inch larger all around than purple piece.

Paint the stirring stick yellow; allow it to dry.

Glue the stitched piece onto yellow felt. Glue the stirring stick to the center back, allowing 7 inches of the pointed end to extend beyond the bottom edge. Center and glue purple felt to the back.

If poking stirring stick into a pumpkin, first cut a slit in the pumpkin using a knife. Then push pointed end of the stick into place.

Goody Basket Trim

As shown on page 28, each repeated design measures 1¾×6⅛ inches.

MATERIALS

FABRICS

6×19-inch piece of 25-count black Lugana fabric

½ yard of 45-inch-wide orange print fabric

6×45-inch piece of black fabric

INSTRUCTIONS

Center design on one end of Lugana fabric strip; begin stitching candy-corn trim motif, *page 36,* about 2 inches from one end. Use three plies of floss to work cross-stitches over two threads of fabric. Work blended needle stitches as shown in key. Work backstitches using two plies. Repeat stitching candy-corn motifs to fit around basket.

Cut cross-stitched fabric strips each 17½ inches long, allowing 1 inch of fabric below design and 1¾ inches of fabric above design. Using one strip as pattern, cut two strips from black fabric.

Trace bottom of basket onto tracing paper. Add ½-inch seam allowance to pattern and cut out. Using pattern, cut lining bottom piece from orange print fabric. For sides of liner, cut two strips 17½ inches long, using the depth of the basket for the width measurement. Taper the short ends of each piece to match the inside curve of the basket. The bottom edge of each basket side lining piece should measure one-half the circumference of the bottom lining piece, plus 1 inch. Sew fabrics right sides facing using ½-inch seam allowances. Join

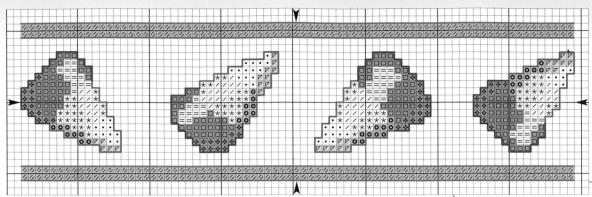

GOODY BASKET TRIM

short ends of side lining pieces, forming a circular band that is wider at the top. Sew bottom lining piece to bottom edge of side lining piece, easing in fullness.

For each cross-stitched strip, sew rickrack along bottom, stitching down center of rickrack positioned ½ inch from fabric edge. Sew matching lining piece to each strip along side and bottom edges. Trim corners; turn right side out. Baste top raw edges together.

With right sides facing, sew each cross-stitched piece to basket lining between side seams. Serge or clean finish all seams. Arrange the lining in the basket.

Make desired bow from ribbons; wire it to the handle, adding bells.

Jack-o'-Lantern Treat Bag

As shown on page 29, bag measures 16½×16½×3 inches.

MATERIALS

FABRICS

14×28-inch piece of 14-count parchment Aida cloth

1 yard of 45-inch-wide black-and-gray-checked (or any other Halloween print) fabric

¾ yard of 45-inch-wide purple print fabric

3 yards of narrow black sew-in piping or braid

THREAD

Cotton flower thread in colors listed in key on page 37

SUPPLIES

Needle; embroidery hoop

Thread to match fabrics

INSTRUCTIONS

Cut Aida cloth in half, making two 14×14-inch pieces. Cut one half into four equal 7×7-inch squares.

Tape or zigzag the edges of each piece of Aida cloth to prevent fraying. Find the center of the pumpkin chart, *page 37,* and the center of the large piece of Aida; begin stitching there. Use four plies of flower thread to work cross-stitches. Work the backstitches using two plies.

Find the center of candy-corn chart, *page 37,* and the center of one small piece of Aida; begin stitching there. Work the cross-stitches and backstitches as for the pumpkin.

Centering stitchery, cut each stitched candy corn to 3½×3½ inches and pumpkin to 11×11 inches.

From checked fabric, cut four 3½×11-inch front piecing strips, a 17×17-inch back piece, and two 3½×16½-inch handle strips. In addition, piece checked fabric as necessary to make a 3½×50-inch boxing strip for bottom and sides of bag.

From purple print, cut two 17×17-inch squares for front and back lining, and piece a 3½×50-inch strip for side and bottom lining.

GOODY BASKET TRIM

ANCHOR		DMC	
002	•	000	White
324	▦	721	Medium bittersweet
323	◪	722	Light bittersweet
295	=	726	Topaz
361	◩	738	Tan
333	❖	900	Burnt orange
292	⁄	3078	Lemon
874	✶	3822	Straw

BLENDED NEEDLE

307	◉	783	Christmas gold (1X) and
1001		976	Golden brown (2X)

BACKSTITCH

323	╱	722	Light bittersweet – border
361	╱	738	Tan – candy-corn tips
307	╱	783	Christmas gold – candy-corn centers
333	╱	900	Burnt orange – candy-corn ends

Stitch count: 22 high x 77 wide
Finished design sizes:
25-count fabric – 1¾ x 6⅛ inches
28-count fabric – 1½ x 5½ inches
36-count fabric – 1¼ x 4¼ inches

Sew seams with right sides facing using ¼-inch seam allowances. For top row of pieced bag front, sew one short end of front piecing strip to right side edge of one candy corn, with candy-corn point in lower right corner. Sew opposite end of strip to left side edge of a second candy corn, with candy-corn point in lower left corner. Repeat to make the bottom row.

For middle section, sew one long edge of a piecing strip to each side of pumpkin stitchery. To complete front, sew bottom edge of top row to top edge of middle section. Turn bottom row upside down and sew to bottom edge of middle section. Points of candy corn should all point toward center.

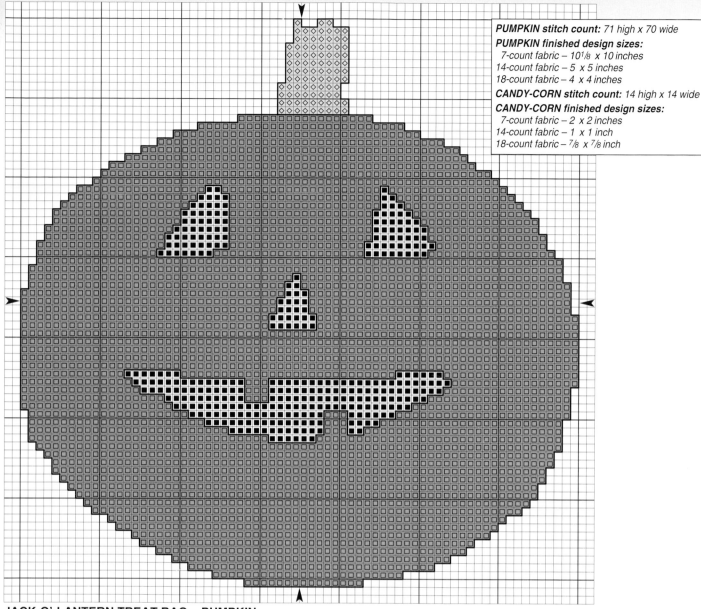

JACK-O'-LANTERN TREAT BAG – PUMPKIN

PUMPKIN stitch count: 71 high x 70 wide
PUMPKIN finished design sizes:
 7-count fabric – 10⅛ x 10 inches
 14-count fabric – 5 x 5 inches
 18-count fabric – 4 x 4 inches
CANDY-CORN stitch count: 14 high x 14 wide
CANDY-CORN finished design sizes:
 7-count fabric – 2 x 2 inches
 14-count fabric – 1 x 1 inch
 18-count fabric – ⅞ x ⅞ inch

Sew the piping around sides and bottom of bag back and front pieces. Sew boxing strip around sides and bottom of front. Sew back piece to boxing strip to complete main part of outer bag. Sew piping around top opening edge.

Sew lining front, back, and side/bottom boxing strip together in same manner. Omit piping, and leave opening for turning in one side seam.

Press under ¼ inch along both of the long edges of each handle strip. Press the strips in half lengthwise, wrong sides facing. Stitch the

pressed edges together. Matching the raw edges, stitch ends of one handle to the bag front, each 3 inches in from opposite sides. Repeat, sewing the second handle to the back.

Slip outer bag into lining, with right sides facing and seams matching. Sew around top edge. Turn bag right side out through opening in lining. Slipstitch opening closed. Press lining to inside and handles upward.

JACK-O'-LANTERN TREAT BAG

ANCHOR	DMC		DMC Flower Thread	
002	000	•	0000	White
403	310	■	2310	Black
324	721	▣	2740	Medium bittersweet
874	3822	✱	2742	Straw
295	726	═	2748	Light topaz
256	704	◇	2788	Chartreuse
333	900	✦	2947	Dark burnt orange
BACKSTITCH				
403	310	/	2310	Black – all backstitches

JACK-O'-LANTERN TREAT BAG – CANDY CORN

Home
Is Where The Heart Is

One of Mary Engelbreit's heartwarming works of art becomes a piece for you to stitch and display in your home—whether you live in a tiny bungalow or a house of grand proportions. Our **Home Sampler** will find a special place in the hearts of your family and everyone who sees it, bringing a sense of warmth and comfort to all around you. Turn the page for more projects inspired by this favorite sentiment. Instructions, charts, and tips for finishing all of the projects begin on *page 44.*

Reach for your house key and smile—it's hanging on your **Favorite–Chair Key Holder.** The **Home Key Chain** and holder both stitch up in a jiffy on plastic canvas using vibrant colors of tapestry wool and floss.

Adorned with sweet stitches and colorful buttons, our **Snuggle–Up–At–Home Pillow** is fun to stitch on black Lugana fabric. We've trimmed this striking piece with a printed ruffle.

You'll always have a kitty in the kitchen when you display our **Kitty Towel Trim** on your favorite towel. We've stitched our design on a towel with an Aida insert and trimmed it with checked fabric and a heart-printed ruffle.

Decorate a chaise or sofa with our **Heart-Of-My-Heart Chaise Pillow.** This striking piece is stitched on black Lugana fabric and adorned with tiny sparkling seed beads.

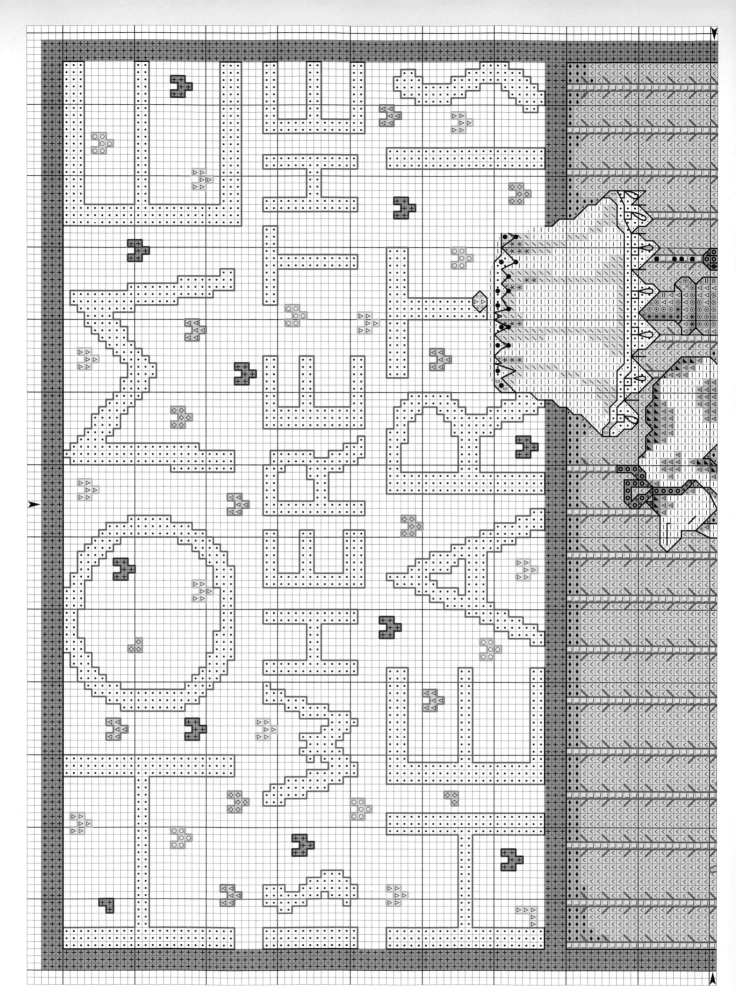

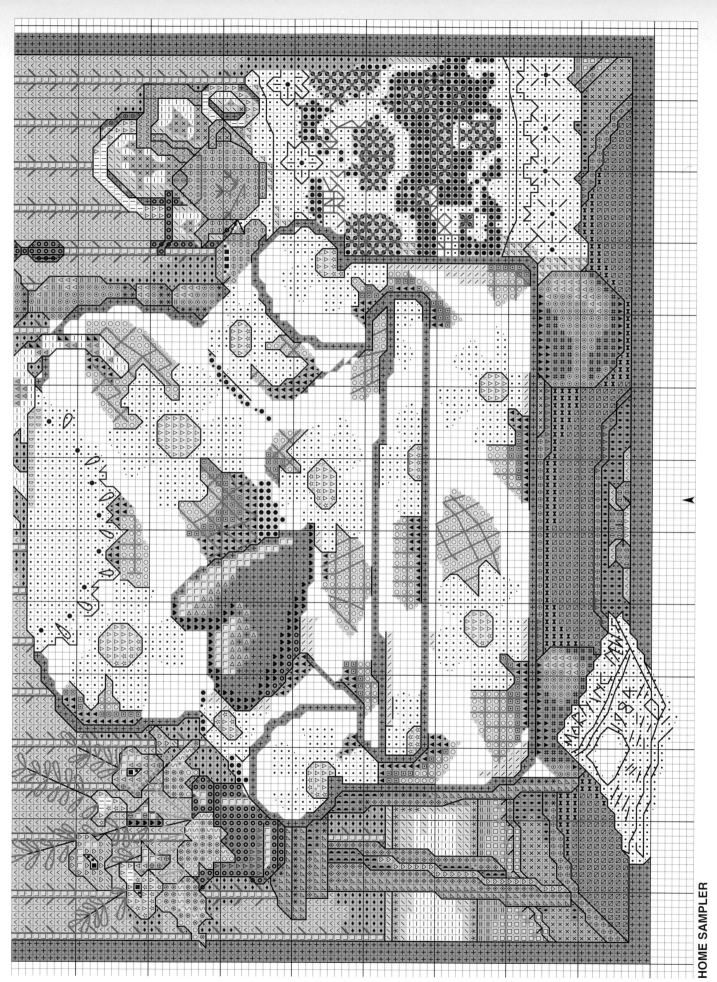

HOME SAMPLER

ANCHOR	DMC	
387		Ecru
002	000	White
342	211	Lavender
352	300	Deep mahogany
1049	301	Medium mahogany
403	310	Black
400	317	Pewter
117	341	Periwinkle
013	349	Dark coral
011	350	Medium coral
010	351	Light coral
008	353	Peach
1014	355	Terra cotta
1047	402	Pale mahogany
398	415	Pearl gray
358	433	Dark chestnut
1046	435	Light chestnut
1045	436	Dark tan
232	452	Shell gray
858	524	Olive drab
936	632	Cocoa
295	726	Topaz
361	738	Light tan
024	776	Pink
161	813	Powder blue
360	839	Dark beige brown
379	840	Medium beige brown
1003	922	Copper
1035	930	Antique blue
269	936	Medium pine green
381	938	Coffee brown
206	966	Baby green
1001	976	Medium golden brown
243	988	Forest green
360	3031	Mocha
292	3078	Lemon
144	3325	Baby blue
264	3348	Yellow green
263	3362	Dark loden
060	3688	Mauve
033	3706	Medium watermelon
1048	3776	Light mahogany
306	3820	Straw
355	3826	Dark golden brown
363	3827	Pale golden brown

BLENDED NEEDLE

ANCHOR	DMC	
358	433	Dark chestnut (2X) and
360	839	Dark beige brown (1X)
1035	930	Antique blue (2X) and
236	3799	Charcoal (1X)
844	3012	Khaki (2X) and
280	733	Olive (1X)
260	3364	Light loden (2X) and
263	3362	Dark loden (1X)

BACKSTITCH

ANCHOR	DMC	
002	000	White – lettering, lace tablecloth
011	350	Medium coral – hearts
1047	402	Pale mahogany – hearts
295	726	Topaz – hearts
861	935	Dark pine green – wallpaper detail
243	988	Forest green – plant stems
144	3325	Baby blue – hearts
264	3348	Yellow green – hearts
033	3706	Medium watermelon – teapot detail
403	310	Black – all remaining backstitches

STRAIGHT STITCH

ANCHOR	DMC	
403	310	Black – plant stems, lampshade pull chain
268	937	True pine green – teapot detail, chair detail (leaves)
033	3706	Watermelon – teapot detail

LAZY DAISY

ANCHOR	DMC	
403	310	Black – chair doily, lampshade, lampshade pull chain, lace tablecloth
268	937	True pine green – plant leaves

FRENCH KNOT

ANCHOR	DMC	
403	310	Black – chair doily, lampshade, lampshade pull chain, lace tablecloth
306	3820	Straw – carpet detail

Stitch count: 187 high x 129 wide

Finished design sizes:
28-count fabric – 13³⁄₈ x 9¹⁄₄ inches
36-count fabric – 10³⁄₈ x 7⁷⁄₈ inches
22-count fabric – 17 x 11³⁄₄ inches

Home Sampler

As shown on page 39, sampler measures 13³⁄₈×9¹⁄₄ inches.

MATERIALS

FABRIC

18×14-inch piece of 28-count black Lugana fabric

FLOSS

Cotton embroidery floss in colors listed in key, above

SUPPLIES

Needle; embroidery hoop

Desired mat and frame

INSTRUCTIONS

Tape or zigzag the edges of the fabric to prevent fraying. Find the center of the chart, *pages 44–45,* and the center of the fabric; begin stitching there. Use three plies of floss to work the cross-stitches over two threads of fabric. Work the blended needle stitches as shown in the key. Work the straight stitches, lazy daisy stitches, and French knots using three plies of floss. Use two plies of floss to work the backstitches.

Press the finished piece from the back. Mat and frame the stitched piece as desired.

Favorite-Chair Key Holder

As shown on page 40, finished key holder measures 10³⁄₄×9¹⁄₄ inches.

MATERIALS

FABRIC

14×12-inch piece of 10-count perforated plastic canvas

THREAD

Tapestry wool in colors listed in key on page 47

SUPPLIES

Needle

1×10×12-inch poplar board

Tracing paper; bandsaw; router

Medium and fine grit sandpaper

Acrylic spray sealer

Acrylic spray varnish

Yellow and barn red acrylic paints

Paintbrushes

Crafts glue

4 brass cup hooks

Mounting hook for hanging

INSTRUCTIONS

Find the center of the chart, *page 47,* and the center of the perforated plastic; begin stitching there. Use one strand of tapestry wool to work the design using half cross-stitches. Work the straight stitches and the

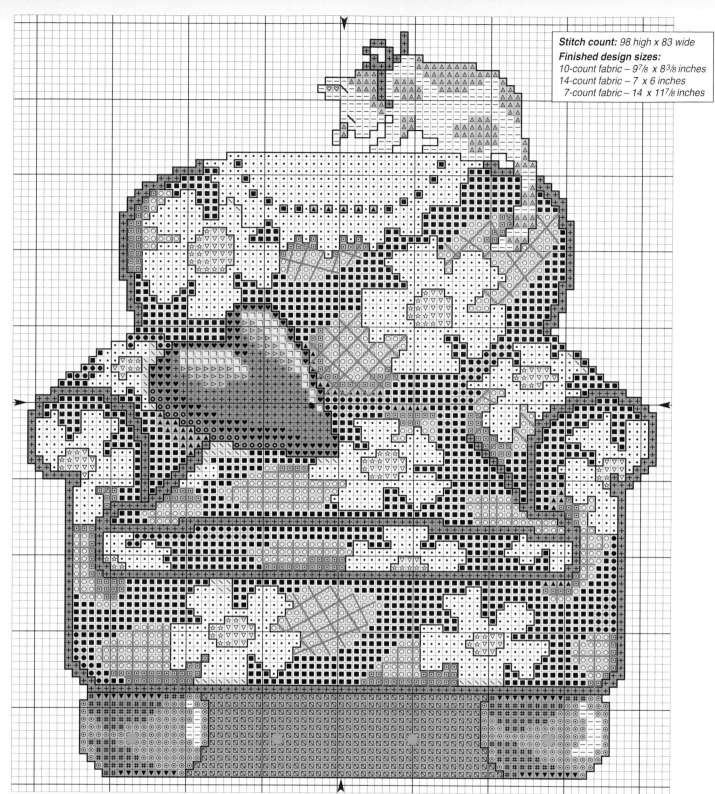

Stitch count: 98 high x 83 wide
Finished design sizes:
10-count fabric – 9⅞ x 8⅜ inches
14-count fabric – 7 x 6 inches
7-count fabric – 14 x 11⅞ inches

FAVORITE-CHAIR KEY HOLDER

FAVORITE-CHAIR KEY HOLDER

ANCHOR	DMC		DMC Tapestry Wool	ANCHOR	DMC		DMC Tapestry Wool	ANCHOR	DMC		DMC Tapestry Wool
387		−	Ecru	352	300	#	7459 Deep mahogany	010	351	▷	7851 Light coral
002	000	•	White	381	938	▼	7533 Coffee brown	024	776	♡	7852 Pink
1014	355	◉	7108 Terra cotta	264	3348	○	7549 Yellow green	1035	930	◨	7930 Antique blue
008	353	⌐	7173 Peach	400	317	●	7594 Pewter	**BACKSTITCH**			
1046	435	△	7176 Light chestnut	013	349	♥	7666 Dark coral	403	310	╱	Black –
403	310	■	7310 Black	398	415	◣	7715 Pearl gray				all backstitches
260	3364	◉	7370 Light loden	295	726	▽	7726 Topaz	**STRAIGHT STITCH**			
263	3362	▲	7427 Dark loden	306	3820	☆	7784 Straw	268	937	╱	True pine green – leaves
1049	301	◎	7457 Medium mahogany	011	350	+	7850 Medium coral	**HOOK PLACEMENT**			

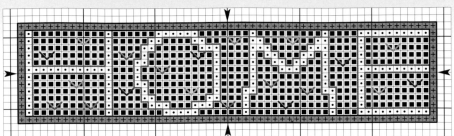

HOME KEY CHAIN

backstitches using four plies of embroidery floss.

Trim around the stitched piece one square beyond stitches.

Trace around the stitched piece onto tracing paper; add ½ inch all around and cut out. Trace shape onto poplar; cut out using bandsaw. Rout edges as desired.

Sand board first with medium grit sandpaper and then with fine grit sandpaper. Spray with acrylic sealer. When sealer is dry, paint board using yellow acrylic paint. Sand lightly and apply second coat of yellow paint. Paint the edges using barn red. Spray with acrylic varnish and let it dry thoroughly.

Center and glue the stitchery onto the top of the painted board.

Screw in four evenly spaced cup hooks along bottom of stitchery as shown in photograph, *page 40.* Affix hanging hook to back.

Home Key Chain

As shown on page 40, finished key chain is 1⅜×5 inches.

MATERIALS
FABRICS
2×6-inch piece of 14-count black perforated plastic
3×6-inch piece of white imitation suede fabric
3×6-inch piece of red imitation suede fabric
FLOSS
Cotton embroidery floss in colors listed in key, above
SUPPLIES
Needle; tacky fabric glue
Pinking shears
Key chain finding with jump ring

INSTRUCTIONS
Find the center of the chart and the center of the perforated plastic; begin stitching there. Use three plies of floss to work the cross-stitches. Work the backstitches using two plies of floss.

Trim the stitched piece of plastic one square beyond the stitching. Glue the stitched piece to the white imitation suede fabric. Using pinking shears, trim the white suede fabric ⅛ inch beyond the plastic. Next, glue the piece to the red suede fabric. Trim to ⅛ inch beyond the white fabric along the top, bottom, and left side edges. On right side edge, cut a point ending ¾ inch beyond the stitched plastic.

Attach the jump ring of the key chain finding to the pointed end of the fabric, ¼ inch from the tip.

Snuggle-Up-At-Home Pillow

As shown on page 41, finished pillow including ruffle measures 15½×21½ inches.

MATERIALS
FABRICS
15×20-inch piece of 25-count black Lugana fabric
1 yard of 45-inch-wide red print fabric
20×18-inch piece of fleece
FLOSS
Cotton embroidery floss in colors listed in key on page 50
SUPPLIES
Needle; embroidery hoop
Twenty-six ⅜-inch to ⅝-inch heart buttons in colors listed in key or desired colors
White sewing thread and threads to match button colors
1½ yards of yellow piping
4 yards of 1-inch-wide flat white cotton lace; polyester fiberfill

INSTRUCTIONS
Tape or zigzag edges of Lugana fabric. Find the center of chart, *pages 50–51,* and of Lugana fabric; begin stitching there. Use three plies of floss to work cross-stitches over two threads of fabric. Work the back-stitches using two plies.

Sew the heart buttons to the stitched design as shown on the chart or at random, using matching thread for each button.

Cut the fleece into two 10×18-inch pieces. Baste one piece to back of the cross-stitched pillow top, stitching around perimeter 1 inch past design. Cut out ½ inch beyond the basting.

Sew piping around the outside edge of the pillow top, right sides facing.

For ruffle, cut three 6×45-inch strips of red print fabric. Sew the short ends together to make a circle. Press the strip in half lengthwise with the wrong sides facing. Sew lace along the folded edge. Sew a gathering thread through both layers of the ruffle close to the raw edges. Pin the ruffle to the pillow top; adjust the gathers evenly. Baste the ruffle in place.

Use the pillow front as a pattern to cut the fleece and the red print pillow back. Baste the fleece to the wrong side of the pillow back.

Sew the pillow front to back, right sides facing, using ½-inch seam allowance. Leave an opening for turning. Trim the seams and corners; turn the pillow right side out and stuff with polyester fiberfill. Slipstitch the opening closed.

Kitty Towel Trim

As shown on page 42, kitty design measures 2×9¼ inches.

MATERIALS
FABRICS
White huck towel with 14-count Aida insert
Printed trim fabrics, if desired
FLOSS
Cotton embroidery floss in colors listed in key on page 51
SUPPLIES
Needle; embroidery hoop
3 small jingle bells

INSTRUCTIONS
Find the center of the chart, *page 51,* and of the Aida insert; begin stitching there. Use three plies of floss to work cross-stitches. Work the backstitches using two plies of floss.

Using the chart as a guide, sew the bells to the kittys' collars.

Press from the back. Trim towel with printed fabrics, if desired.

Heart-Of-My-Heart Chaise Pillow

As shown on page 43, finished pillow including ruffle measures 14½×16 inches.

MATERIALS
FABRICS
15×17-inch piece of 25-count black Lugana fabric
1¼ yard of 45-inch-wide yellow print fabric
Two 14×16-inch pieces of fleece
FLOSS
Cotton embroidery floss in colors listed in key on page 52
SUPPLIES
Needle; embroidery hoop
Beads in colors listed in key
Graph paper
White chalk fabric marker
1½ yards of red piping
4 yards of black narrow sew-in braid
Yellow and black sewing threads
Polyester fiberfill

INSTRUCTIONS
Tape or zigzag Lugana fabric to prevent fraying. Find the center of the chart, *pages 52–53,* and of the Lugana fabric; begin stitching there. Use three plies of floss to work cross-stitches over two threads of fabric. Work the straight stitches and backstitches using two plies.

Sew buttercup beads to yellow cross-stitches and gold beads to gold cross-stitches in flower centers. Using a single strand of DMC 937 green floss, work straight stitches diagonally across each leaf ¼ inch apart as shown on chart. Repeat stitching in opposite direction to make a grid pattern. Attach a bead that matches background stitches to each intersection of threads.

Enlarge heart shape, *page 52,* onto graph paper; cut out. Centering stitched design within heart, draw around heart shape onto fabric using chalk marker. Baste fleece to back of cross-stitch, stitching ½ inch inside heart outline. Cut out along outline. Sew piping to outside edge of pillow top, right sides facing.

For ruffle, cut six 4×45-inch strips from yellow print. Sew short ends of three strips together to make a circle. Repeat for remaining three strips. Pin braid to one edge of one ruffle circle. With right sides facing and using a ½-inch seam allowance, sew ruffle pieces together with braid between layers. Press the ruffle right side out. Sew a gathering thread through both layers close to the raw edges. Pin the ruffle to the pillow top; adjust the gathers evenly. Baste the ruffle in place.

Use the pillow top as a pattern to cut the fleece and the yellow print pillow back. Baste the fleece to the wrong side of the pillow back. Sew the pillow front to back, right sides facing, using ½-inch seam allowance. Leave an opening for turning. Trim the seams and clip the corners. Turn pillow right side out and stuff it with fiberfill. Slipstitch the opening closed.

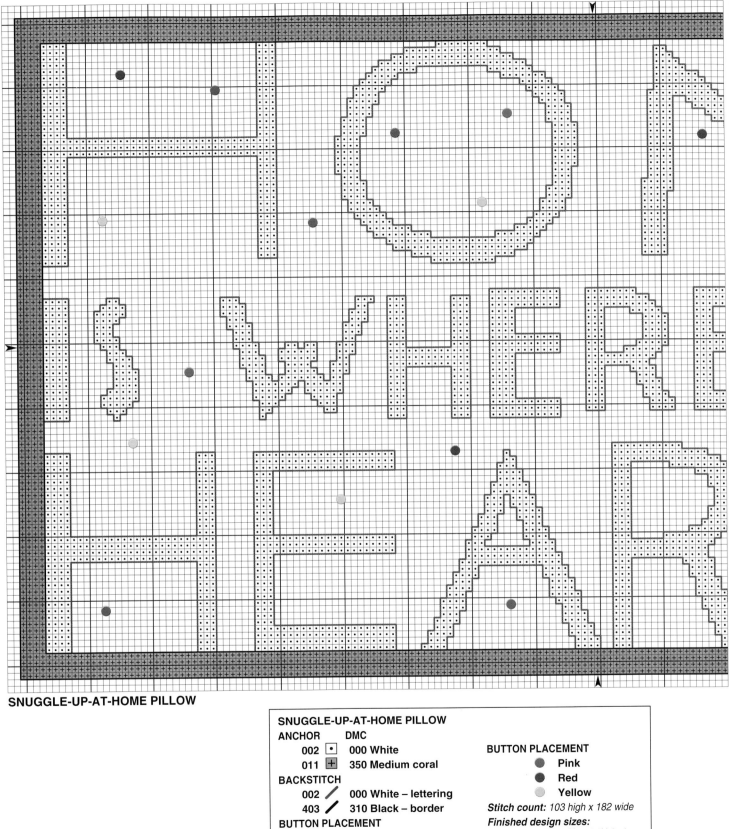

SNUGGLE-UP-AT-HOME PILLOW

SNUGGLE-UP-AT-HOME PILLOW

ANCHOR		DMC	
002	•	000 White	
011	+	350 Medium coral	

BACKSTITCH

002	/	000 White – lettering
403	/	310 Black – border

BUTTON PLACEMENT

- ● Blue
- ● Green
- ● Orange

BUTTON PLACEMENT

- ● Pink
- ● Red
- ● Yellow

Stitch count: 103 high x 182 wide
Finished design sizes:
25-count fabric – 8 1/4 x 14 1/2 inches
28-count fabric – 7 3/8 x 13 inches
36-count fabric – 5 3/4 x 10 1/8 inches

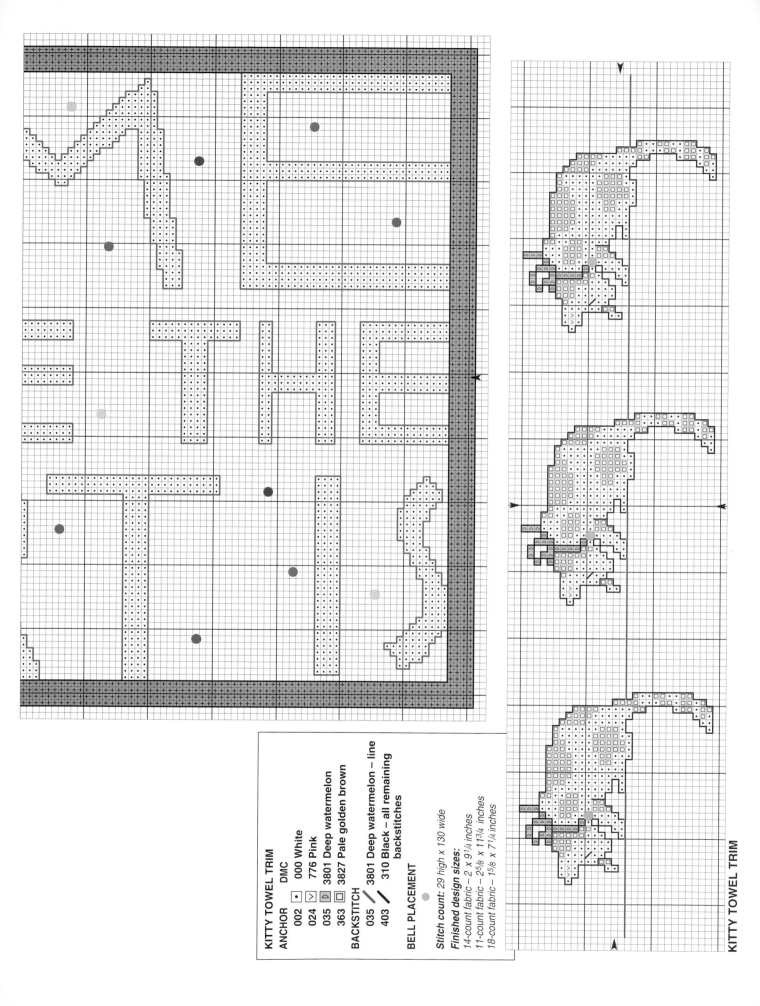

KITTY TOWEL TRIM

KITTY TOWEL TRIM
ANCHOR   DMC
002   ⊡   000 White
024   ⋎   776 Pink
035   ᴅ   3801 Deep watermelon
363   ☐   3827 Pale golden brown
BACKSTITCH
035   ╱   3801 Deep watermelon – line
403   ╲   310 Black – all remaining
                backstitches

BELL PLACEMENT ●

Stitch count: 29 high x 130 wide

Finished design sizes:
14-count fabric – 2 x 9¼ inches
11-count fabric – 2⅝ x 11¾ inches
18-count fabric – 1⅝ x 7¼ inches

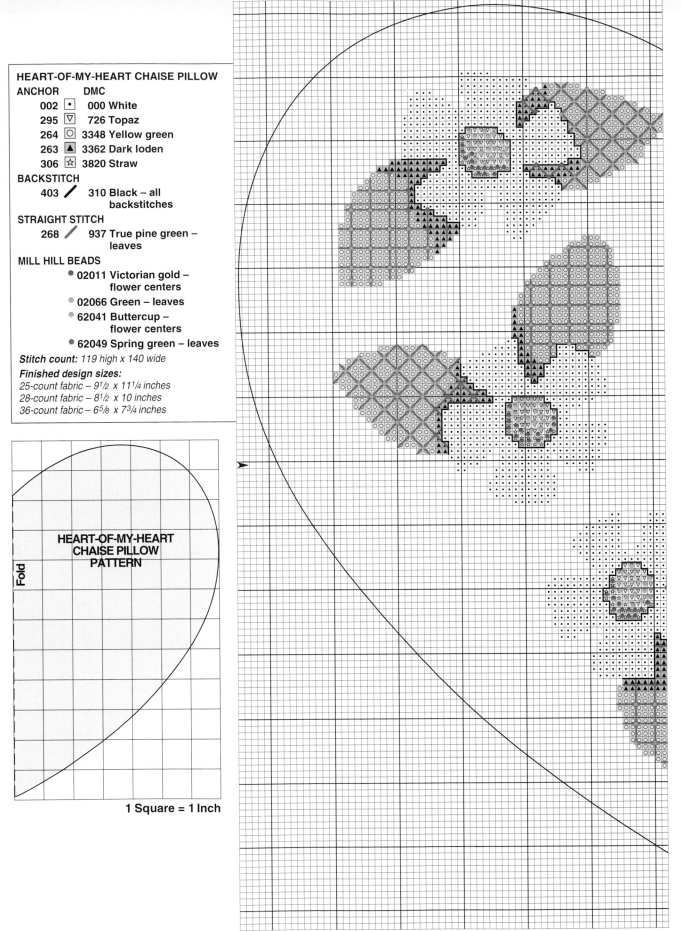

HEART-OF-MY-HEART CHAISE PILLOW

ANCHOR		DMC	
002	•	000	White
295	▽	726	Topaz
264	◎	3348	Yellow green
263	▲	3362	Dark loden
306	☆	3820	Straw

BACKSTITCH

403	/	310 Black – all backstitches

STRAIGHT STITCH

268	/	937 True pine green – leaves

MILL HILL BEADS

- 02011 Victorian gold – flower centers
- 02066 Green – leaves
- 62041 Buttercup – flower centers
- 62049 Spring green – leaves

Stitch count: 119 high x 140 wide
Finished design sizes:
25-count fabric – 9 1/2 x 11 1/4 inches
28-count fabric – 8 1/2 x 10 inches
36-count fabric – 6 5/8 x 7 3/4 inches

HEART-OF-MY-HEART CHAISE PILLOW PATTERN

Fold

1 Square = 1 Inch

HEART-OF-MY-HEART CHAISE PILLOW

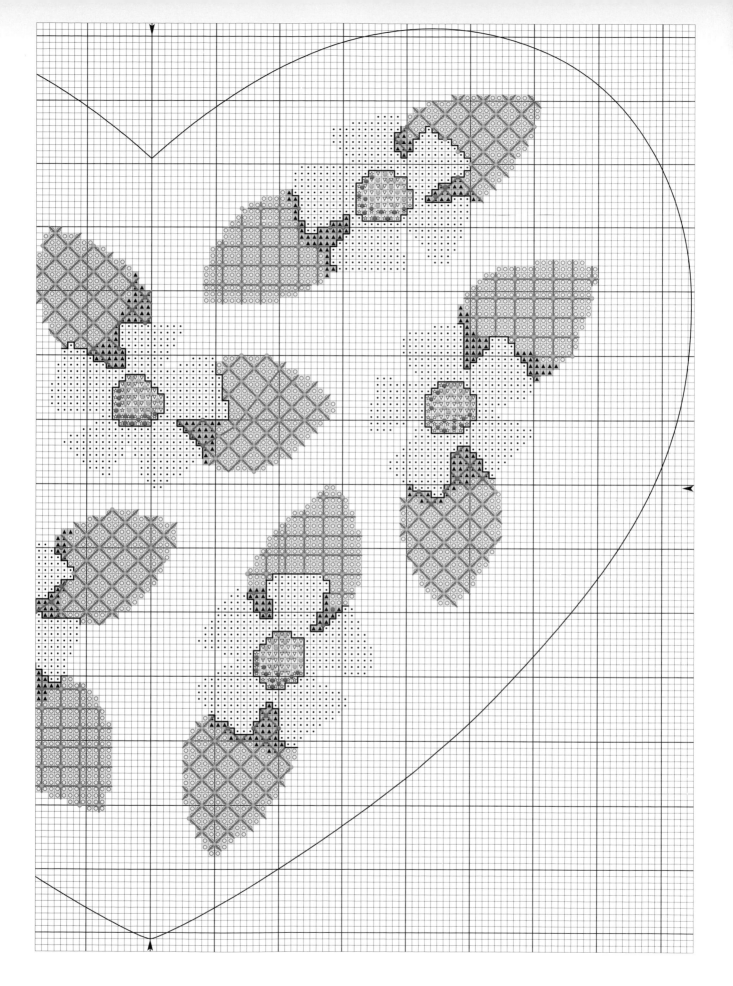

"Breit" Ideas
for Autumn

Everyone Needs Their Own Spot

Cuddle up for the cooler autumn weather in a warm sweatshirt adorned with a parade of favorite furry friends stitched across the front.

Any dog lover would be delighted with any one of these frolicking pups stitched as a lapel pin.

In addition to our pillowcase trim, these fun-to-stitch puppies would also make cute-as-a-button curtain trims or tiebacks, a decorative bed pillow, or a darling addition to the front of a special little boy's pajamas.

Worked on fabric instead of vinyl weave, the place mat design doubles as a bedroom accent when stitching a little boy's or girl's name in the center.

Trick or Treat

If you'd like a complete set of Halloween jewelry, stitch up a couple of extra button covers and glue earring posts to the backs.

Any little goblin would appreciate the trick-or-treater design stitched on a treat bag to carry when going out to collect goodies!

If you're stitching the pumpkin design on a trick-or-treat goody bag, try combining floss with glow-in-the-dark blending filament (instead of using flower thread) for an extra safety precaution come Halloween night.

Use the face on the pumpkin motif as inspiration for carving your own jack-o'-lantern.

Home Is Where The Heart Is

Using just the sentiment, "Home Is Where The Heart Is," stitch a sampler piece and give it to someone special the next time there's a housewarming party.

Stitch the kitty design on perforated plastic, attach it to a wooden skewer, and you have a quick-stitch, kitty-lover's plant poke.

The tiny heart motifs that surround the lettering have a multitude of uses. Use them to embellish doll clothing, the bib on a girl's jumper—even for towel inserts, bookmarks, and sachets.

Stitch just the daisy motif and create a pin for your favorite gardener to enjoy any time of the year.

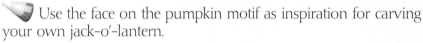

Winter

Snowy days are perfect to cuddle and stitch snowmen and favorite motifs of Christmas. This chapter is filled with gift-giving stitches. We've collected all kinds of ideas and put them in your winter wonderland of designs. Try our tree toppers, ornaments, mittens, and more. What a pleasant way to spend the winter!

Cozy up for Winter Stitching!

Believe

Stitched with love and able to make a believer out of Scrooge himself, our **Believe Sampler** is a work of art. Stitched on 28-count silvery moon linen, the piece is worked with a variety of specialty stitches, three-dimensional ribbon and charm embellishments, and mohair and nylon yarn. A happy challenge to stitch, this sampler is sure to become an heirloom for your Christmas-loving family. Turn the page for more festive projects to make your season bright. Charts and instructions for all of the projects begin on *page 62.*

57

Destined to be a cherished part of every Christmas season, our **Believe Ornaments** include eight of Mary Engelbreit's charming motifs stitched into treasured trims for your holiday tree. Stitch just one of the lovable designs or create the entire set to enjoy yourself or to give as gifts. Fill the branches with our sweet **Heart–And–Star Garland** stitched on perforated plastic and tied together with colorful ribbon.

    Display your love for Santa by wearing your **Sweet St. Nick Pin** proudly during the holiday season. Stitched on Hardanger fabric, Santa is embellished with tiny sparkling seed beads.

Designed to hold a heavenly Christmas gift, our **Star-And-Moon Gift Bag** is stitched on linen with just six colors of floss. Lined with gold lamé fabric and tied together with a shiny gold cord, the bag will hold favorite treasures even after the holidays are over.

Set a magical holiday table with our **Sparkling Place Mat** stitched and couched with metallic threads. Tiny jingle bells sewn to the edges of the mat make the piece dance with holiday fun.

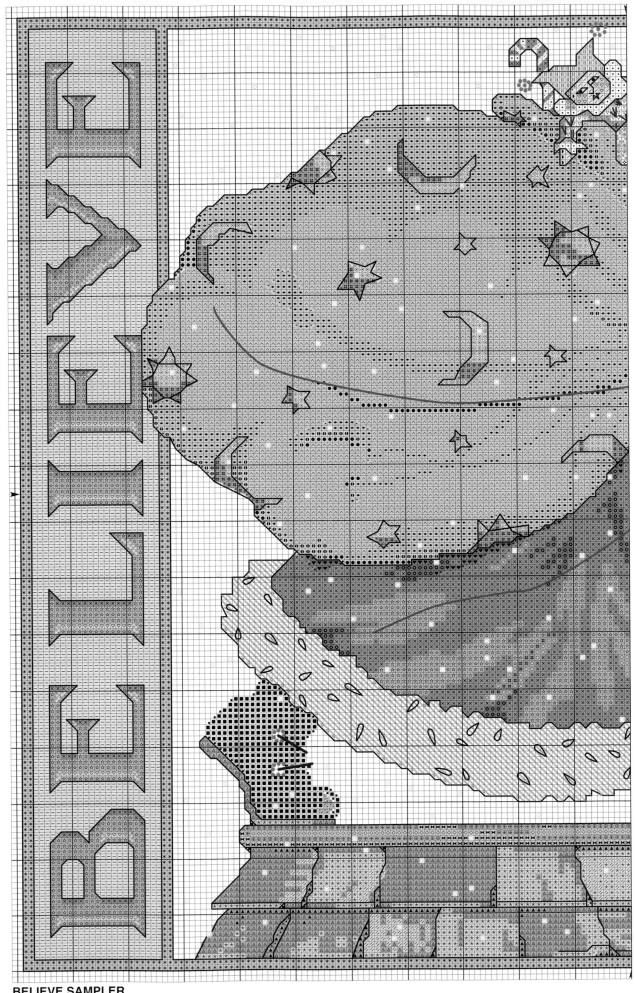

62
BELIEVE SAMPLER

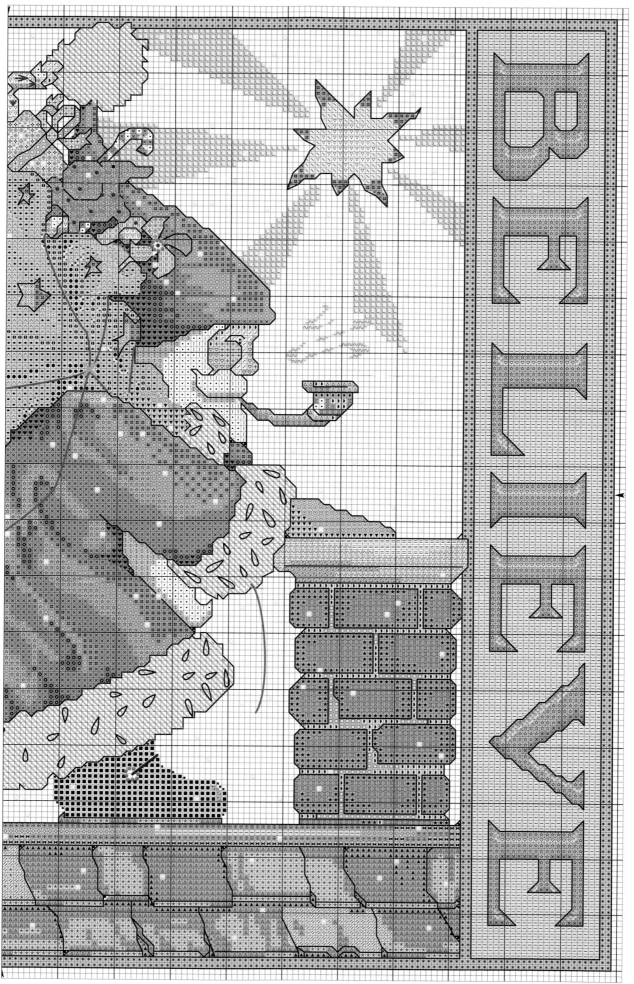

ANCHOR		DMC	
002	·	000	White
403	■	310	Black
117	⁞	341	Light periwinkle
013	☒	349	Dark coral
010	◎	351	Light coral
362	▢	437	Medium tan
267	▣	470	Avocado
162	❖	517	Dark wedgwood blue
1038	⊕	519	Sky blue
891	△	676	Old gold
226	−	702	Light Christmas green
256	‖	704	Chartreuse
323	S	722	Light bittersweet
361	✶	738	Light tan
303	⊙	742	Light tangerine
302	▽	743	True yellow
360	◆	839	Dark beige brown
268	▼	937	Pine green
292	‖	3078	Pale lemon
031	♡	3708	Light watermelon
868	╱	3779	Pale terra-cotta
1050	▲	3781	Mocha
875	◇	3817	Celadon green
306	✳	3820	Dark straw
874	═	3822	Light straw
5975	⊠	3830	True terra-cotta

BLENDED NEEDLE

400	◨	317 True pewter (2X) and
1041		535 Ash gray (1X)
119	◈	333 Deep periwinkle (1X) and
176		792 Dark cornflower blue (2X)
038	⊞	335 Rose (2X) and
1023		3712 Salmon (1X)
011	☆	350 Medium coral (2X) and
035		3705 Dark watermelon (1X)
010	⊞	351 Light coral (1X) and
314		741 Medium tangerine (2X)
401	◐	413 Dark pewter (2X) and
176		792 Dark cornflower blue (1X)
398	⌒	415 Light pearl gray (2X) and
234		762 Pale pearl gray (1X)
683	⋈	500 Deep blue green (2X) and
236		3799 Charcoal (1X)
878	⊞	501 Dark blue green (2X) and
212		561 Seafoam (1X)
832	◭	612 Drab brown (1X) and
379		840 Medium beige brown (2X)
936	★	632 Deep cocoa (2X) and
360		839 Dark beige brown (1X)
1040	◫	647 True beaver gray (1X) and
397		3024 Brown gray (2X)
361	⊘	738 Light tan (2X) and
882		758 Light terra-cotta (1X)
303	◺	742 Light tangerine (1X) and
302		743 True yellow (2X)

ANCHOR		DMC	

BLENDED NEEDLE

234	⌐	762 Pale pearl gray (1X) and
274		928 Gray blue (2X)
178	●	791 Deep cornflower blue (1X) and
236		3799 Charcoal (2X)
380	♥	838 Deep beige brown (2X) and
897		902 Garnet (1X)
360	◉	839 Dark beige brown (1X) and
896		3721 Shell pink (2X)
379	▸	840 Medium beige brown (1X) and
1007		3772 Dark cocoa (2X)
1030	∧	3746 Dark periwinkle (2X) and
177		3807 True cornflower blue (1X)

HALF CROSS-STITCH
(stitch in direction of symbol)

	╲	W88 Rainbow Gallery Wisper white – coat trim and hat

BACKSTITCH

013	╱	349 Dark coral – jester's mouth
226	╱	702 Light Christmas green – elephant
403	╱	310 Black – all remaining backstitches (2X)

STRAIGHT STITCH

013	╱	349 Dark coral – jester's shirt
	╱	Red silk ribbon – Santa's boots

FRENCH KNOT

002	○	000 White – detail on heart
403	●	310 Black – jester's eyes and elephant's eyes
013	●	349 Dark coral – flowers on elephant, pinwheel center
226	●	702 Light Christmas green – elephant (2X)

LAZY DAISY

	⬭	W99 Rainbow Gallery Wisper black – detail on coat trim

BEADS

	●	00557 Mill Hill Gold seed beads – jester's hat, pinwheel, and Santa's boots
	○	4-31 Gick Rock candy 11/0 beads – background
	●	4-95 Gick Eggshell 11/0 beads – heart and star attached to sampler

TWISTED CORD AND TASSEL

310	╱	434 Medium chestnut and
1046		435 Light chestnut – bag tie

COUCHING

	✕	Green silk ribbon and
226		702 Light Christmas green – bag tie

Stitch count: 170 high x 218 wide
Finished design sizes:
28-count fabric – 12⅛ x 15⅝ inches
22-count fabric – 15½ x 19⅞ inches
36-count fabric – 9½ x 12⅛ inches

Believe Sampler

As shown on page 56, sampler measures 12⅛×15⅝ inches.

MATERIALS
FABRICS
20×24-inch piece of 28-count silvery moon linen; two 2×2-inch pieces of 14-count clear perforated plastic
THREADS
Cotton embroidery floss in colors listed in key, left
Wisper thread in colors listed in key
White sewing thread
SUPPLIES
Needle; embroidery hoop
⅛-inch-wide red silk ribbon
Beads in colors listed in key
24-inch length of ⅛-inch-wide green satin ribbon; one red wood bead

INSTRUCTIONS
Tape or zigzag edges of linen. Find center of chart, *pages 62–63,* and of fabric; begin stitching there. Use three plies of floss to work cross-stitches over two threads of fabric. Work the lazy daisy stitches, straight stitches, and French knots using two plies. Work the backstitches using one ply. Use one strand of each color for twisted cord and tassel, securing threads by couching with three plies of medium chestnut (DMC 434). Use one ply of Wisper thread to work half-cross stitches. Use sewing thread to attach beads. Press finished piece from the back.

Find center of heart chart, *page 68,* and of one piece of plastic; begin stitching there. Use three plies to work cross-stitches and French knots, two plies for backstitches. Use thread to attach beads. Repeat for star.

Secure green ribbon as indicated on chart, leaving one tail 10 inches long. Thread wood bead on the end of 10-inch tail and secure it to the center of bottom coat trim using red and yellow floss. Tack star below red bead. Thread heart on long tail of ribbon; tack in place with green floss using photograph, *page 56*, as a guide.

Mat and frame as desired.

Believe Ornaments

As shown on page 58, ornaments measure from 3⅛×4 inches to 5×4⅛ inches.

MATERIALS *for one ornament*

FABRICS

8×10-inch piece of 14-count white Aida cloth; 6×7-inch piece of red felt

FLOSS

Cotton embroidery floss in colors listed in key on page 67

SUPPLIES

Needle; embroidery hoop

Water-erasable fabric marker

6×7-inch piece of self-stick mounting board with foam

Tracing paper; crafts knife

18-inch piece of ⅜-inch-wide gold flat trim

18-inch piece of ¼-inch-wide flat braid in desired color

18-inch piece of ⅛-inch-wide satin ribbon to match braid

Crafts glue

INSTRUCTIONS

Tape or zigzag edges of Aida fabric to prevent fraying. Find center of desired chart, *pages 65–68*, and of fabric; begin stitching there. Use two plies of floss to work the cross-stitches. Work the remaining stitches as indicated in the key.

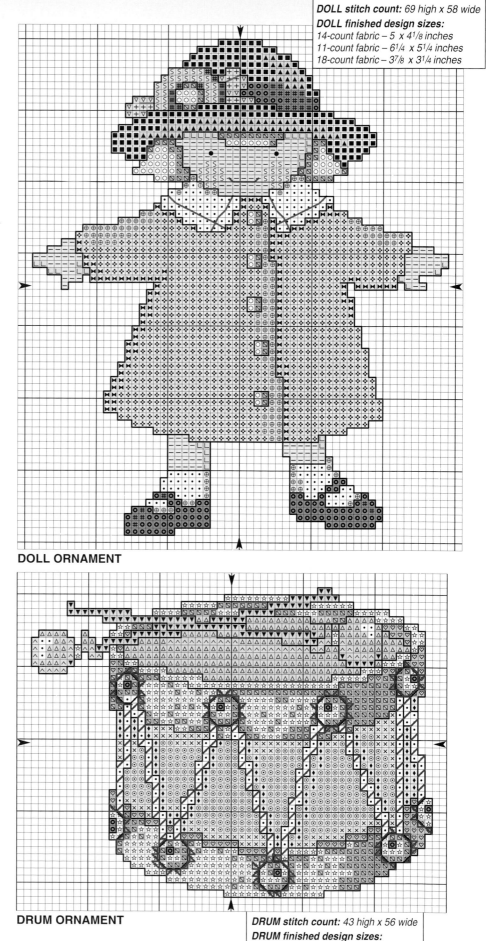

DOLL ORNAMENT

DRUM ORNAMENT

DOLL stitch count: 69 high x 58 wide
DOLL finished design sizes:
14-count fabric – 5 x 4⅛ inches
11-count fabric – 6¼ x 5¼ inches
18-count fabric – 3⅞ x 3¼ inches

DRUM stitch count: 43 high x 56 wide
DRUM finished design sizes:
14-count fabric – 3⅛ x 4 inches
11-count fabric – 4 x 5⅛ inches
18-count fabric – 2⅜ x 3⅛ inches

65

Using fabric marker, draw an oval or circular outline as desired around stitchery. Place tracing paper over stitchery and trace outline; cut out. Place pattern on mounting board and draw around shape; cut out with crafts knife. Cut matching back from felt.

Add a 1-inch seam around drawn outline of stitchery; cut out. Peel protective paper from mounting board. Center foam side of mounting board on back of stitchery; press. Fold raw edges of fabric to back; glue in place, clipping as necessary.

Glue braid around edge, overlapping ends at bottom. Glue gold trim behind braid. For hanger, fold ribbon in half. Glue center fold of ribbon to top center of ornament. Glue felt to ornament back.

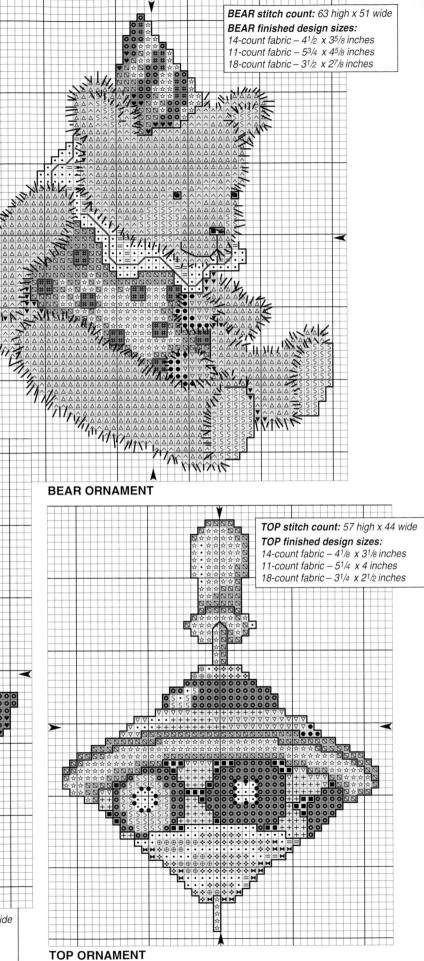

BEAR ORNAMENT

BEAR stitch count: 63 high x 51 wide
BEAR finished design sizes:
14-count fabric – 4½ x 3⅝ inches
11-count fabric – 5¾ x 4⅝ inches
18-count fabric – 3½ x 2⅞ inches

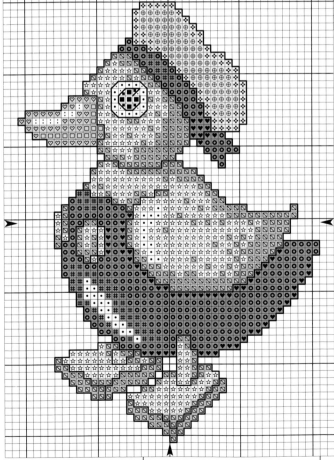

DUCK ORNAMENT

DUCK stitch count: 61 high x 42 wide
DUCK finished design sizes:
14-count fabric – 4⅜ x 3 inches
11-count fabric – 5½ x 3⅞ inches
18-count fabric – 3⅜ x 2⅜ inches

TOP stitch count: 57 high x 44 wide
TOP finished design sizes:
14-count fabric – 4⅛ x 3⅛ inches
11-count fabric – 5¼ x 4 inches
18-count fabric – 3¼ x 2½ inches

TOP ORNAMENT

66

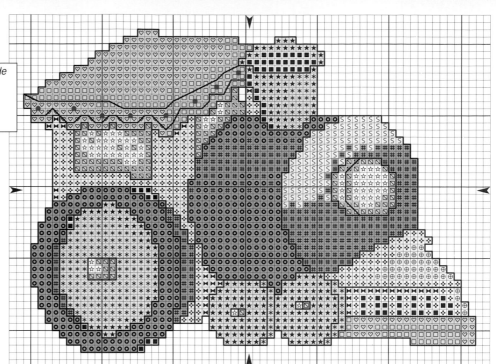

TRAIN stitch count: *45 high x 63 wide*
TRAIN finished design sizes:
14-count fabric – 3¼ x 4½ inches
11-count fabric – 4⅛ x 5¾ inches
18-count fabric – 2½ x 3½ inches

SOLDIER stitch count: *74 high x 28 wide*
SOLDIER finished design sizes:
14-count fabric – 5¼ x 2 inches
11-count fabric – 6¾ x 2½ inches
18-count fabric – 4⅛ x 1½ inches

TRAIN ORNAMENT

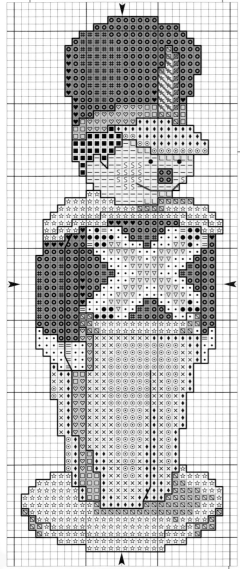

SOLDIER ORNAMENT

BELIEVE ORNAMENTS

ANCHOR		DMC
002	•	000 White
289	☆	307 True lemon
403	■	310 Black
978	✕	322 Navy
1025	◉	347 Deep salmon
008	S	353 Peach
401	▲	413 Dark pewter
1045	⋀	436 Dark tan
228	●	700 Medium Christmas green
226	▽	702 Light Christmas green
256	＋	704 Chartreuse
293	○	727 Pale topaz
361	∟	738 Light tan
275	╱	746 Off white
130	⊙	809 Delft blue
1005	♥	816 Garnet
164	◆	824 Bright blue
160	＝	827 Powder blue
1001	▢	976 Medium golden brown
1002	♡	977 Light golden brown
1024	⊞	3328 Dark salmon
1009	−	3770 Ivory
851	★	3808 Deep turquoise
779	✳	3809 Dark turquoise

BLENDED NEEDLE

1045	▼	436 Dark tan (1X) and
8581		646 Beaver gray (1X)
362	△	437 Medium tan (1X) and
292		3078 Pale lemon (1X)
1039	❖	518 Wedgwood blue (1X) and
433		996 Medium electric blue (1X)
1038	⊕	519 Sky blue (1X) and
167		3766 Light peacock blue (1X)
8581	◈	646 Medium beaver gray (1X) and
361		738 Light tan (1X)
305	◨	725 True topaz (1X) and
307		783 Christmas gold (1X)

ANCHOR		DMC
BLENDED NEEDLE		
410	⋈	995 Dark electric blue (1X) and
170		3765 Deep peacock blue (1X)
292	⦂	3078 Pale lemon (1X) and
386		3823 Pale yellow (1X)

BACKSTITCH

002	╱	000 White – elephant's eye and bear's nose (2X)
1025	╱	347 Deep salmon – doll's mouth, bear's collar, and soldier's mouth (1X); drum, bear's shirt and hearts on elephant (2X); elephant (6X)
228	╱	700 Medium Christmas green – leaves on doll's hat (2X)
403	╱	310 Black – all remaining backstitches (2X)

BLENDED BACKSTITCH

1039	╱	518 Light wedgwood blue (1X) and
433		996 Medium electric blue (1X) – doll's collar

STRAIGHT STITCH

403	╱	310 Black – bear's fur (1X) and elephant's head piece (2X)
1001	╱	976 Medium golden brown – soldier's hat detail (2X)

BLENDED STRAIGHT STITCH

403	╱	310 Black (1X) and
361		738 Light tan (1X) – elephant's tail

LAZY DAISY

226	⬭	702 Light Christmas green – elephant's blanket (3X)

FRENCH KNOT

002	●	000 White – bear's eyes (2X)
403	●	310 Black – top (2X); doll's eyes and soldier's eyes (3X)
1025	●	347 Deep salmon – train (3X)

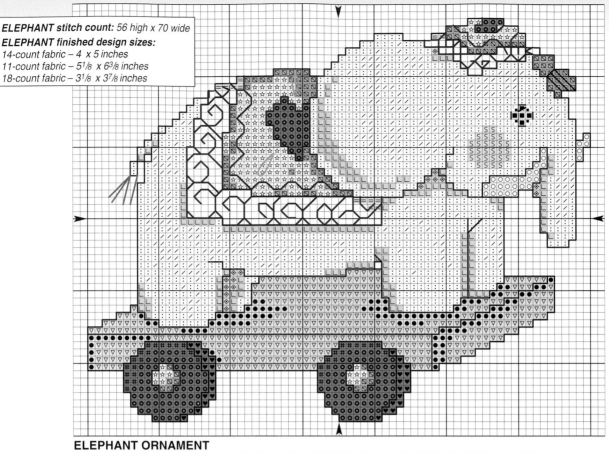

ELEPHANT stitch count: 56 high x 70 wide
ELEPHANT finished design sizes:
14-count fabric – 4 x 5 inches
11-count fabric – 5⅛ x 6⅜ inches
18-count fabric – 3⅛ x 3⅞ inches

ELEPHANT ORNAMENT

Heart-And-Star Garland

As shown on page 58, finished garland is 72 inches long.

MATERIALS

For one star and one heart

FABRIC

Two 8×10-inch pieces of 10-count clear perforated plastic

FLOSS

Cotton embroidery floss in colors listed in key, right

SUPPLIES

Needle; fifteen 2.5-mm pearl beads

2¼ yards of ⅛-inch-wide blue satin ribbon; white thread

HEART-AND-STAR GARLAND

INSTRUCTIONS

Cut plastic into 2×2-inch pieces. For each heart and star, find center of chart and of plastic; begin stitching there. Use three plies of floss to work cross-stitches and French knots. Work backstitches using two plies. Use thread to attach beads. Stitch as many motifs as desired; trim one square beyond stitching.

Thread ribbon through hearts and stars as follows: Leaving a 6-inch tail, knot one end of ribbon. Thread unknotted end from front side edge of one star to back, across back of

HEART-AND-STAR GARLAND		
ANCHOR	**DMC**	
002	•	000 White
013	✕	349 Dark coral
011	◖	350 Medium coral
010	○	351 Light coral
323	S	722 Light bittersweet
302	▽	743 True yellow
031	♡	3708 Light watermelon
BACKSTITCH		
403	╱	310 Black – all backstitches
FRENCH KNOTS		
002	○	000 White – hearts
BEADS		
	●	White pearls

STAR stitch count: 16 high x 18 wide
STAR finished design sizes:
10-count plastic – 1⅝ x 1⅞ inches
8-count plastic – 2 x 2¼ inches
14-count plastic – 1⅛ x 1¼ inches
HEART stitch count: 15 high x 16 wide
HEART finished design sizes:
10-count plastic – 1½ x 1⅝ inches
8-count plastic – 1¾ x 2 inches
14-count plastic – 1⅛ x 1⅛ inches

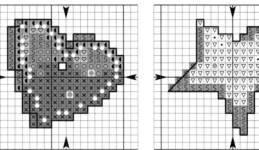

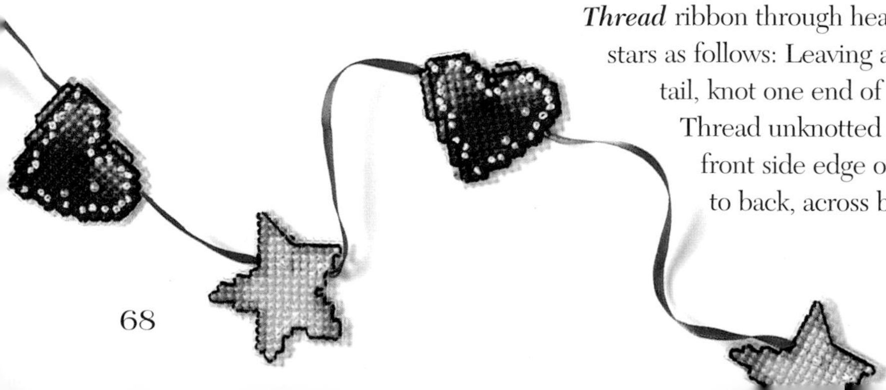

star, then up through a hole along opposite edge to front. Push star almost to knot in ribbon. Tie a second knot 6 to 8 inches from the first, and thread a heart onto ribbon in same manner. Knot ribbon and continue to thread motifs, alternating hearts and stars, and knotting ribbon in between.

Sweet St. Nick Pin

As shown on page 59, brooch is 2½ inches in diameter.

MATERIALS

FABRICS
6×6-inch piece of 22-count light blue Hardanger fabric

6×6-inch piece of fusible interfacing

2½-inch-diameter circle of light blue felt

FLOSS
Cotton embroidery floss in colors listed in key, right

SUPPLIES
Needle; embroidery hoop;

Beads in color listed in key

2½-inch-diameter circle of self-stick mounting board with foam

9-inch-long piece of ¼-inch-wide gold metallic flat trim

Crafts glue

1-inch-long pin back

INSTRUCTIONS

Tape or zigzag edges of fabric. Find center of chart *above right,* and of fabric; begin stitching there. Use two plies of floss to work cross-stitches. Work blended needle stitches as specified in key. Work backstitches using one ply. Use one ply of matching floss to attach beads.

Center interfacing on back of stitchery and fuse, following the manufacturer's instructions.

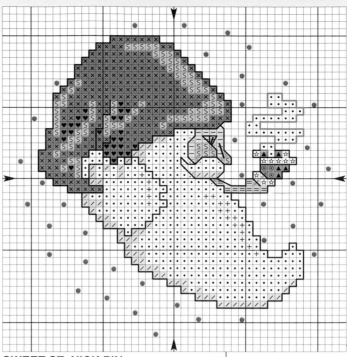

SWEET ST. NICK PIN

Center motif over mounting board circle; trim fabric ½ inch beyond edge. Peel protective paper from mounting board. Center foam side of mounting board on back of stitchery and press. Fold raw edges of fabric to back; glue in place, clipping as necessary.

Glue gold trim around edge of pin. Glue felt to back. Glue pin back to felt, ⅓ of the way down from top.

Star-And-Moon Gift Bag

As shown on page 60, bag is 12 inches tall and 6 inches in diameter.

MATERIALS

FABRICS
½ yard of 45-inch-wide 28-count Dutch blue cashel linen

½ yard of 45-inch-wide cotton batiste underlining fabric

½ yard of 45-inch-wide gold metallic print lining fabric

THREADS
Cotton embroidery floss in colors listed in key on page 70

Sewing thread to match linen

SWEET ST. NICK PIN		
ANCHOR		DMC
002	•	000 White
013	✕	349 Dark coral
290	☆	444 Medium lemon
288	+	445 Light lemon
361	=	738 Light tan
355	▲	975 Deep golden brown
1001	◉	976 Medium golden brown
1015	♥	3777 Deep terra-cotta
868	–	3779 Pale terra-cotta
BLENDED NEEDLE		
010	S	351 Light coral (1X) and
324		721 Medium bittersweet (1X)
1040	╱	647 True beaver gray (1X) and
397		3024 Brown gray (1X)
BACKSTITCH		
002	╱	000 White – Santa's eye and nose
403	╱	310 Black – Santa and pipe
1040	╱	647 True beaver gray – smoke
BEADS		
●		40557 Mill Hill Gold petite beads

Stitch count: 44 high x 44 wide
Finished design sizes:
22-count fabric – 2 x 2 inches
28-count fabric – 1½ x 1½ inches
36-count fabric – 1¼ x 1¼ inches

SUPPLIES

Needle; embroidery hoop

2 yards of narrow gold metallic sew-in piping

1 yard of ¼-inch-diameter gold metallic cord

Two 1×1-inch gold star charms

Crafts glue

STAR-AND-MOON GIFT BAG

STAR-AND-MOON GIFT BAG		
ANCHOR	DMC	
303	742	Light tangerine
130	809	Delft blue
306	3820	Dark straw
BLENDED NEEDLE		
010	351	Light coral (1X) and
314	741	Medium tangerine (2X)

ANCHOR	DMC	
BACKSTITCH		
403	310	Black – stars, moons and border
STRAIGHT STITCH		
130	809	Delft blue – rays

Stitch count: 112 high x 84 wide
Finished design sizes:
28-count fabric – 8 x 6 inches
22-count fabric – 10¼ x 7⅝ inches
36-count fabric – 6¼ x 4⅝ inches

INSTRUCTIONS

Cut a piece of blue linen 18 inches long and 26 inches wide. Tape or zigzag the edges to prevent fraying. Mark a point 10⅛ inches down from top and 7¾ inches in from left edge of linen rectangle. Find the center of the chart, *page 70*, and the marked point on the fabric; begin stitching there. Use three plies of floss to work the cross-stitches. Work the blended needle stitches as indicated in the key. Work the straight stitches and backstitches using two plies.

Cut 2½ inches from each side of linen to make final measurement 13×21 inches. Cut the same size rectangle from both underlining and lining. Set lining aside. Baste underlining to wrong side of linen.

Draw a 7-inch-diameter circle on leftover piece of linen. Back the linen with underlining fabric; baste together along circle outline. Sew gold piping around circle along basting line. Cut out circle ½ inch beyond piping to allow for seam allowance. Use circle as pattern to cut lining piece. Set lining aside.

Sew the short edges of linen rectangle together, right sides facing, using ½-inch seam allowance. Sew piping around top edge. Sew underlined linen circle to bottom.

Sew lining rectangle and circle together in the same manner, omitting piping; leave an opening in the side seam for turning. With the right sides facing, sew the lining to linen bag. Match side seams and join top edge using ½-inch seam allowance. Trim the seam allowance; turn to right side through lining. Slip-stitch the opening closed. Press top edge.

To make casing, stitch around the bag 1⅝ inches below the top edge and again ½ inch below first

stitching. Open the outer side seam between the rows of stitching. Insert the gold cord through the opening and run it through the casing to make the drawstring.

Glue a star charm to each end of the cord.

Sparkling Place Mat

As shown on page 61, place mat measures 14¾×18½ inches.

MATERIALS

For one place mat

FABRICS

18×24-inch piece of 28-count white Jobelan fabric

18×24-inch piece of white cotton fabric

18×24-inch piece of fleece

THREADS

Cotton embroidery floss in colors listed in key, below right

Metallic gold #16 braid as listed in key

Metallic copper sewing thread

White sewing thread

SUPPLIES

Needle; embroidery hoop

Quilt-marking pencil

2 yards of narrow gold metallic piping

Forty ⁵⁄₁₆-inch-diameter gold jingle bells

INSTRUCTIONS

Tape or zigzag edges of Jobelan fabric. Find top left stitch of "Believe" border on sampler chart, *pages 62–63*. On Jobelan fabric, measure in 3 inches from top left corner of fabric; begin stitching there. Use two plies of floss to work cross-stitches. Work blended needle stitches as indicated in key. Work backstitches using one ply. Stitch "Believe" band on left side. Continue stitching by *increasing* the stitch count of the borders between

the "Believe" bands from 164 stitches to 198 stitches. Stitch the "Believe" band on the right side.

Baste fleece to back of stitched piece, ½ inch beyond cross-stitching. Use marking pencil to draw a 1-inch diagonal grid onto fabric within cross-stitched frame. With copper sewing thread on spool and white thread on bobbin, use a medium long, very narrow machine zigzag stitch to couch over gold braid along grid lines. Pull all threads to wrong side and knot.

Trim excess fabric ½ inch beyond basting. Sew gold piping around perimeter along basting line. Using stitched piece as pattern, cut backing from white cotton.

With right sides facing, sew front to back along piping seam lines. Leave an opening for turning. Trim seam allowance and clip corners. Turn right side out; sew opening closed.

Sew 20 jingle bells to each end of the place mat between the piping and cross-stitching.

Refer to chart on pages 62–63.

SPARKLING PLACE MAT

ANCHOR		DMC	
013	☒	349	Dark coral
226	⊟	702	Light Christmas green
031	♡	3708	Light watermelon
306	✳	3820	Dark straw

BLENDED NEEDLE

011	★	350	Medium coral (1X) and
035		3705	Dark watermelon (1X)

BACKSTITCH

403	╱	310	Black – all backstitches

COUCHING

	╱	002	Metallic copper sewing thread couched over Kreinik #16 gold braid – background

JINGLE BELLS

	●		Gold – left and right edges

Stitch count: 170 high x 252 wide

Finished design sizes:
28-count fabric – 12⅛ x 18 inches
22-count fabric – 15½ x 23 inches
36-count fabric – 9½ x 14 inches

Let It Snow

The weather outside is cold and snowy and perfect for building a family of snowmen—or for cuddling inside and stitching one! Our **Let It Snow Sampler** is stitched on peach Aida cloth and features a happy snowman family and a checkered border. The finished piece sports a bright polka-dot mat made using a paper punch. For more fun-to-stitch snowmen projects, turn the page. Instructions and charts for all projects begin on *page 77*.

Year after year our **Country Snowmen Stocking** will welcome the Christmas season hanging from the mantel for everyone to admire. Stitched on Hardanger fabric, the stocking is trimmed in holiday plaid.

Get ready for fun in the snow with our **Wintry–Warm Scarf and Mittens** set. Stitched on polar fleece using waste canvas, the message and motifs stand out proudly against the plain backgrounds. A blanket–stitch border and floss fringe complete the set.

Using a simple holiday motif and perforated paper, these **Clever Christmas Cards** are fun to stitch. The cards work up in the wink of an eye and then are trimmed with floss, ribbons, and colored papers. Add a handwritten message for one-of-a-kind holiday cards and gift tags.

Let It Snow Sampler

As shown on page 72–73, finished sampler measures 11⅝×19⅝ inches.

MATERIALS

FABRIC

20×28-inch piece of 14-count light peach Aida cloth

FLOSS

Cotton embroidery floss in colors listed in key, below

SUPPLIES

Needle; embroidery hoop

Approximately 19 small white pom-poms

Crafts glue

Desired mats and frame

INSTRUCTIONS

Tape or zigzag edges of the Aida cloth to prevent fraying. Find the center of the chart, *right* and *pages* 78–79, and the center of the fabric; begin stitching there. Use two plies of embroidery floss to work the cross-stitches over one square of the Aida cloth. Work the French knots, straight stitches, and backstitches as indicated in the key.

Press the finished piece from the back.

To attach the pom-poms, apply a small dot of glue to the back of each pom-pom and carefully press onto the fabric where desired. Let the glue dry.

Mat and frame the stitched piece as desired.

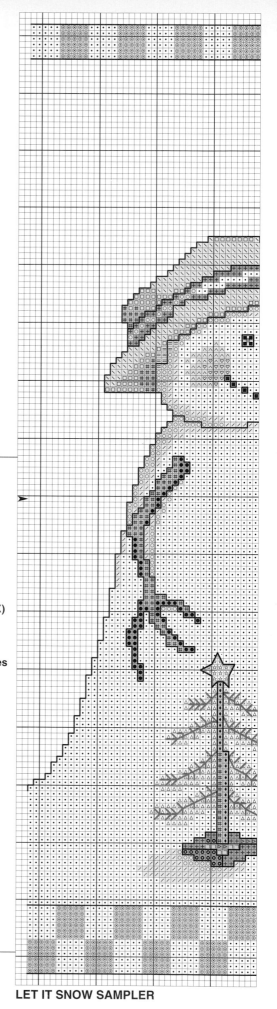

LET IT SNOW SAMPLER

ANCHOR		DMC
002	·	000 White
403	■	310 Black
399	═	318 Steel
218	▲	319 Pistachio
117	○	341 Light periwinkle
011	+	349 Dark coral
401	◨	413 Pewter
374	#	420 Hazel
310	♦	434 Chestnut
1045	□	436 Dark tan
362	◁	437 Medium tan
891	▽	676 Light old gold
256	◇	704 Chartreuse
305	☆	725 Topaz
890	✳	729 Medium old gold
316	⊕	740 Dark tangerine
303	▽	742 Light tangerine
013	◎	817 Deep coral
360	●	898 Coffee brown
332	✳	946 Burnt orange
073	△	963 Rose pink
206	─	966 Baby green
246	◉	986 Dark forest green
244	×	987 Medium forest green
036	♡	3326 Rose
033	⊓	3706 Medium watermelon
120	╱	3747 Pale periwinkle
035	▷	3801 Deep watermelon
278	△	3819 Moss green
386	▯	3823 Yellow
9575	◠	3824 Melon

BACKSTITCH

002	╱	000 White–noses (2X)
399	╱	318 Steel–coal button highlights (2X)
218	╱	319 Pistachio–holly leaf veins (2X); wreath (1X)
011	╱	349 Dark coral–broom (2X); apron (1X)
374	╱	420 Hazel–broom straws (1X)
360	╱	898 Coffee brown–oak leaf veins (2X)
244	╱	987 Medium forest green– Christmas tree and leaves on apron (2X)
386	╱	3823 Yellow–star points (2X)
403	╱	310 Black–all remaining stitches (1X)

STRAIGHT STITCH

403	╱	310 Black–comb (1X)

FRENCH KNOT

002	●	000 White–eyes, holly berries (2X); wreath (1X)
403	●	310 Black–broom, mouth (1X)
011	●	349 Dark coral–bow polka dots (2X); apron (1X)

Stitch count: 163 high x 275 wide

Finished design sizes:
14-count fabric – 11⅝ x 19⅝ inches
11-count fabric – 14⅞ x 10 inches
18-count fabric – 11¾ x 7¾ inches

LET IT SNOW SAMPLER

Country Snowmen Stocking

As shown on page 74, finished stocking measures 18 inches long.

MATERIALS

FABRICS

24×18-inch piece of 22-count red Hardanger fabric

¾ yard of 45-inch-wide plaid taffeta fabric

14×20-inch piece of fleece

14×20-inch piece of fusible interfacing

½ yard of 45-inch-wide lining fabric

2×3-inch piece of royal blue ultra suede

FLOSS

Cotton embroidery floss in colors listed in key, right

SUPPLIES

Needle; embroidery hoop

Tracing paper; 3 red seed beads

Two ¼-inch black shank buttons

Three ⅜-inch black buttons

Seven 6-mm black faceted beads

11 red pebble beads

Five 8-mm red faceted beads

½-inch-wide yellow star button

6-inch piece of red satin ribbon

Fusible interfacing

1½ yards of metallic gold sew-in piping

¾ yard of ½-inch-wide flat trim

¼ yard of red cord

½ yard of ¼-inch-wide red flat braid

INSTRUCTIONS

Tape or zigzag edges of the Hardanger fabric to prevent fraying. Find the center of the chart, *page 81*, and the center of the Hardanger fabric; begin stitching there. Use three plies of floss to work cross-stitches over two threads of fabric. Work the French knots and backstitches using two plies of floss.

Sew on the beads and the buttons using two plies of matching floss. Tie the piece of red satin ribbon into a small bow and tack it to the bottom of the wreath; trim the ribbon ends if needed. Press the finished stitchery from the back.

Trace the scarf pattern, *page 81*, onto tracing paper; cut out. Cut one scarf from blue ultra suede and machine-stitch to snowman, referring to photograph on *page 74* as a guide.

Enlarge and trace stocking pattern; cut out. Center the cross-stitched design on the stocking pattern with the design 5 inches down from the top edge of the stocking pattern; cut out. Also cut a back from taffeta and two lining pieces; set aside.

Line the stocking front with fleece. Trace the heel and toe shapes onto fusible interfacing following the manufacturer's instructions. Fuse to the plaid fabric; cut out. Fuse the toe and heel shapes to the stocking front. Machine-zigzag over the raw edges of the heel and toe. Top-stitch the red trim over the zigzag stitching.

Sew metallic gold piping along the outside edge of the stocking, except at the top.

For cuff, cut a 9×18½-inch rectangle from the plaid fabric. Fuse interfacing to the stocking back and cuff.

Sew the stocking front to back along the piped edge using a ½-inch seam allowance and with the right sides facing. Clip the seam allowance; turn right side out.

Press the cuff in half, matching the raw edges. Stitch the gold trim around the folded edge. Baste the raw edges together and the cuff around the top edge of the stocking.

COUNTRY SNOWMEN STOCKING		
ANCHOR		**DMC**
002	·	000 White
403	■	310 Black
399	⊟	318 Steel
218	▲	319 Pistachio
117	○	341 Light periwinkle
011	⊞	349 Dark coral
401	◨	413 Pewter
374	⊞	420 Hazel
310	◆	434 Chestnut
1045	□	436 Dark tan
362	◩	437 Medium tan
256	◇	704 Chartreuse
316	⊕	740 Dark tangerine
303	◿	742 Light tangerine
013	◉	817 Deep coral
360	●	898 Coffee brown
332	✱	946 Burnt orange
073	◿	963 Rose pink
246	◎	986 Dark forest green
244	✕	987 Medium forest green
036	♡	3326 Rose
033	◰	3706 Medium watermelon
120	◿	3747 Pale periwinkle
278	△	3819 Moss green
386	⊡	3823 Yellow
BACKSTITCH		
218	╱	319 Pistachio—leaf veins, wreath, Christmas tree
403	╱	310 Black—all remaining stitches (1X)
FRENCH KNOT		
403	●	310 Black—mouth
BEADS		
	○	Black—small snowman's eyes and buttons
	●	05025 Red pebble beads—wreath
	○	02063 Red seed beads—holly berries in small snowman's hat
	○	Red 8-mm—Christmas tree ornaments
BUTTONS		
	✕	Black ¼-inch—large snowman's buttons
	✕	Black ⅜-inch—large snowman's eyes
	✕	Yellow ½-inch—star Christmas tree topper

Stitch count: 122 high x 68 wide

Finished design sizes:
22-count fabric – 11 x 6⅛ inches
28-count fabric – 8¾ x 4⅞ inches
36-count fabric – 6⅞ x 3⅞ inches

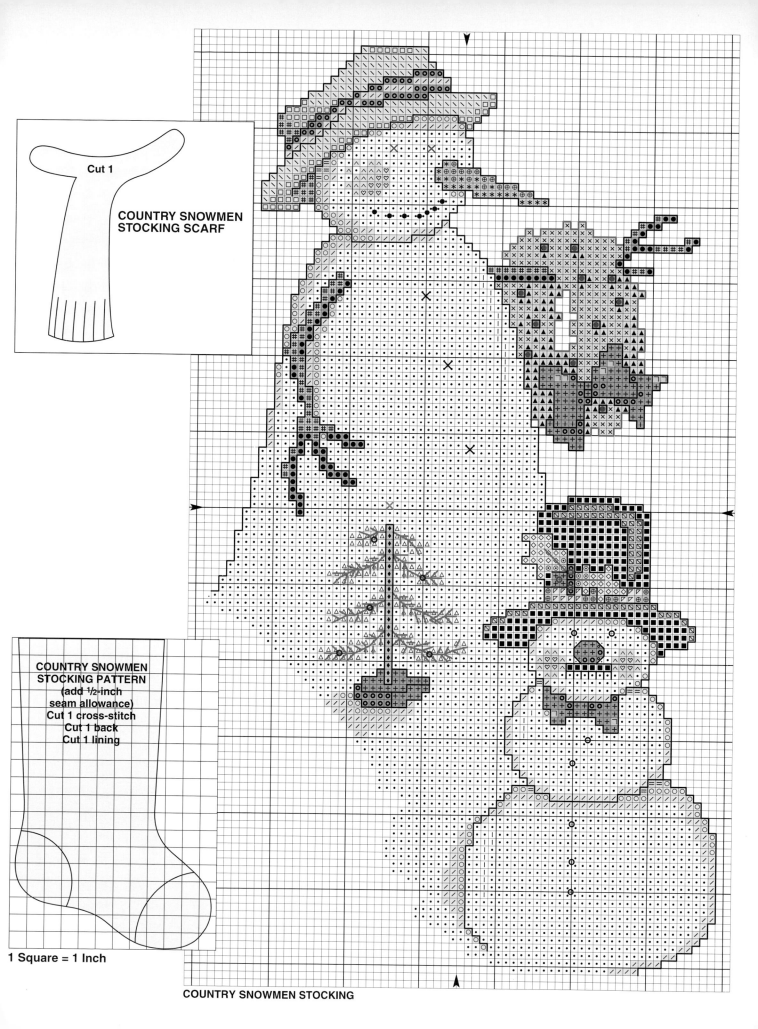

Cut 1

COUNTRY SNOWMEN
STOCKING SCARF

**COUNTRY SNOWMEN
STOCKING PATTERN**
(add ½-inch
seam allowance)
Cut 1 cross-stitch
Cut 1 back
Cut 1 lining

1 Square = 1 Inch

COUNTRY SNOWMEN STOCKING

Tack the ends of the red cord to the upper left corner of the cuff for a hanging loop.

Slip the stocking through the cuff with the right sides facing and the seams matching. Stitch around the top edge. Clip the seam and turn the stocking through the opening in the lining. Slip-stitch the opening closed.

Press the lining to the inside. Top-stitch through the stocking and the lining around the top edge, leaving the cuff free. Turn the cuff down.

Wintry-Warm Mittens

As shown on page 75, snowman designs each measure 4³⁄₈×2³⁄₈ inches on the adult mittens.

MATERIALS

FABRICS
½ yard of red polar fleece

Two 6×4-inch pieces of 14-count waste canvas

½ yard of plaid flannel lining

¼ yard of green corduroy

FLOSS
Cotton embroidery floss in colors listed in key, right

2 additional skeins of white floss (DMC 000)

SUPPLIES
Tracing paper; needle

1 yard of ¼-inch-wide elastic

INSTRUCTIONS

Enlarge and trace the pattern pieces, page 83, onto tracing paper; cut out. Cut two sets of mitten pieces from polar fleece and from lining (reversing shapes for the opposite mitten); set lining aside.

Baste a piece of waste canvas on each mitten back, aligning centers.

Find the center of the chart, *right*, and the center of the waste canvas; begin stitching there. Use three plies of embroidery floss to work the cross-stitches. Work the satin stitches, French knots, and backstitches using two plies of floss.

To remove the waste canvas, remove basting threads and trim within ½ inch from stitching. Gently pull the waste canvas threads loose, using tweezers if necessary.

Using the patterns, cut the remaining mitten pieces. Stitch all seams with the right sides facing and using ¼-inch seam allowance.

Stitch the thumb to the thumb gusset around the curved edge from A to B. Stitch the inner seam of thumb and palm, tapering to a point at A. Machine-zigzag over the elastic stretched on the wrong side of the palm/thumb, 3 inches down from the top edge.

Stitch mitten palm to back along side and finger curve. Turn right side out.

Repeat for the lining, leaving an opening for turning in the side seam of the lining.

Cut two cuffs from the corduroy, each 6½×12½ inches. Stitch the short ends of the cuff together. Press the seams open. Fold the cuff in half with the wrong sides facing and matching the raw edges.

Work the blanket stitch, *page 20*, along the folded edge of the mitten cuff using six plies of black floss. Ease-stitch along the top edge of the cuff and baste to the mitten, matching the center back seams.

Slip the mitten into the lining, matching the side seams and the thumb. Stitch around the top edge. Slip-stitch the opening in the lining closed. Tuck the lining into the mitten and turn the cuff down.

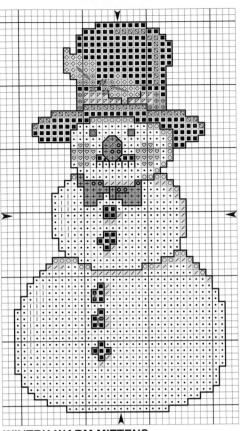

WINTRY-WARM MITTENS

WINTRY-WARM MITTENS		
ANCHOR		DMC
002	⊡	000 White
403	■	310 Black
117	○	341 Light periwinkle
011	⊞	349 Dark coral
401	◩	413 Pewter
256	◇	704 Chartreuse
316	⊕	740 Dark tangerine
303	▽	742 Light tangerine
013	◉	817 Deep coral
246	◎	986 Dark forest green
036	♡	3326 Rose
120	⧄	3747 Pale periwinkle
386	Ⅰ	3823 Yellow
BACKSTITCH		
002	╱	000 White – nose
399	╱	318 Steel – button highlights
218	╱	319 Pistachio – leaf veins
403	╱	310 Black – all remaining stitches
SATIN STITCH		
013	❘	349 Dark coral – holly berries
FRENCH KNOT		
002	●	000 White – eyes, holly berries

Stitch count: 61 high x 33 wide

Finished design sizes:
14-count fabric – 4³⁄₈ x 2³⁄₈ inches
18-count fabric – 3³⁄₈ x 1⁷⁄₈ inches
11-count fabric – 5½ x 3 inches

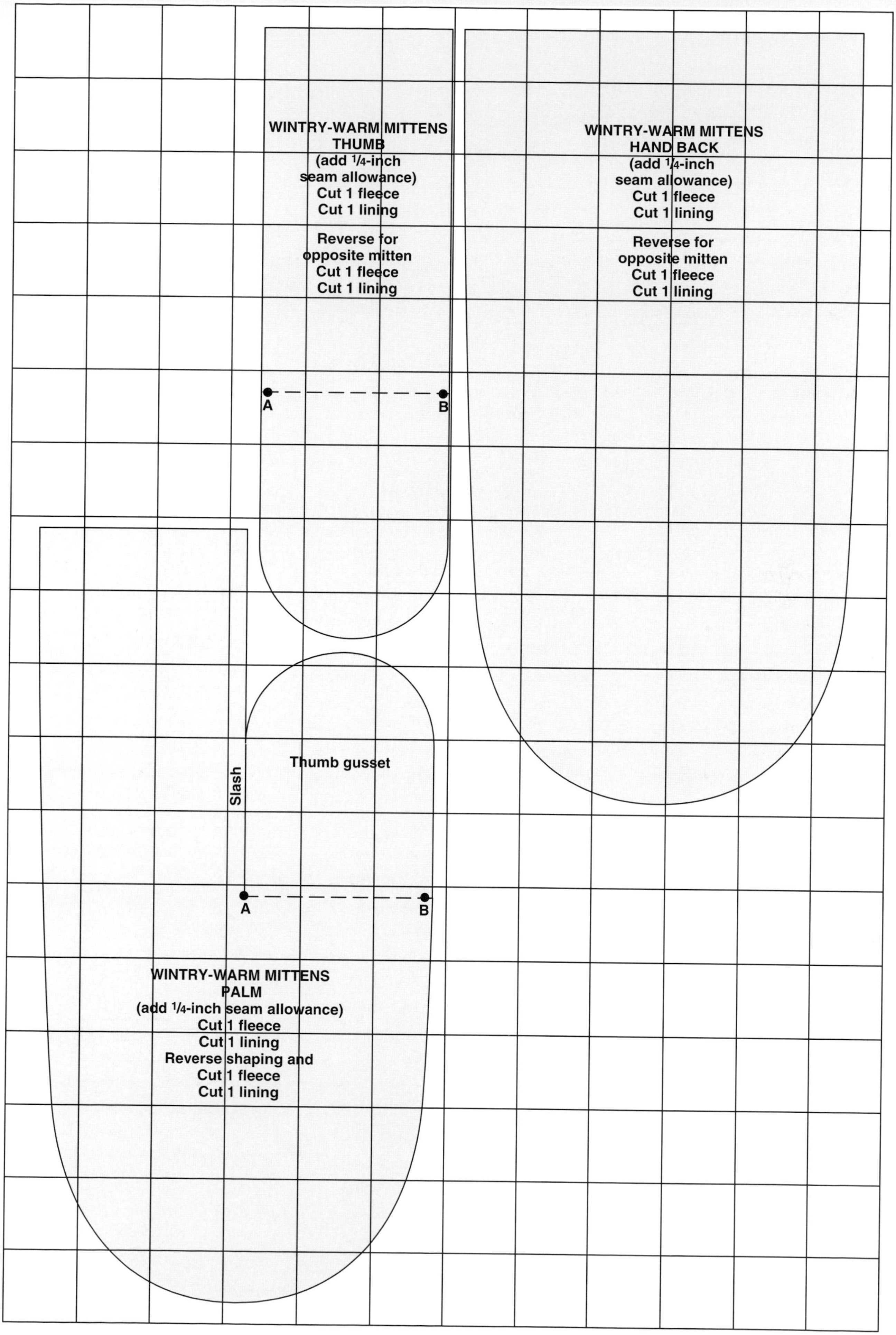

WINTRY-WARM MITTENS
THUMB
(add ¼-inch
seam allowance)
Cut 1 fleece
Cut 1 lining

Reverse for
opposite mitten
Cut 1 fleece
Cut 1 lining

WINTRY-WARM MITTENS
HAND BACK
(add ¼-inch
seam allowance)
Cut 1 fleece
Cut 1 lining

Reverse for
opposite mitten
Cut 1 fleece
Cut 1 lining

A ●------------● B

Slash

Thumb gusset

A ●------------● B

WINTRY-WARM MITTENS
PALM
(add ¼-inch seam allowance)
Cut 1 fleece
Cut 1 lining
Reverse shaping and
Cut 1 fleece
Cut 1 lining

1 Square = 1 Inch

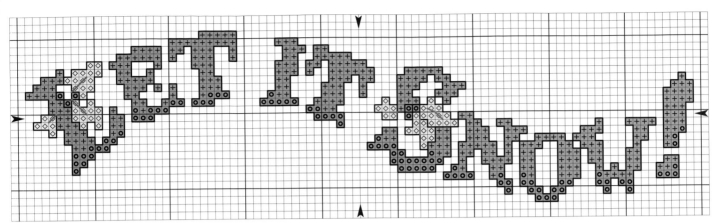

WINTRY-WARM SCARF

Wintry-Warm Scarf

As shown on page 75, finished scarf measures 10¼×64 inches.

MATERIALS

FABRICS

Two 4×10-inch pieces of 10-count waste canvas

14×68-inch piece of white Arctic fleece

FLOSS

Cotton embroidery floss in colors listed in key, above right

2 additional skeins of black (DMC 310) floss

4 additional skeins each of deep coral (DMC 817), dark coral (DMC 349), dark forest green (DMC 986), and chartreuse (DMC 704)

SUPPLIES

Needle; awl; crochet hook

INSTRUCTIONS

Baste each piece of waste canvas 5 inches from each end of the fleece. Find the center of the chart, *above*, and the center of the waste canvas; begin stitching there. Use four plies of embroidery floss to work the cross-stitches. Work the backstitches using two plies of floss.

WINTRY-WARM SCARF

ANCHOR		DMC
011	+	349 Dark coral
256	◇	704 Chartreuse
013	◉	817 Deep coral
BACKSTITCH		
218	/	319 Pistachio–leaf veins
403	/	310 Black–all remaining stitches

Stitch count: 23 high x 88 wide
Finished design sizes:
10-count fabric – 2⅓ x 8⅞ inches
14-count fabric – 1⅝ x 6¼ inches
18-count fabric – 1¼ x 4⅞ inches

To remove the waste canvas, remove basting thread and trim within ½ inch of stitching. Gently pull the waste canvas thread loose, using tweezers if necessary.

Trim the fleece along the long edges 1 inch from the stitching. Trim the fabric 2 inches below the lettering on each short end.

Top-stitch a ⅜-inch hem all the way around the scarf. Use six plies of black floss to work blanket stitches, *page 20*, on the two long edges of the scarf.

For floss fringe, remove the floss labels and cut one end of the floss skein using scissors. Divide the floss into two equal sections. Use an awl to pierce the holes for the fringe, approximately ½ inch apart and ½ inch in from the edge. Use a crochet hook to pull one floss section through the fabric. Tie over hand

knots to secure floss. Repeat, alternating the four floss colors. If necessary, trim the floss ends even.

Clever Christmas Cards

As shown on page 76, star measures 1⅛×1 inch, holly leaf measures 2×2½ inches, and Christmas tree measures 3⅝×5⅝ inches.

MATERIALS

FABRIC

14-count brown perforated paper

FLOSS

Cotton embroidery floss in colors listed in key, page 85

SUPPLIES

Needle

Seed beads in color listed in key

Assorted papers or blank note cards

Crafts glue; narrow ribbons

Decorative-edge scissors, paper punch, and markers, if desired

INSTRUCTIONS

Find the center of the desired chart, *page 85*, and the center of a desired size piece of perforated paper; begin stitching there. Use two plies of floss to work cross-stitches. Work the

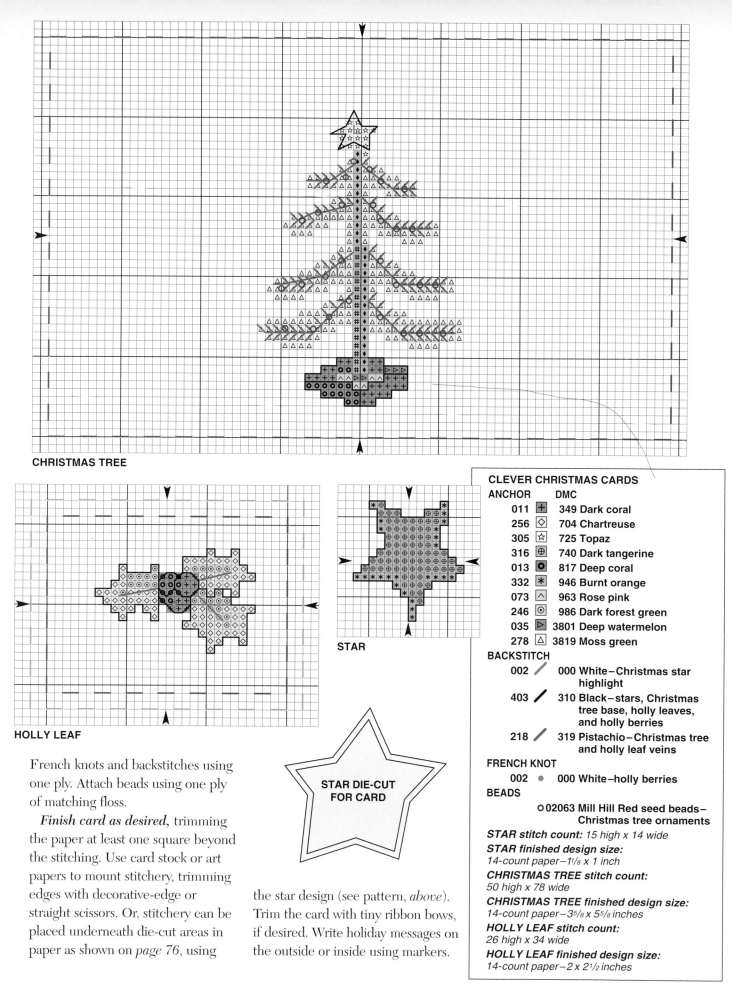

CHRISTMAS TREE

HOLLY LEAF

STAR

STAR DIE-CUT FOR CARD

French knots and backstitches using one ply. Attach beads using one ply of matching floss.

Finish card as desired, trimming the paper at least one square beyond the stitching. Use card stock or art papers to mount stitchery, trimming edges with decorative-edge or straight scissors. Or, stitchery can be placed underneath die-cut areas in paper as shown on *page 76*, using

the star design (see pattern, *above*). Trim the card with tiny ribbon bows, if desired. Write holiday messages on the outside or inside using markers.

Peace

Designed to bring beauty and grace to your home at Christmastime, our **Peace Sampler** combines the charm of Mary Engelbreit with the elegance of fine needlework, creating a memorable holiday framed piece. The message and motif are stitched on 28–count blue linen and embellished with glistening seed beads. Turn the page for more heavenly angel projects to make in time for Christmas. Instructions and charts for all projects begin on *page 90*.

What a beautiful way to send the message of

peace—proudly displayed upon the mantel. Our

Peace Christmas Stocking is designed with the stitching on the cuff and beautiful golden

beads quilting the body of the stocking. Display your **Happy Angel Ornaments**, stitched on

16-count Aida cloth, on the tree or make them the focal point for a centerpiece filled with

holiday greens and colorful glass balls.

Our **Heavenly Angel Tree Topper** is the crowning glory to an already lovely tree.

Stitched with half cross-stitches using wool yarn, the piece offers an elegant display of stitching

possibilities. The piece is finished by surrounding it with folded gold ribbons.

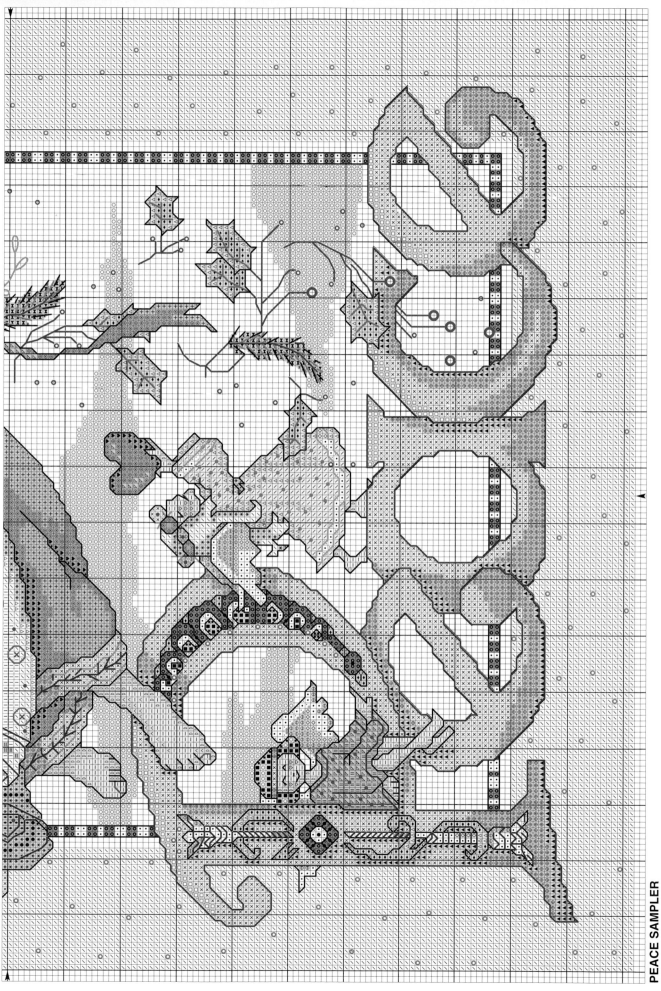

PEACE SAMPLER

Peace Sampler

As shown on page 86, sampler measures 16×12⅛ inches.

MATERIALS

FABRIC
24×20-inch piece of 28-count Nordic blue linen

FLOSS
Cotton embroidery floss in colors listed in key, below

SUPPLIES
Needle; embroidery hoop
Beads as listed in key
Desired mats and frame

INSTRUCTIONS

Tape or zigzag edges of the linen fabric to prevent fraying. Find the center of the chart, *pages 90–91,* and the center of the fabric; begin stitching there. Use three plies of embroidery floss to work the cross-stitches over two threads of the linen fabric. Work the lazy daisy stitches, French knots, and straight stitches using two plies of embroidery floss. Work the satin stitches and backstitches using one ply of floss, unless otherwise noted in the key. Attach beads using two plies of matching floss.

Press the finished stitchery from the back. Mat and frame as desired.

Peace Christmas Stocking

As shown on page 88, finished stocking measures 17½ inches long.

MATERIALS

FABRICS
12×24-inch piece of 25-count Victorian green Lugana fabric
¾ yard of 45-inch-wide red velveteen
¾ yard of 45-inch-wide green satin fabric
½ yard of 45-inch-wide fleece

PEACE SAMPLER

ANCHOR	DMC	Color
002	000	White
403	310	Black
9046	321	Christmas red
358	433	Dark chestnut
253	472	Avocado
281	580	Dark moss green
280	581	True moss green
923	699	Dark Christmas green
227	701	True Christmas green
256	704	Chartreuse
326	720	Bittersweet
361	738	Tan
314	741	Tangerine
302	743	Yellow
275	746	Off white
1022	760	True salmon
259	772	Loden
024	776	Medium pink
307	783	Christmas gold
271	819	Light pink
907	832	Bronze
1011	948	Peach
298	972	Canary
888	3045	Yellow beige
292	3078	Lemon
1024	3328	Dark salmon
1023	3712	Medium salmon
1020	3713	Pale salmon
1027	3722	Shell pink
1031	3753	Antique blue
928	3761	Sky blue
167	3766	Peacock blue
1050	3781	Mocha
1019	3802	Antique mauve
874	3822	Light straw
1048	3826	Golden brown

BLENDED NEEDLE

306	3820	Dark straw (2X) and
890	729	Medium old gold (1X)

BACKSTITCH

002	000	White – "Peace"
9046	321	Christmas red – lettering (4X); dress trim (3X); "P" detail, gown trim, shawl trim (2X)
310	434	Medium chestnut – holly stems, pine branches (3X); eyebrows (2X); eye detail (1X)
280	581	True moss green – shawl trim (2X)
923	699	Dark Christmas green – holly (2X)
227	701	True Christmas green – vine (3X)
256	704	Chartreuse – vine (3X); dress (2X)
1022	760	True salmon – toenail (2X)
1031	3753	Antique blue – pine branch detail
403	310	Black – all remaining backstitches

STRAIGHT STITCH

169	3760	Wedgwood blue – eye corners

LAZY DAISY

256	704	Chartreuse – small leaves

FRENCH KNOT

403	310	Black – letter "P" and pupils
9046	321	Christmas red – shawl and dress, sitting angel's dress, angel's wreath
227	701	True Christmas green – dress
298	972	Canary – angel's wreath

SATIN STITCH

9046	321	Christmas red – mouth
169	3760	Wedgwood blue – eye iris

BEADS

02059	Mill Hill Yellow glass seed beads
02063	Mill Hill Red glass seed beads
03049	Mill Hill Red antique glass beads
05025	Mill Hill Ruby pebble beads
62014	Mill Hill Black frosted beads
62044	Mill Hill Autumn frosted beads
72052	Mill Hill Red velvet small bugle beads

Stitch count: 224 high x 170 wide

Finished design sizes:
28-count fabric – 16 x 12⅛ inches
36-count fabric – 12½ x 9½ inches
22-count fabric – 20⅜ x 15½ inches

THREADS

Cotton embroidery floss in colors listed
   in key, right

Metallic red ribbon floss

Metallic gold machine-quilting thread

SUPPLIES

Needle

Embroidery hoop

Seed beads in color listed in key

3 yards of red sew-in piping

Approximately 100 metallic gold
   6-mm beads

6-inch-piece of gold cord for hanging

¾ yard of 1½-inch-wide metallic gold
   flat lace

INSTRUCTIONS

Tape or zigzag the edges of the
Lugana fabric. Find the center of
chart, *below,* and of Lugana fabric;
begin stitching there. Use three plies
of floss to work cross-stitches over
two threads of fabric. Work the

PEACE CHRISTMAS STOCKING

ANCHOR		DMC	
002	·	000	White
403	■	310	Black
9046	◉	321	Christmas red
227	◆	701	True Christmas green
256	△	704	Chartreuse
326	▲	720	Bittersweet
314	⊕	741	Tangerine
302	▢	743	Yellow
1022	◺	760	True salmon
259	＼	772	Loden
1011	—	948	Peach
298	✕	972	Canary
1024	‖	3328	Dark salmon
928	◇	3761	Sky blue
167	⊖	3766	Peacock blue
1019	♥	3802	Antique mauve

BLENDED NEEDLE

| 306 | ✳ | 3820 | Dark straw (2X) and |
| 890 | | 729 | Medium old gold (1X) |

BACKSTITCH

| 403 | ╱ | 310 | Black – angels, holly leaves, and letter "P" |
| 310 | ╱ | 434 | Medium chestnut– holly leaf stems |

ANCHOR		DMC	
BACKSTITCH			
256	╱	704	Chartreuse– angel in green dress
314	╱	741	Tangerine– angel in red dress
298	╱	972	Canary–angel in red dress
9046	╱	321	Christmas red– all remaining stitches
STRAIGHT STITCH			
923	╱	699	Dark Christmas green– holly leaves (2X)
FRENCH KNOT			
403	●	310	Black–letter "P" (4X)
9046	●	321	Christmas red–halo (2X)
227	●	701	True Christmas green– angel in green dress (2X)
298	●	972	Canary–halo (2X)
BEADS			
	○	02013	Mill Hill Red red seed beads

Stitch count: 63 high x 110 wide
Finished design sizes:
25-count fabric – 5 x 8⅞ inches
28-count fabric – 4½ x 7⅞ inches
36-count fabric – 3½ x 6⅛ inches

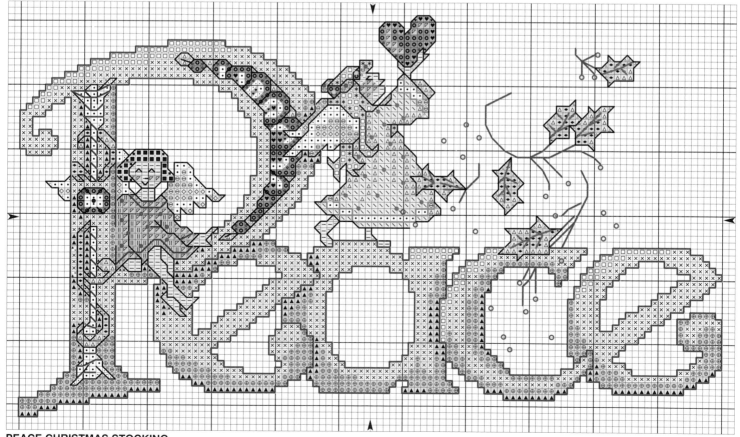

PEACE CHRISTMAS STOCKING

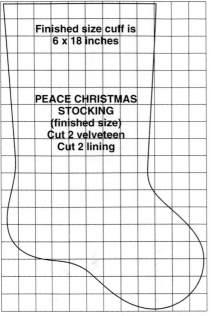

Finished size cuff is 6 x 18 inches

PEACE CHRISTMAS STOCKING (finished size) Cut 2 velveteen Cut 2 lining

1 Square = 1 Inch

blended needle stitches, straight stitches, and French knots as noted in key. Work backstitches using two plies. Attach beads using two plies of matching floss.

Enlarge and trace the stocking pattern, *above,* onto tracing paper; cut out. Use the pattern to cut two shapes each from the velveteen, satin, and fleece. Cut one from interfacing.

To machine-quilt the stocking front, line velveteen with a piece of fleece. Mark a 1-inch grid on the bias. Machine-zigzag with metallic gold thread couched over one strand of metallic red ribbon floss on grid lines. Sew a gold bead to each quilted intersection. Stitch the interfacing to the wrong side of the stocking back.

With the stitchery centered, trim the Lugana fabric to measure 7×19 inches. Cut one 7×19-inch piece from fleece and one from satin lining fabric.

Stitch piping along sides and bottom edge of stocking front, clipping as necessary. Stitch stocking front to back with right sides facing, using a ½-inch seam allowance. Trim and clip the seam. Turn right side out.

Line cuff with fleece and baste on seam line. Stitch center back seam. Stitch piping around bottom edge of cuff. Trim all fleece from seam allowance. Sew seam in center back of the cuff lining.

Stitch lining to cuff around bottom edge, with right sides facing and matching back seams. Stitch lining to cuff around bottom edge. Trim and clip the seam allowance. Turn right side out. Press and baste the raw edges together.

Center the cuff design on the front of the stocking and stitch around the top edge. Stitch the piping around the top edge.

Tack the ends of the hanging loop to the upper left corner of the stocking cuff.

Stitch the lining pieces together, leaving top open and an opening for turning. Slip the stocking into lining, matching seams. Stitch around top edge. Trim and clip seam allowance. Pull stocking through lining opening. Slip-stitch the opening closed.

Press lining to inside. Hand-stitch gold lace around bottom edge of cuff.

Happy Angel Ornaments

As shown on page 88, finished ornaments measure 6½×6½ inches and 7×6¼ inches.

MATERIALS
For both ornaments
FABRICS
Two 8×7-inch pieces of 16-count cherub pink Aida cloth
Two 6×5-inch pieces of white felt
FLOSS
Cotton embroidery floss in colors listed in keys on page 95

SUPPLIES
Needle
Embroidery hoop
Seed beads in colors listed in key
Two 6×5-inch pieces of matboard
Two 6×5-inch pieces of extra-loft fleece
Fusible interfacing
Crafts glue
½ yard of ½-inch-wide flat gold braid
1 yard of 1½-inch-wide red satin ribbon
1 yard of 1½-inch-wide green satin ribbon
Two 10-inch pieces of gold cord

INSTRUCTIONS
Tape or zigzag the edges of the Aida cloth pieces. Find the center of one angel chart, *page 95,* and of one piece of Aida cloth; begin stitching there. Use two plies of floss to work cross-stitches. Work the backstitches using one ply. Attach beads using two plies of matching floss. Repeat for remaining angel design.

Enlarge and trace the oval and circular patterns, *page 95,* onto tracing paper; cut out. Use patterns to cut one shape each from matboard, fleece, and felt. Set felt pieces aside. Cover matboard shapes with fleece using fusible interfacing, following the manufacturer's directions.

Center and trace oval pattern on the back of the stitched piece; cut out ½ inch beyond marking. Center and glue stitched piece to fleece-covered matboard. Clip edges of Aida cloth and glue to back side of matboard.

Glue braid around outside edge of each ornament. Gather one edge on each piece of satin ribbon. Glue ribbons to outside edges of ornaments, adjusting the gathers as needed.

Make a hanging loop from each piece of gold cord. Glue the ends of the cord to the top of each ornament. Glue the felt pieces to the backs of each ornament.

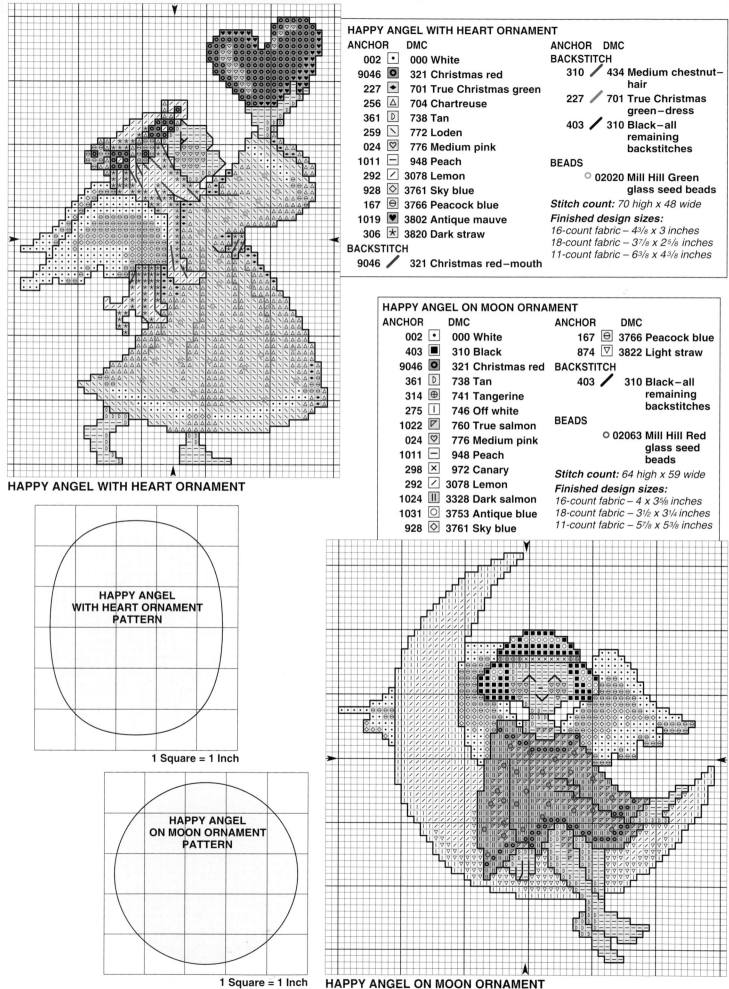

HAPPY ANGEL WITH HEART ORNAMENT

ANCHOR		DMC	
002	·	000	White
9046	◉	321	Christmas red
227	◆	701	True Christmas green
256	△	704	Chartreuse
361	D	738	Tan
259	＼	772	Loden
024	♡	776	Medium pink
1011	—	948	Peach
292	╱	3078	Lemon
928	◇	3761	Sky blue
167	⊖	3766	Peacock blue
1019	♥	3802	Antique mauve
306	✶	3820	Dark straw

BACKSTITCH

9046	╱	321 Christmas red—mouth

ANCHOR	DMC
BACKSTITCH	
310 ╱	434 Medium chestnut—hair
227 ╱	701 True Christmas green—dress
403 ╱	310 Black—all remaining backstitches

BEADS

◎ 02020 Mill Hill Green glass seed beads

Stitch count: 70 high x 48 wide

Finished design sizes:
16-count fabric – 4⅜ x 3 inches
18-count fabric – 3⅞ x 2⅝ inches
11-count fabric – 6⅜ x 4⅜ inches

HAPPY ANGEL WITH HEART ORNAMENT

**HAPPY ANGEL
WITH HEART ORNAMENT
PATTERN**

1 Square = 1 Inch

**HAPPY ANGEL
ON MOON ORNAMENT
PATTERN**

1 Square = 1 Inch

HAPPY ANGEL ON MOON ORNAMENT

ANCHOR		DMC	
002	·	000	White
403	■	310	Black
9046	◉	321	Christmas red
361	D	738	Tan
314	⊕	741	Tangerine
275	I	746	Off white
1022	▽	760	True salmon
024	♡	776	Medium pink
1011	—	948	Peach
298	×	972	Canary
292	╱	3078	Lemon
1024	‖	3328	Dark salmon
1031	○	3753	Antique blue
928	◇	3761	Sky blue

ANCHOR		DMC	
167	⊖	3766	Peacock blue
874	▽	3822	Light straw

BACKSTITCH

403	╱	310 Black—all remaining backstitches

BEADS

◎ 02063 Mill Hill Red glass seed beads

Stitch count: 64 high x 59 wide

Finished design sizes:
16-count fabric – 4 x 3⅝ inches
18-count fabric – 3½ x 3¼ inches
11-count fabric – 5⅞ x 5⅜ inches

HAPPY ANGEL ON MOON ORNAMENT

Heavenly Angel Tree Topper

As shown on page 89, finished tree topper measures 11¼×14½ inches.

MATERIALS

FABRICS

14×17-inch piece of 14-count light blue Aida cloth

Two 10×13-inch pieces of ivory felt

THREAD

Patternayan wool in colors listed in key on page 97

SUPPLIES

Needle; embroidery hoop

Seed beads in colors listed in key

10×13-inch piece of matboard

Two 10×13-inch pieces of extra-loft fleece

Two 10×13-inch pieces of fusible interfacing; crafts glue

1 yard of ½-inch-wide flat metallic gold-and-red braid

3 yards of 2½-inch-wide metallic gold ribbon; ivory thread

1 yard of ⅜-inch-wide red satin ribbon

7 metallic green sew-on holly leaf gems; 6 red pebble beads

1¾-inch-wide gold French horn charm

INSTRUCTIONS

Tape or zigzag edges of Aida cloth to prevent fraying. Find center of chart, *right and page 97*, and of Aida cloth; begin stitching there. Use one ply of wool to work half cross-stitches. Work backstitches, French knots, and straight stitches using three plies of floss. Attach beads using matching floss.

Enlarge and trace the oval pattern, *page 97*, onto tracing paper; cut out. Use oval pattern to cut one shape from matboard, two from fleece, and two from felt. Set felt pieces aside. Cover matboard shape with two layers of fleece using fusible interfacing and following manufacturer's directions.

Center and trace oval pattern on back of stitchery. Cut out ¾ inch beyond marking; center and glue stitchery to matboard. Clip edges of Aida cloth and glue to back of matboard. Glue braid around outside edge.

To make prairie points, cut about thirty-six 2½-inch squares from gold ribbon. Using diagrams, *below,* fold ribbons in half diagonally, then in half again. Stitch points together in a chain, tucking each point halfway inside the next. Glue the length of prairie points around the outside edge behind braid.

Stitch the felt pieces together using a ¼-inch seam allowance; leave 6 inches open at center of one long side of oval. Glue felt to back of matboard.

Use photo, *page 89*, as a guide to tack red ribbon atop stitchery and through charm. Glue charm to fabric. Sew on holly leaves and bead berries. Tie gold ribbon into a bow; tack at top of topper.

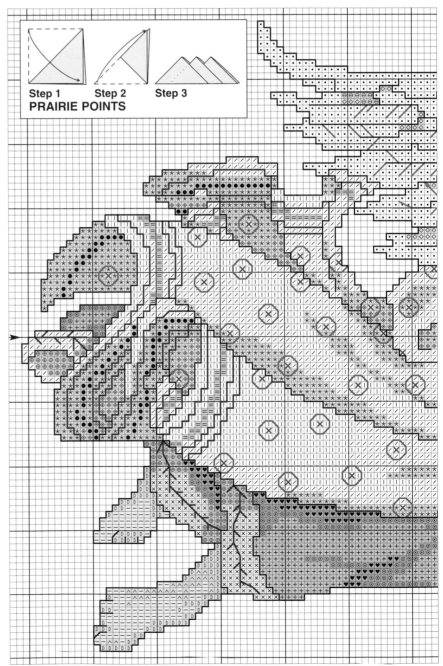

Step 1 Step 2 Step 3
PRAIRIE POINTS

HEAVENLY ANGEL TREE TOPPER

HEAVENLY ANGEL TREE TOPPER

ANCHOR	DMC		PATTERNAYAN	
002	000	•	260	White
275	746	I	263	Off white
358	433	⊠	401	Dark chestnut
1050	3781	▼	423	Mocha
928	3761	◇	555	Sky blue
167	3766	⊖	584	Peacock blue
281	580	●	612	Dark moss green
280	581	=	653	True moss green
253	472	◿	694	Avocado
227	701	◆	697	True Christmas green
307	783	⊗	700	Christmas gold
306	3820	✳	702	Dark straw
292	3078	◺	714	Lemon
888	3045	∩	742	Yellow beige
314	741	⊕	812	Tangerine
298	972	✕	814	Canary
1048	3826	#	872	Golden brown
361	738	◨	875	Tan

ANCHOR	DMC		PATTERNAYAN	
1019	3802	♥	910	Antique mauve
1020	3713	∧	915	Pale salmon
1027	3722	⊙	932	Shell pink
1023	3712	+	933	Medium salmon
024	776	♡	946	Medium pink
1011	948	−	947	Peach

ANCHOR	DMC			
BACKSTITCH				
9046	321	/	Christmas red−shawl stripes and gown detail	
310	434	/	Medium chestnut−face detail	
281	580	/	Dark moss green−shawl	
923	699	/	Dark Christmas green−holly	
928	3761	/	Sky blue−wing detail and eye highlights	
403	310	/	Black−all remaining backstitches	

ANCHOR	DMC			
STRAIGHT STITCH				
9046		/	321	Christmas red−mouth
FRENCH KNOT				
928		●	3761	Sky blue− eyes
BEADS				
		○	02013	Mill Hill Red red seed beads
		✕	02063	Mill Hill Red glass seed beads

Stitch count: 98 high x 153 wide
Finished design sizes:
14-count fabric − 7 x 11 inches
18-count fabric − 5½ x 8½ inches
11-count fabric − 9 x 14 inches

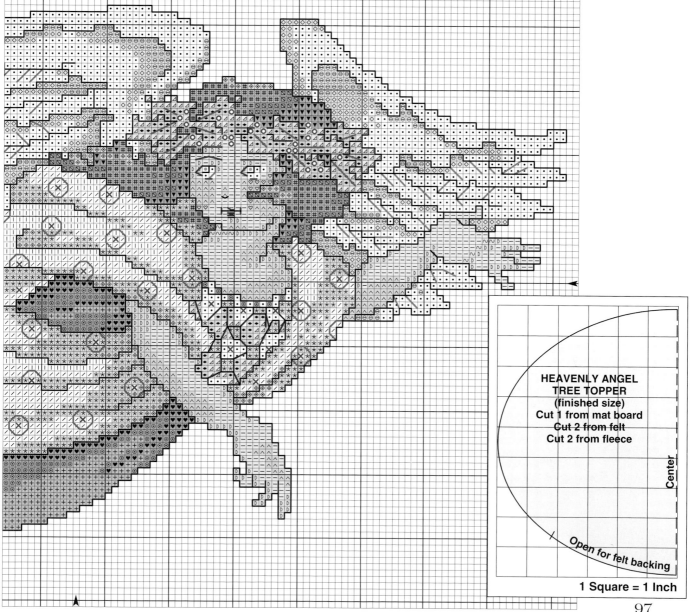

HEAVENLY ANGEL
TREE TOPPER
(finished size)
Cut 1 from mat board
Cut 2 from felt
Cut 2 from fleece

Center

Open for felt backing

1 Square = 1 Inch

"Breit" Ideas
for Winter

Believe

Using the instructions for the place mat, lengthen the area between the ends to make a festive table runner to grace the center of your holiday table or buffet.

Share your needlework talents! Stitch the Sweet St. Nick Pin design and use it to create a one-of-a-kind Christmas card. Simply mount it behind a cut out circle on a blank note card.

Stitch the sentiment, "Believe," as a striking message to adorn your holiday home. (Used to create a stocking cuff, it would surely make Santa put in an extra goody or two!)

Any one of our whimsical ornament designs could be stitched on perforated plastic to make package trims for friends.

Let It Snow

Stitch one of these friendly fellows on 7-count Klostern fabric, sew on a backing fabric, and stuff with fiberfill to make a huggable pal for a special child on your holiday gift list.

To make a spectacular garland for your Christmas tree, stitch several of the stars from the card design on perforated plastic. String them together using floss, with colorful beads between the stitched pieces.

If you prefer not to sew your winter accessories, keep an eye out for mittens, hats, and scarves in solid-colored felt, fleece, or wool that match your cold-weather jacket. Most of these can be easily embellished with cross-stitches using waste canvas.

Add a whimsical touch to your kitchen this holiday season by stitching these fun snowmen motifs on towels, pot holders, and table linens!

Peace

For an extra-special greeting card, stitch one of the small angels on perforated plastic and attach it to a blank note card. The recipient can remove the lovingly stitched angel and use it as an ornament—making it a Christmas card and gift all in one!

Stitch the stocking cuff design on a smaller-count fabric and finish as a glorious accent pillow.

Imagine the large heavenly angel adorning a tree skirt. Finish the edge with prairie points as we did on the tree topper. This lovely Christmas tree skirt would add an elegant touch beneath your holiday evergreen.

Create a festive wearable using a small-count piece of waste canvas to stitch "Peace" or one of the small angels on a pocket, shirt, or fine-knit sweater.

Spring

We all wait for spring–and it never disappoints us! All things are bright and beautiful, and everything seems new again. Butterflies, flowers, gardens, birds, warm sunshine, and events of joy–you'll find them all in this chapter filled with the wonders of spring.

Welcome Spring Stitching!

Felicitations

Welcome a precious baby into the world with these ever-so-sweet nursery rhyme designs from Mary Engelbreit. The charming characters in our **Felicitations Sampler** come to life stitched over two threads of blueberry Annabelle fabric. Destined to be treasured for a lifetime, this personalized keepsake includes several specialty stitches for added detail. Our collection of memory-making projects continues on the next page. Instructions and charts for all projects begin on *page 105*.

Standing proud, our **Mother Goose Doorstop** will merrily hold the nursery room door ajar. Stitched on Jobelan fabric, the cheerful design is trimmed with crisp checked piping and a striped ruffle.

To keep the little bundle of joy snug, stitch this dear **Storybook Afghan** on soft Davosa fabric. Create **Cow-Jumped-Over-The-Moon Tiebacks** for a fun accent. The set is stitched on perforated plastic and finished with colorful covered wire and suede.

103

Here's a clever way to turn your stitchery into bright accents for a child's furniture. To create this fun **Storybook Table Set**, simply paint an unfinished table and chairs in the vibrant colors shown or select colors to match your nursery decor. Then make color copies of the pieces you have stitched from this chapter, clip out the motifs you like, and decoupage them onto the tabletop and chair seats—or on a dresser or toy box!

Felicitations Sampler

As shown on page 101, finished sampler measures 16½×10 inches.

MATERIALS

FABRIC

24×18-inch piece of 28-count blueberry Annabelle fabric

FLOSS

Cotton embroidery floss in colors listed in key on page 108

SUPPLIES

Needle; embroidery hoop; graph paper
Petite beads in color listed in key
Desired mat and frame

INSTRUCTIONS

Chart name and date on graph paper using chart, *below*. Tape or zigzag edges of fabric. Find center of chart, *pages 106–107*, and of fabric; begin stitching there. Use two plies of floss to work cross-stitches over two threads of fabric. Work blended needle stitches, blended backstitches, straight stitches, couching, lazy daisy stitches, and backstitches as specified in key. Use one ply to work satin stitches and French knots, and to attach beads.

Press stitchery; frame as desired.

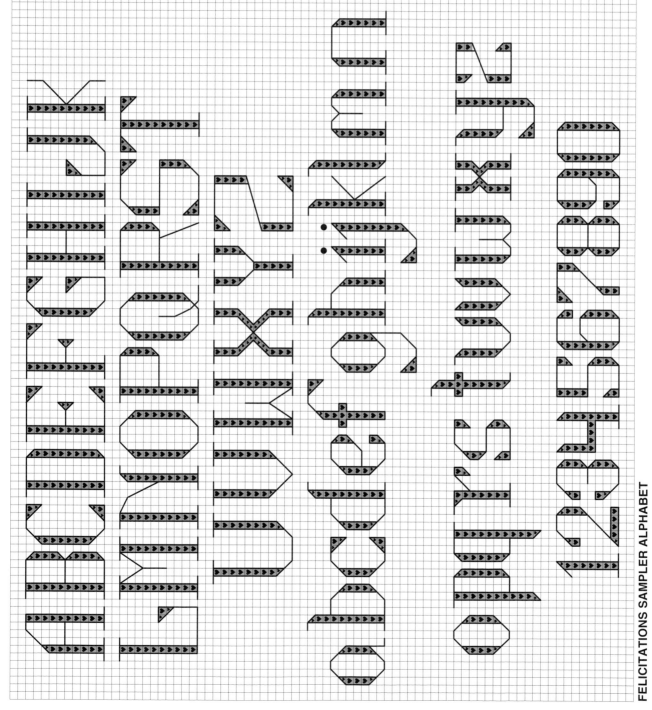

FELICITATIONS SAMPLER

ANCHOR	DMC	
387		Ecru
002	000	White
352	300	Deep mahogany
1049	301	Medium mahogany
403	310	Black
215	319	Dark pistachio
038	335	Medium rose
013	349	Dark coral
1014	355	Dark terra-cotta
398	415	Light pearl gray
310	434	Chestnut
1045	436	Dark tan
232	452	Shell gray
858	524	Olive drab
361	738	Light tan
303	742	Tangerine
275	746	Off white
882	758	Light terra-cotta
1022	760	True salmon
234	762	Pale pearl gray
128	775	Baby blue
176	793	Medium cornflower blue
175	794	Light cornflower blue
162	825	Dark bright blue
161	826	Medium bright blue
380	838	Deep beige brown
379	840	Medium beige brown
388	842	Light beige brown
944	869	Dark hazel
218	890	Deep pistachio
052	899	Light rose
333	900	Dark burnt orange
850	926	Medium gray blue
332	946	Medium burnt orange
314	970	Pumpkin
298	972	Canary
1001	976	Golden brown
846	3011	Khaki
905	3021	Brown gray
886	3047	Yellow beige
292	3078	Lemon
266	3347	Yellow green
059	3350	Dusty rose
382	3371	Black brown
1023	3712	Medium salmon
869	3743	Pale antique violet
1036	3750	Deep antique blue
035	3801	Watermelon
305	3821	Straw
386	3823	Yellow

BLENDED NEEDLE

ANCHOR	DMC	
400	317	Pewter (1X) and
176	793	Medium cornflower blue (1X)
013	349	Dark coral (1X) and
1014	355	Dark terra-cotta (1X)
008	353	Peach (1X) and
1020	3713	Pale salmon (1X)
1014	355	Dark terra-cotta (1X) and
380	838	Deep beige brown (1X)
310	434	Chestnut (1X) and
1045	436	Dark tan (1X)
1045	436	Dark tan (1X) and
378	841	True beige brown
683	500	Deep blue green (1X) and
877	3815	Celadon green (1X)
936	632	Deep cocoa (1X) and
380	838	Deep beige brown (1X)
936	632	Deep cocoa (1X) and
360	839	Dark beige brown (1X)
256	704	Chartreuse (1X) and
266	3347	Yellow green (1X)
890	729	Old gold (1X) and
373	3828	True hazel (1X)
945	834	Bronze (1X) and
886	3047	Yellow beige (1X)
379	840	Medium beige brown (1X) and
1007	3772	Dark cocoa (1X)
378	841	True beige brown (1X) and
1008	3773	Rose beige (1X)
204	913	Nile green (1X) and
877	3815	Celadon green (1X)
851	924	Deep gray blue (1X) and
779	3768	Dark gray blue (1X)
862	934	Deep pine green (1X) and
269	936	Medium pine green (1X)
261	3053	Gray green (1X) and
260	3364	Loden (1X)

BACKSTITCH

ANCHOR	DMC	
400	317	Pewter – detail on spoon (1X)
1014	355	Dark terra-cotta – cat's vest (1X)
310	434	Chestnut – goose's bonnet (1X)
011	817	Deep coral – border curls (1X)
162	825	Dark bright blue – house windows (1X)
380	838	Deep beige brown – goose's bonnet (1X)
052	899	Light rose – stripes on dish's dress (1X)
269	936	Medium pine green – stripes on cat's clothing (1X)
266	3347	Yellow green – house windows (1X)
059	3350	Dusty rose – dish's bow (1X)
403	310	Black – all remaining backstitches (1X)

BLENDED BACKSTITCH

ANCHOR	DMC	
403	310	Black (1X) and
1014	355	Dark terra-cotta (2X) – spoon's mouth

STRAIGHT STITCH

ANCHOR	DMC	
002	000	White – highlights on flowers and highlight on "felicitations" ribbon (2X)
013	349	Dark coral – dish's mouth (2X)
1014	355	Dark terra-cotta – cat's buttons (2X)
878	501	Dark blue green – grass blades (2X)
875	502	Medium blue green – grass blades (2X)
161	826	Medium bright blue – stripes on goose's bonnet (1X)
388	842	Light beige brown – dish's face (2X)
1023	3712	Medium salmon – cow's ears (2X)

SATIN STITCH

ANCHOR	DMC	
403	310	Black – glasses and nose of mice
379	840	Medium beige brown – eyebrows on cat
059	3350	Dusty rose – "felicitations" banner

COUCHING

ANCHOR	DMC	
002	000	White (2X) and
013	349	Dark coral (1X) – wand in cow's mouth
403	310	Black – violin strings (1X) and bow (2X)

LAZY DAISY

ANCHOR	DMC	
403	310	Black – spoon's mustache (1X)
400	317	Pewter – design on spoon handle (2X)
256	704	Chartreuse – flowers by gate (2X)

FRENCH KNOT

ANCHOR	DMC	
002	000	White – flowers, cow's nose, moon's eyes, goose's eye, cat's eyes and buttons, spoon's eyes and chin, and "felicitations" ribbon
403	310	Black – violin, cow's eyes, cat's mouth, goose's mouth, mice noses and belly buttons, and personalization
013	349	Dark coral – spoon's hatband
298	972	Canary – spoon's coat
059	3350	Dusty rose – exclamation points in "felicitations" banner

BEADS

O 40479 Mill Hill White petite glass beads – stars

Stitch count: 230 high x 139 wide
Finished design sizes:
28-count fabric – 16½ x 10 inches
22-count fabric – 21 x 12⅝ inches
36-count fabric – 12¾ x 7¾ inches

Mother Goose Doorstop

As shown on page 102, finished doorstop measures 16×10×6 inches.

MATERIALS

FABRICS
21×18-inch piece of 20-count white Jobelan fabric

½ yard of 45-inch-wide green-and-white-checked fabric

¼ yard of 45-inch-wide pink-and-white-striped fabric

FLOSS
Cotton embroidery floss in colors listed in key, below

SUPPLIES
Needle; embroidery hoop

Erasable fabric marker

½ yard of fleece; white sewing thread

2 yards of narrow piping cord

½ yard of fusible interfacing

7×11-inch piece of matboard

7×11-inch piece of paper-backed iron-on adhesive

Polyester fiberfill

Balloon filled with sand, or other sand weight

½ yard of ½-inch-wide country blue satin ribbon

Gold heart charm

INSTRUCTIONS

Tape or zigzag the edges of the Jobelan fabric to prevent fraying. Find the center of the chart, *page 110*, and the center of the Jobelan fabric; begin stitching there. Use three plies of floss to work cross-stitches over two threads of fabric. Work blended needle stitches as indicated in key, *below.* Use two plies to work straight stitches, French knots, and backstitches.

Use erasable marker to draw a simplified curved shape ½ inch beyond the stitched design as shown in photograph, *page 102.* Baste fleece to back of stitchery, sewing along outline. Cut out ½ inch beyond basting. Using stitched front piece as pattern, cut doorstop back from green-and-white-checked fabric.

Cut enough 1½-inch-wide bias strips of checked fabric to total 75 inches in length. Sew short ends together to make one long strip. Center piping cord lengthwise on wrong side of fabric strip. Fold fabric around cording, bringing raw edges together. Use a zipper foot to sew through both layers of fabric close to cording. Matching raw edges, sew piping around sides and top of stitchery along basting line.

For ruffle, cut two 2½×44-inch strips of pink-and-white-striped fabric. Sew two short ends together. Press strip in half lengthwise with wrong sides facing. Sewing through both layers, run a gathering stitch ½ inch from raw edges. Pin ruffle around stitchery on top of piping, matching raw edges and adjusting gathers evenly.

Sew doorstop front to back, leaving bottom open. Trim seam to ¼ inch and clip curves. Turn right side out. Sew the remaining piping around the bottom edge.

Enlarge and trace oval bottom pattern, *page 110,* onto tracing paper; cut out. Cut oval from matboard. Following manufacturer's directions, fuse iron-on adhesive to back of 7×11-inch piece of green-and-white-checked fabric. Lay matboard on back of fabric and draw oval 1 inch beyond matboard edges. Cut out fabric oval, remove backing, and fuse to matboard. Fuse or glue edges to back side, clipping fabric as necessary.

Stuff doorstop firmly with fiberfill, adding sand weight near bottom. Whipstitch bottom piece to piping around opening edges.

Tie ribbon into a bow and tack to neck. Tack heart securely to bow.

MOTHER GOOSE DOORSTOP

ANCHOR		DMC	
002	•	000	White
403	■	310	Black
038	⊕	335	Medium rose
013	♥	349	Dark coral
008	▽	353	Peach
398	∼	415	Light pearl gray
1045	▣	436	Dark tan
232	≡	452	Shell gray
361	○	738	Light tan
303	+	742	Tangerine
1022	♡	760	True salmon
234	▯	762	Pale pearl gray
128	／	775	Baby blue
176	△	793	Medium cornflower blue
175	‖	794	Light cornflower blue
052	◇	899	Light rose
333	⋈	900	Dark burnt orange

ANCHOR		DMC	
204	◿	913	Nile green
332	⊛	946	Medium burnt orange
314	▷	970	Light pumpkin
298	☆	972	Canary
266	✤	3347	Yellow green
1023	⊙	3712	Medium salmon
877	◎	3815	Celadon green
386	◣	3823	Yellow

BLENDED NEEDLE

400	▮	317	Pewter (1X) and
176		793	Medium cornflower blue (2X)
008	⌐	353	Peach (1X) and
1020		3713	Pale salmon (2X)
945	⌂	834	Bronze (1X) and
886		3047	Yellow beige (2X)
378	△	841	True beige brown (1X) and
1045		436	Dark tan (2X)

ANCHOR		DMC	
BACKSTITCH			
403	／	310	Black – all backstitches
STRAIGHT STITCH			
002	／	000	White – highlights on flowers, goose's face
310	／	434	Chestnut – goose's bonnet
176	／	793	Medium cornflower blue – goose's bonnet
FRENCH KNOT			
002	○	000	White – flower highlights
298	●	972	Canary – stars
ATTACHMENT			
	✕		Blue satin ribbon bow and heart charm

Stitch count: 150 high x 118 wide

Finished design sizes:
20-count fabric – 15 x 11⅞ inches
28-count fabric – 10¾ x 8½ inches
36-count fabric – 8⅜ x 6½ inches

MOTHER GOOSE DOORSTOP

MOTHER GOOSE
DOORSTOP BOTTOM

1 Square = 1 Inch

Cow-Jumped-Over-The-Moon Tiebacks

As shown on page 103, each finished tieback measures 6×7 inches.

MATERIALS *for two sets*

FABRICS

Two 6×6-inch pieces of 14-count black perforated plastic

Two 5×5-inch pieces of 14-count black perforated plastic

6×12-inch piece of pink felted imitation-suede fabric

4×8-inch piece of white felted imitation-suede fabric

FLOSS

Cotton embroidery floss in colors listed in key, below right

SUPPLIES

Needle

Fabric glue

30 inches of pink plastic-coated fine copper wire

30 inches of purple plastic-coated fine copper wire

Pencil

Pink and white sewing threads

Sewing needle

3 yards of 1½-inch-wide wire-edged ribbon in desired color

INSTRUCTIONS

Find the center of one moon chart, *below,* and the center of one 6-inch piece of perforated plastic; begin stitching there. Use four plies of floss to work cross-stitches over two squares. Work the French knots and backstitches using two plies of floss. Repeat for the other moon chart.

Find the center of one cow chart, *below,* and the center of one 5-inch piece of perforated plastic; begin stitching there. Repeat for the other cow chart.

Trim each plastic piece one square beyond stitching. Glue moons to pink suede fabric and cows to white suede fabric. Cut out around pieces, allowing ⅛ inch of fabric to show beyond plastic.

Cut each wire into two 15-inch-long pieces. For each tieback, coil one pink and one purple wire around the pencil. Holding the wire ends together, whipstitch one end of wires to back of moon and the remaining wire to the back of cow.

Arrange ribbon around curtain or drape and tie loosely. Tack moon to ribbon and arrange pieces as shown in photograph, *page 103.*

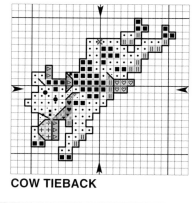

COW TIEBACK

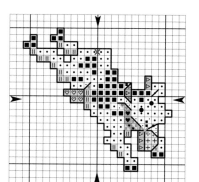

COW TIEBACK

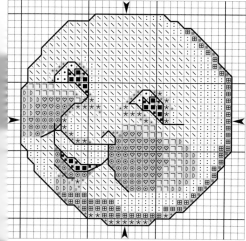

MOON TIEBACK

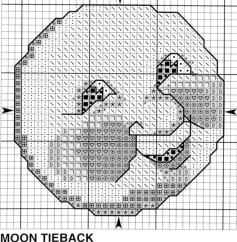

MOON TIEBACK

COW-JUMPED-OVER-THE-MOON TIEBACKS		
ANCHOR		DMC
002	•	000 White
403	■	310 Black
013	♥	349 Dark coral
303	+	742 Tangerine
882	D	758 Light terra-cotta
1022	♡	760 True salmon
175	‖	794 Light cornflower blue
388	✶	842 Light beige brown
314	▷	970 Light pumpkin
292	:	3078 Lemon
1023	⊙	3712 Medium salmon
1020	⬑	3713 Pale salmon
305	⊞	3821 Straw
386	◰	3823 Yellow
BACKSTITCH		
403	/	310 Black – all backstitches
FRENCH KNOT		
002	●	000 White – moon's eyes
403	●	310 Black – cow's eyes
ATTACHMENTS		
002	✕	000 White – tail
	✕	Bell – cow bell

MOON stitch count: 31 high x 31 wide
MOON finished design sizes:
14-count plastic – 4½ x 4½ inches
COW stitch count: 21 high x 22 wide
COW finished design sizes:
14-count plastic – 3 x 3⅛ inches

Storybook Afghan

As shown on page 103, finished afghan measures 36×40½ inches.

MATERIALS

FABRIC

40×44-inch piece of 18-count white Davosa fabric

THREAD

Flower thread in colors listed in key on page 113

SUPPLIES

Needle; embroidery hoop; white thread

Three 5-yard packages of 7-mm-wide yellow silk embroidery ribbon

INSTRUCTIONS

Tape or zigzag edges of fabric. Baste a 19¼×13¼-inch rectangle in the center of the fabric, continuing the basting lines to the edges of the fabric.

Find center of chart, *page 115,* and of fabric; begin stitching there. Use three plies of flower thread to work cross-stitches over two threads of fabric. Work blended needle stitches as indicated in key. Use two plies to work straight stitches, satin stitches, French knots, and backstitches. Stitch remaining motifs, *pages 112–114,* where desired.

Stitch around outside edges using a long, narrow zigzag stitch, 6 inches beyond outside edges of stitching. Cut fabric 2 inches beyond zigzag stitching.

Thread needle with doubled length of ribbon. Weave ribbon under and over three threads of fabric from edge to edge where basted. Remove basting. Knot ribbon ends just past zigzag stitching; trim. Fringe edges of fabric.

Storybook Table Set

As shown on page 104, motifs were color-copied from our stitched afghan.

MATERIALS

SUPPLIES

Child's unfinished wood table and chairs

Very fine grit sandpaper; tack cloth

Acrylic spray sealer

2-ounce bottles of Palmer Prism acrylic paints: one *each* of leaf green, snow, boysenberry, and golden yellow; two bottles of wheat; paint brushes

Newspaper; acrylic spray matte varnish

Stitched Storybook Afghan, left

Decoupage medium

INSTRUCTIONS

Lightly sand table and chairs; wipe with tack cloth. Spray with sealer.

Paint table legs and chair spindles green. Sand lightly; apply second coat. Paint table edge, edges of chair seats, and chair backs boysenberry, mixed with a few drops of snow. Mix one part yellow with three parts wheat; paint table top, chair seats, and legs. Cover table top and chair seats with paper; spray remaining surfaces with varnish.

Color-copy desired cross-stitched designs from afghan; cut out designs.

Using decoupage medium, glue designs as desired onto table top and

chair seats. Allow to dry. Apply several coats of decoupage medium to paper-covered surfaces, allowing to dry and sanding lightly between coats. When dry, spray lightly with varnish.

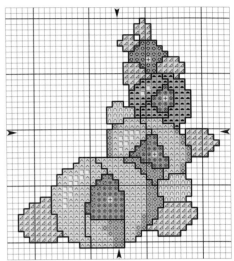

FLOWERS – BOTTOM RIGHT CORNER

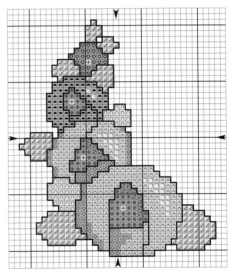

FLOWERS – BOTTOM LEFT CORNER

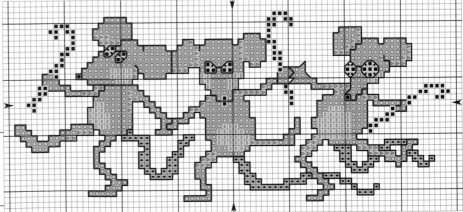

MICE stitch count: 35 high x 78 wide
MICE finished design sizes:
  7-count fabric – 5 x 11⅛ inches
  10-count fabric – 3½ x 7⅞ inches
  14-count fabric – 2½ x 5½ inches

MICE

STORYBOOK AFGHAN

ANCHOR	DMC Flower Thread		DMC	
387		−		Ecru
002		•	000	White
352	2400	◉	300	Mahogany
403	2310	■	310	Black
013	2666	♥	349	Dark coral
1014	2354	✳	355	Dark terra-cotta
914	2407	⊔	407	Medium cocoa
310	2434	⁄	434	Chestnut
362	2436	▢	437	Tan
232	2318	＝	452	Medium shell gray
256	2788	∩	704	Chartreuse
303	2748	＋	742	Tangerine
882	2758	◨	758	Light terra-cotta
1022	2761	♡	760	True salmon
024	2776	∧	776	Pink
161	2322	⊖	826	Bright blue
380	2801	◪	838	Deep beige brown
378	2841	▷	841	True beige brown
388	2842	✴	842	Light beige brown
944	2829	⌗	869	Hazel
052	2899	◇	899	Light rose
204	2912	◺	913	Nile green
269	2937	▼	936	Pine green
381	2898	▲	938	Coffee brown
332	2946	⊗	946	Medium burnt orange
316	2947	◁	971	True pumpkin
298	2742	☆	972	Canary
1001	2766	◈	976	Golden brown
846	2730	⌷	3011	Khaki
905	2610	◖	3021	Brown gray
292	2743	⁝	3078	Lemon
087	2719	◤	3607	Fuchsia
1020	2225	⬒	3713	Pale salmon
869	2415	⬓	3743	Antique violet
120	2933	▷	3747	Periwinkle
1036	2590	◆	3750	Antique blue

ANCHOR	DMC Flower Thread		DMC	
035	2350	◰	3801	Watermelon
063	2309	◲	3805	Cyclamen
305	2726	⊞	3821	Straw
386	2745	◳	3823	Yellow

BLENDED NEEDLE

936	2632	◆	632	Deep cocoa (1X) and
360	2840		839	Dark beige brown (2X)
882	2758	◷	758	Light terra-cotta (1X) and
1020	2225		3713	Pale salmon (2X)
1007	2405	☒	3772	Dark cocoa (1X) and
379	2841		840	Medium beige brown (2X)
1008	2407	▽	3773	Rose beige (1X) and
388	2842		842	Light beige brown (2X)

STRAIGHT STITCH

403	2310	／	310	Black – violin strings and bow
1014	2354	／	355	Dark terra-cotta – cat's buttons

SATIN STITCH

013	2666	／	349	Dark coral – dish and spoon's mouths

BACKSTITCH

352	2400	／	300	Mahogany – cat's vest
013	2666	／	349	Dark coral – dish's bow and collar
233	2414	／	451	Dark shell gray – cow's tail, spoon
360	2840	／	839	Dark beige brown – cat's eyebrows
052	2899	／	899	Light rose – dish's dress
269	2937	／	936	Pine green – cat's clothing
298	2742	／	972	Canary – stars
403	2310	／	310	Black – all remaining backstitches

FRENCH KNOT

403	2310	•	310	Black – cow's eyes, cat's violin
013	2666	•	349	Dark coral – spoon's hatband

BOTTOM RIGHT FLOWERS stitch count:
41 high x 36 wide
BOTTOM RIGHT FLOWERS finished design sizes:
 7-count fabric – 5⁷⁄₈ x 5¼ inches
10-count fabric – 4⅛ x 3⅝ inches
14-count fabric – 2⅞ x 2⅝ inches

BOTTOM LEFT FLOWERS stitch count:
42 high x 35 wide
BOTTOM LEFT FLOWERS finished design sizes:
 7-count fabric – 6 x 5 inches
10-count fabric – 4¼ x 3½ inches
14-count fabric – 3 x 2½ inches

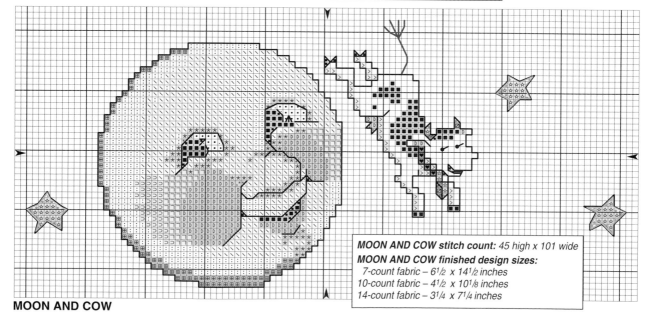

MOON AND COW stitch count: 45 high x 101 wide
MOON AND COW finished design sizes:
 7-count fabric – 6½ x 14½ inches
10-count fabric – 4½ x 10⅛ inches
14-count fabric – 3¼ x 7¼ inches

MOON AND COW

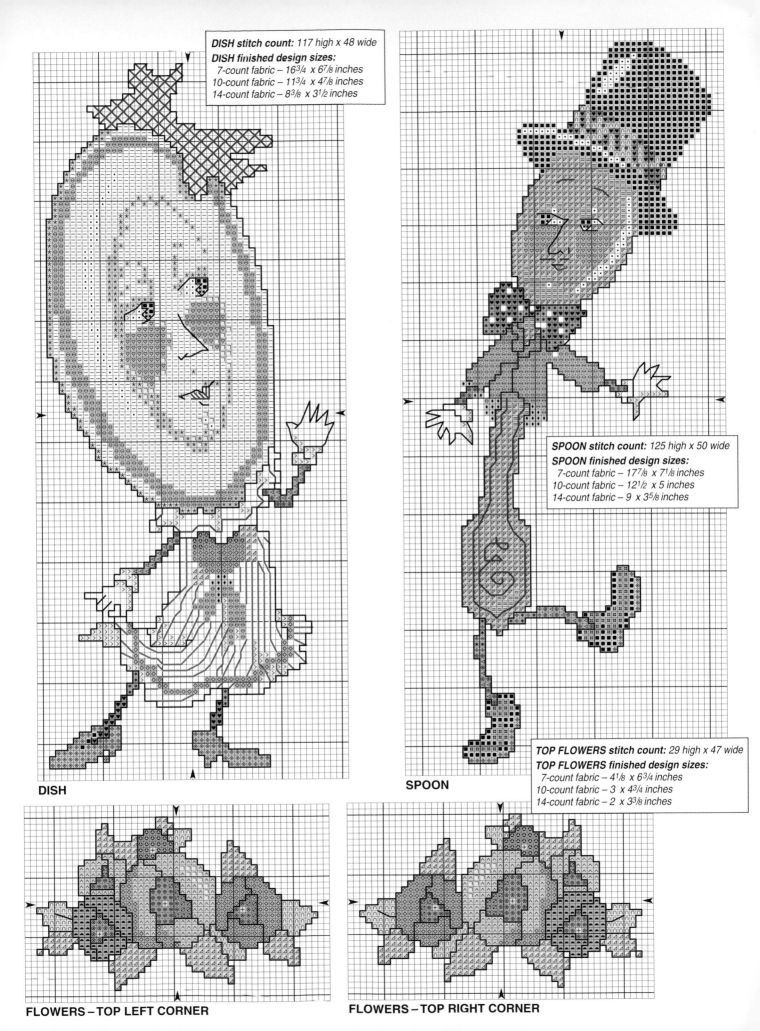

DISH stitch count: 117 high x 48 wide
DISH finished design sizes:
 7-count fabric – 16¾ x 6⅞ inches
 10-count fabric – 11¾ x 4⅞ inches
 14-count fabric – 8⅜ x 3½ inches

DISH

SPOON stitch count: 125 high x 50 wide
SPOON finished design sizes:
 7-count fabric – 17⅞ x 7⅛ inches
 10-count fabric – 12½ x 5 inches
 14-count fabric – 9 x 3⅝ inches

SPOON

TOP FLOWERS stitch count: 29 high x 47 wide
TOP FLOWERS finished design sizes:
 7-count fabric – 4⅛ x 6¾ inches
 10-count fabric – 3 x 4¾ inches
 14-count fabric – 2 x 3⅜ inches

FLOWERS – TOP LEFT CORNER

FLOWERS – TOP RIGHT CORNER

CAT stitch count: 152 high x 125 wide
CAT finished design sizes:
  7-count fabric – 21³/₄ x 17⁷/₈ inches
  10-count fabric – 15¹/₄ x 12¹/₂ inches
  14-count fabric – 10⁷/₈ x 9 inches

CAT

The Happy Gardener

The long-awaited signs of spring are abloom at last on our **Happy Gardener Sampler.** Stitched with a rainbow of colors on 28-count ice blue Jubilee fabric, the flowers and garden bounty seem real enough to pick and savor. The three sections of this design could also be stitched and framed separately for an interesting arrangement. For more fresh-as-spring projects, turn the page. Instructions and charts for all projects begin on *page 121.*

Keep all of your secret green thumb tips in this cheerful book that features a hand-stitched **Gardener's Journal Cover.** Stitched on Edinborough linen, the fanciful band sits atop the checked-fabric background. The **Garden Hat Pin** stitches up in an evening and is the perfect accent for any spring outfit.

Tea in the garden will be oh, so enchanting while wearing this striking **Garden Party Pinafore** stitched on water lily Jobelan fabric and trimmed with printed-fabric ruffles, ties, and binding.

Add a personal touch to an otherwise ordinary clay pot by stitching our **Flowerpot Band** featuring some tiny warm-weather friends. You can easily adjust the size of your band for any-size pot. For more fun in the sun, trim a favorite straw hat with our **Fun Flower Hat Band** stitched on linen and trimmed with bright jumbo rickrack.

Gather your veggies while sporting these bibs accented with our appliquéd **Gardener's Bib Pocket Trim** worked on Jobelan fabric.

120

HAPPY GARDENER SAMPLER

ANCHOR		DMC	
002	·	000	White
108	⌃	210	Lavender
352	▦	300	Deep mahogany
1049	⊙	301	Medium mahogany
218	▲	319	Dark pistachio
013	♥	349	Dark coral
009	S	352	Pale coral
235	⊿	414	Steel
374	Φ	420	Medium hazel
1045	☆	436	Dark tan
288	I	445	Lemon
267	▶	469	Avocado
063	⊘	602	Cranberry
324	⊠	721	Medium bittersweet
314	▢	741	Medium tangerine
303	○	742	Light tangerine
144	═	800	Delft blue
379	▣	840	Medium beige brown
218	●	890	Deep pistachio
333	◕	900	Burnt orange
897	★	902	Garnet
862	✤	934	Deep pine green
268	◇	937	True pine green
881	−	945	Ivory
1001	⊕	976	Golden brown
244	◈	987	Forest green
410	◓	995	Dark electric blue
433	⊠	996	Medium electric blue
883	+	3064	Light cocoa
266	Ⅱ	3347	Medium yellow green
264	⁚	3348	Light yellow green
262	▽	3363	Medium loden
260	✶	3364	Light loden
382	■	3371	Black brown
1020	∼	3713	Salmon
1007	▨	3772	Dark cocoa
1015	◆	3777	Terra-cotta
1050	▼	3781	Dark mocha
236	✕	3799	Charcoal
062	♡	3806	Cyclamen
306	✳	3820	Straw
9575	⟋	3824	Melon
328	⌐	3825	Pale bittersweet

BLENDED NEEDLE

1046	△	435	Chestnut (2X) and
890		729	Medium old gold (1X)
891	⊘	676	Light old gold (2X) and
362		437	Medium tan (1X)
907	◀	832	Bronze (2X) and
306		3820	Straw (1X)
380	⋈	838	Deep beige brown (2X) and
360		3031	Deep mocha (1X)
944	◈	869	Dark hazel (2X) and
1050		3781	Dark mocha (1X)
256	◘	906	Medium parrot green (2X) and
257		905	Dark parrot green (1X)
1035	⊖	930	Dark antique blue (2X) and
176		793	Medium cornflower blue (1X)
1034	▽	931	Medium antique blue (2X) and
176		793	Medium cornflower blue (1X)

BLENDED NEEDLE

1033	▨	932	True antique blue (2X) and
175		794	Light cornflower blue (1X)
267	⊛	3346	Hunter green (2X) and
846		3011	Khaki (1X)
266	⊞	3347	Medium yellow green (2X) and
846		3011	Khaki (1X)
263	✤	3362	Dark loden (2X) and
861		935	Dark pine green (1X)
236	◧	3799	Charcoal (2X) and
1035		930	Dark antique blue (1X)

BACKSTITCH

013	╱	349	Dark coral – collar, sock trim, chimney (2X)
235	╱	414	Steel – fence (2X)
897	╱	902	Garnet – flowers on shirt (1X)
257	╱	905	Dark parrot green – tomato stems (1X); top of tomato (2X)
268	╱	937	True pine green – house windows, door frame (3X)
244	╱	987	Forest green – stem of pea pod on seed packet (1X)
360	╱	3031	Deep mocha – border (1X)
403	╱	310	Black – all remaining backstitches (1X)

SATIN STITCH

013	╱	349	Dark coral – mouth (1X)

STRAIGHT STITCH

002	╱	000	White – tomato highlights, radishes (1X); ME (2X)
218	╱	319	Dark pistachio – stems (1X)
1046	╱	435	Chestnut – hat detail (1X)
891	╱	676	Light old gold – border on ME marker (1X)
324	╱	721	Medium bittersweet – carrot on seed packet (2X)
256	╱	906	Medium parrot green – carrot-top stems (1X)
244	╱	987	Forest green – grass blades, stems (2X)
260	╱	3364	Light loden – stems (1X)

BLENDED STRAIGHT STITCH

403	╱	310	Black (1X) and
1046		435	Chestnut (1X) – cabbage detail

FRENCH KNOT

002	●	000	White – sunflower detail, flower highlights, seeds (1X)
403	●	310	Black – barn windows (1X); seeds (2X); seeds being tossed (3X)
013	●	349	Dark coral – flowers (1X)
257	●	905	Dark parrot green – peas on seed packet (1X)
1015	●	3777	Terra-cotta – seeds (2X)

BLENDED FRENCH KNOT

403	●	310	Black (2X) and
324		721	Medium bittersweet (1X) – seeds

Stitch count: 125 high x 171 wide

Finished design sizes:
28-count fabric – 9 x 12¼ inches
36-count fabric – 7 x 9½ inches
22-count fabric – 11⅜ x 15½ inches

HAPPY GARDENER SAMPLER

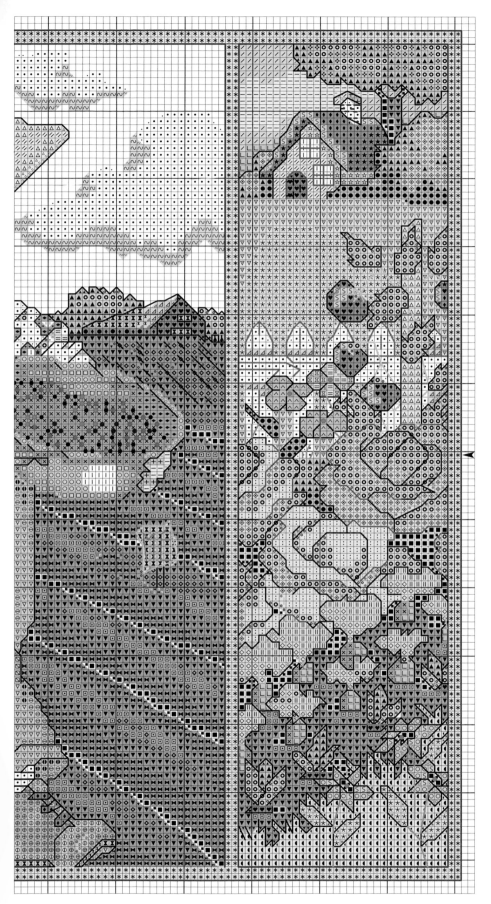

Happy Gardener Sampler

As shown on page 116, finished sampler measures 9×12¼ inches.

MATERIALS

FABRIC

15×18-inch piece of 28-count ice blue Jubilee fabric

FLOSS

Cotton embroidery floss in colors listed in key on page 121

SUPPLIES

Needle

Embroidery hoop

Desired mat and frame

INSTRUCTIONS

Tape or zigzag edges of the fabric to prevent fraying. Find the center of the chart, *left*, and the center of the fabric; begin stitching there. Use two plies of floss to work cross-stitches over two threads of fabric. Work the blended needle stitches, satin stitches, straight stitches, blended straight stitches, French knots, blended French knots, and backstitches as specified in the key.

Press stitchery from the back. Mat and frame as desired.

Gardener's Journal Cover

As shown on page 118, finished cover fits an 8½×12-inch purchased journal.

MATERIALS

FABRICS

16×4½-inch piece of 36-count antique white Edinborough linen

¾ yard of 45-inch-wide green-and-white-checked fabric

FLOSS

Cotton embroidery floss in colors listed in key, right

SUPPLIES

Needle; antique white sewing thread

8½×12-inch journal

18×24-inch piece of fleece

2 yards of piping cord

28-inch piece of red trim

INSTRUCTIONS

Tape or zigzag edges of linen. Begin stitching left end of chart, *below,* 2 inches from left end of linen. Use two plies of floss to work cross-stitches over two threads of fabric. Work blended needle stitches as indicated in key. Work French knots and backstitches using one ply. Trim stitched piece to measure 14×3¼ inches. Turn under ½ inch along both long edges; press. Sew red trim to long edges.

Measure dimensions of journal opened flat. Add ½ inch all around for seam allowance. Cut fabric and fleece to measurements.

Baste fleece to the wrong side of the fabric, stitching ¼ inch from the edges. With the fabric rectangle positioned horizontally, pin the band vertically down the right side, 3½ inches from the edge; topstitch in place.

To make piping, cut 1½-inch-wide bias strips to total 2 yards. Sew short ends together to make one long strip. Center piping cord lengthwise on wrong side of strip. Fold fabric around cording, bringing raw edges together. Use zipper foot to sew through both layers of fabric close to cording. Matching raw edges, sew piping around perimeter of fabric cover rectangle.

Cut lining piece to match outer piece, omitting seam allowance on short sides. Cut two 7×13-inch end flaps. To hem, turn under ¼ inch twice along one long edge of each end flap. Matching raw edges, baste one end flap to each end of cover. Sew lining to cover, right sides facing, along top and bottom long edges. Trim seams and clip corners.

Turn cover right side out through opening at one end. Turn the flaps to the right side; fit the cover over journal.

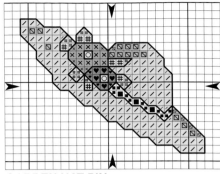

GARDEN HAT PIN

GARDENER'S JOURNAL COVER		
ANCHOR		DMC
002	·	000 White
108	⌃	210 Lavender
403	■	310 Black
013	♥	349 Dark coral
324	✕	721 Medium bittersweet
303	O	742 Light tangerine
175	▽	794 Light cornflower blue
257	#	905 Dark parrot green
144	+	3325 Baby blue
1031	ꟷ	3753 Antique blue
062	♡	3806 Cyclamen
373	◨	3828 Hazel
BLENDED NEEDLE		
891	⁄	676 Light old gold (2X) and
885		739 Tan (1X)
256	◎	906 Medium parrot green (2X) and
257		905 Dark parrot green (1X)
FRENCH KNOT		
403	●	310 Black – watering can spout
257	●	905 Dark parrot green – seed packet
BACKSTITCH		
013	⁄	349 Dark coral – seed packet
257	⁄	905 Dark parrot green – tendrils
403	⁄	310 Black – all remaining backstitches

Stitch count: 26 high x 114 wide

Finished design sizes:
36-count fabric – 1½ x 6⅜ inches
28-count fabric – 1⅞ x 8⅛ inches
22-count fabric – 2⅜ x 10⅜ inches

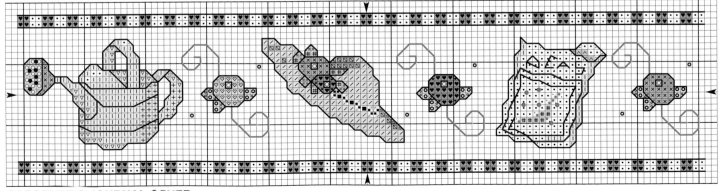

GARDENER'S JOURNAL COVER

GARDEN HAT PIN

ANCHOR		DMC	
403	■	310	Black
013	♥	349	Dark coral
324	✕	721	Medium bittersweet
303	○	742	Light tangerine
257	⊞	905	Dark parrot green
373	⊠	3828	Hazel
BLENDED NEEDLE			
891	⁄	676	Light old gold (2X) and
885		739	Tan (1X)
BACKSTITCH			
403	╱	310	Black – all backstitches

Stitch count: 17 high x 23 wide
Finished design sizes:
14-count plastic – 2½ x 3¼ inches

Garden Hat Pin

As shown on page 118, finished pin without charms measures 3×3¾ inches.

MATERIALS

FABRICS

4×6-inch piece of 14-count clear plastic canvas

3×5-inch piece of brown felted imitation-suede fabric

3×5-inch piece of red felted imitation-suede fabric

FLOSS

Cotton embroidery floss in colors listed in key, above

SUPPLIES

Needle; tacky fabric glue

Scissors; pinking shears

Three 1½-inch-long miniature garden tool charms

Brown sewing thread; pin back

INSTRUCTIONS

Find center of plastic canvas and of chart, *page 124*; begin stitching there. Use three plies of floss to work cross-stitches. Work blended needle stitches as indicated in key. Work backstitches using two plies.

Trim plastic one square beyond the stitching. Glue hat to brown

fabric; cut out ⅛ inch beyond the plastic using regular scissors. Next, glue to the red fabric. Using pinking shears, cut out ⅛ inch beyond the brown fabric.

Tack garden charms to hang evenly spaced, from bottom of hat.

Glue pin back to back of hat.

Garden Party Pinafore

As shown on page 119, pinafore is made from a purchased adult pattern.

MATERIALS

FABRICS

2 yards of 45-inch-wide water lily Jobelan fabric

Light green print fabric for ruffles, ties, waistband, and skirt binding, in amounts indicated on pattern envelope

Light green cotton bib lining fabric in amount indicated on pattern envelope

FLOSS

Cotton embroidery floss in colors listed in key on page 127

SUPPLIES

Needle; embroidery hoop

Apron pattern with bib and ruffles

Notions as indicated on pattern envelope

INSTRUCTIONS

Cut out bib pattern. Baste bib pattern shape onto Jobelan fabric. From Jobelan fabric, cut apron skirt 45 inches wide by length indicated in pattern instructions.

Tape or zigzag edges of the Jobelan fabric cut for bib. Using the small motifs for the bib, *page 126*, stitch randomly on bib fabric as desired. Use three plies of floss to work cross-stitches over two threads of fabric. Work blended needle stitches

as indicated in key. Use two plies to work the French knots, straight stitches, and backstitches.

For apron skirt, tape or zigzag the edges of the Jobelan fabric. Find the center of skirt chart, *pages 126–127*, and of skirt width 6½ inches above bottom edge; begin stitching there.

Cut out stitched bib along basting lines. Cut bib lining from light green lining fabric. Cut all remaining pieces from green print. If desired, bind apron skirt bottom and side edges. Cut a 2½-inch-wide strip long enough to bind each edge. Beginning with side edges, sew binding to right side using ½-inch seam allowance. Press under ½ inch along remaining raw edge, turn to wrong side, and slip-stitch in place along seamline. Repeat for bottom edge, turning under raw edges at ends.

Complete apron according to the pattern instructions.

Gardener's Bib Pocket Trim

As shown on page 120, finished pocket trim is 3⅝×7⅜ inches.

MATERIALS

FABRICS

6×12-inch piece of 28-count light blue Jobelan fabric

6×12-inch piece of light blue cotton lining fabric

FLOSS

Cotton embroidery floss in colors listed in key on page 128

SUPPLIES

Needle

Embroidery hoop

6×12-inch piece of lightweight fusible interfacing

¾ yard of ½-inch-wide red flat trim

Continued on page 127

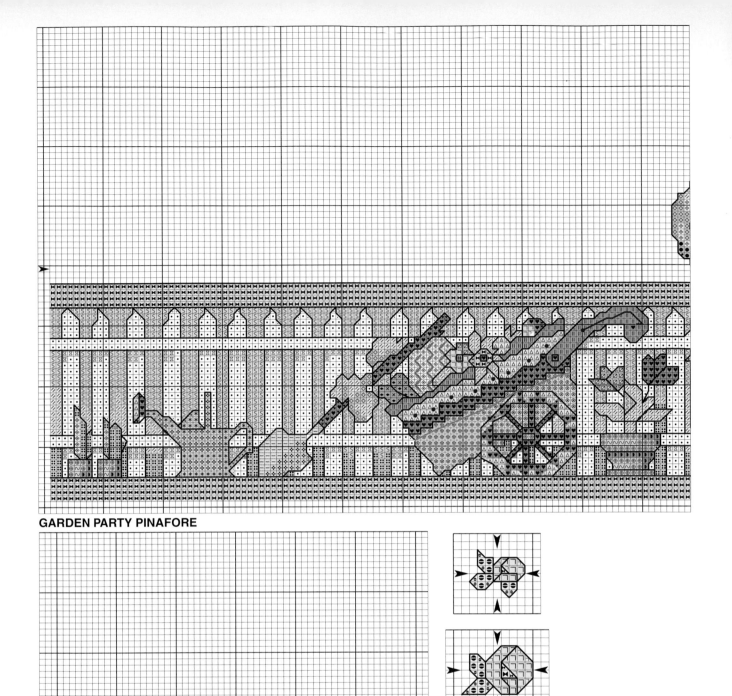

GARDEN PARTY PINAFORE

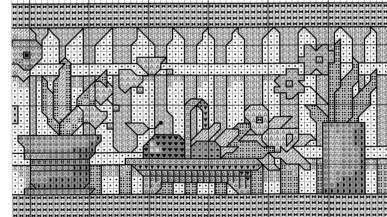

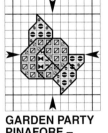

**GARDEN PARTY
PINAFORE –
FLORAL BIB MOTIFS**

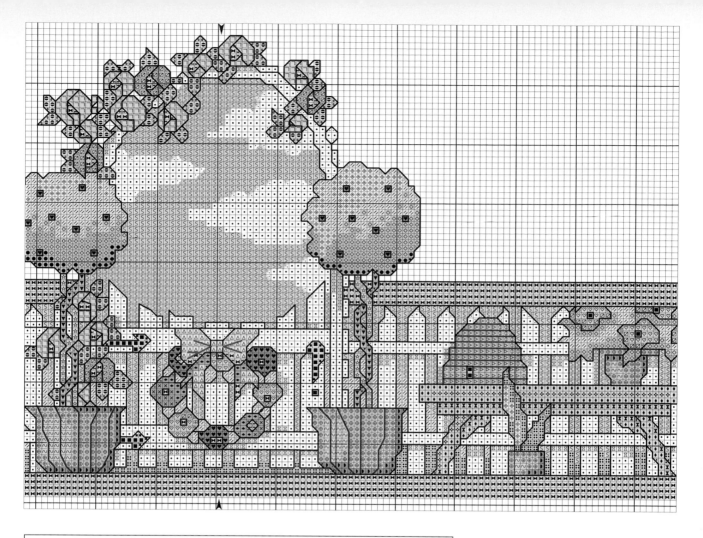

GARDEN PARTY PINAFORE

ANCHOR		DMC	
002	⚫	000	White
108	⌃	210	Lavender
352	⊞	300	Mahogany
403	■	310	Black
013	♥	349	Coral
5975	⊕	356	Medium terra cotta
855	◫	370	Pecan
373	▷	422	Hazel
233	❖	451	Dark shell gray
231	━	453	Light shell gray
859	◈	523	Olive drab
1041	✳	535	Ash gray
280	╱	581	Moss green
167	⩂	598	Medium turquoise
063	⬰	602	Cranberry
324	☒	721	Bittersweet
305	△	725	Topaz
882	∿	758	Light terra cotta
378	☆	841	Beige brown
333	◆	900	Burnt orange
258	▦	904	Parrot green
861	●	935	Dark pine green
269	⊛	936	Medium pine green
268	◇	937	True pine green
1002	▯	977	Golden brown
244	⬯	987	Forest green
433	△	996	Electric blue
025	⅃	3716	Rose pink

ANCHOR		DMC	
1032	⊠	3752	Antique blue
1050	▼	3781	Mocha
236	⊠	3799	Charcoal
062	♡	3806	Cyclamen
851	◆	3808	Deep turquoise
306	⋈	3820	Straw

BLENDED NEEDLE

936	◨	632 Cocoa (2X) and
1015		918 Red copper (1X)

FRENCH KNOTS

403	●	310 Black – apple leaf
013	●	349 Coral – cart

STRAIGHT STITCH

002	╱	000 White – cart
333	╱	900 Burnt orange – ribbon detail

BACKSTITCH

013	╱	349 Coral – cart
861	╱	935 Dark pine green – watermelon
1050	╱	3781 Mocha – pots, bee skeep, and basket
403	╱	310 Black – all remaining backstitches

Stitch count: 77 high x 279 wide
Finished design sizes:
25-count fabric – 6 1/8 x 22 3/8 inches
28-count fabric – 5 1/2 x 20 inches
36-count fabric – 4 1/4 x 15 1/2 inches

INSTRUCTIONS

Tape or zigzag edges of Jobelan fabric to prevent fraying. Find the center of the chart, *page 128*, and the center of the Jobelan fabric; begin stitching there. Use two plies of floss to work cross-stitches over two threads of fabric. Work the French knots and backstitches using one ply of floss.

Fuse interfacing to wrong side of stitchery, following manufacturer's instructions. Sew trim, finished edge toward center, around perimeter of design 1/8 inch past stitching.

Sew the lining to the stitchery, right sides facing, along trim seam line. Leave an opening for turning. Trim the seam allowance to 1/4 inch; clip the corners. Turn right side out and sew the opening closed.

Hand-sew trim to the front pocket of overalls.

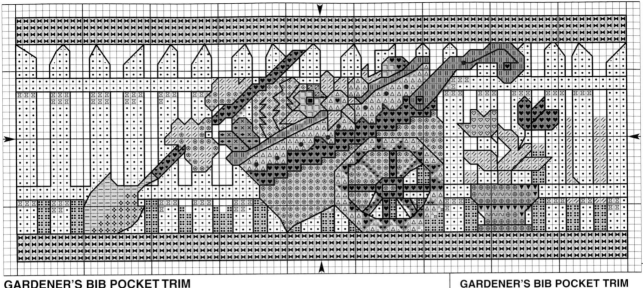

GARDENER'S BIB POCKET TRIM

Flowerpot Band

As shown on page 120, finished band measures 1¾×30 inches.

MATERIALS *for a 30-inch pot*

FABRICS

32×4-inch piece of 36-count dirty Edinborough linen; ½ yard of 45-inch-wide fabric in desired print

FLOSS

Cotton embroidery floss in colors listed in key on page 129

SUPPLIES

Needle; tracing paper

Sewing thread to match fabric

Rickrack or flat trim in desired color

INSTRUCTIONS

Tape or zigzag edges of linen. Find the center of chart, *page 129*, and of linen; begin stitching there. Use two plies of floss to work cross-stitches over two threads of fabric. Work French knots using two plies and backstitches using one ply of floss.

Cut print fabric as follows: Measure circumference of flowerpot and add 1 inch for fabric width. Measure height of flowerpot, plus the width of cross-stitched band, and add 1 inch for fabric length. Trace bottom of pot onto tracing paper; add ½-inch seam allowance all around and cut out. Cut circle from fabric for bottom of pot cover.

Trim cross-stitched fabric strip to 1⅞ inches wide, and length of fabric rectangle. Sew rickrack or trim along bottom edge of strip. Trim seam allowance to ½ inch. Press under edge along rickrack or trim seam. Serge or hem one long edge of the fabric rectangle. Lay the band right side up onto the right side of the fabric, matching the trimmed edge of the strip to the finished edge of the fabric. Slip-stitch edges together, allowing rickrack trim to extend beyond edge. Turn under the raw edge of stitched strip ¼ inch and slip-stitch to fabric.

Join the short ends of the fabric rectangle using ½-inch seam allowance. Sew gathering thread around perimeter of bottom circle, ½ inch from edges. Gather evenly to fit raw edge of fabric rectangle; stitch.

GARDENER'S BIB POCKET TRIM

ANCHOR		DMC	
002	•	000	White
403	■	310	Black
013	♥	349	Dark coral
5975	⊕	356	Medium terra-cotta
233	✤	451	Dark shell gray
231	−	453	Light shell gray
859	◈	523	Olive drab
280	⁄	581	Moss green
063	⊠	602	Cranberry
936	▼	632	Cocoa
324	✕	721	Medium bittersweet
305	△	725	Topaz
882	∼	758	Light terra-cotta
333	◆	900	Burnt orange
258	▦	904	Parrot green
269	✳	936	Pine green
1002	‖	977	Golden brown
433	◿	996	Medium electric blue
025	⊓	3716	Rose pink
1032	⊠	3752	Antique blue
062	♡	3806	Cyclamen
306	⋈	3820	Straw

FRENCH KNOT

| 013 | ● | 349 | Dark coral – cart |
| 305 | ● | 725 | Topaz – flower center |

BACKSTITCH

| 013 | ╱ | 349 | Dark coral – cart handle and detail |
| 403 | ╱ | 310 | Black – all remaining backstitches |

Stitch count: 36 high x 90 wide
Finished design sizes:
28-count fabric – 2⅝ x 6½ inches
36-count fabric – 2 x 5 inches
22-count fabric – 3¼ x 8⅛ inches

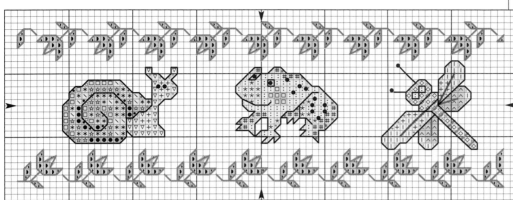

FLOWERPOT BAND

Fun Flower Hat Band

As shown on page 120, finished hat band measures 1¾×50 inches.

MATERIALS

FABRICS

5×54-inch piece of 32-count star sapphire linen

2¼×54-inch piece of yellow-and-white-checked cotton fabric

FLOSS

Cotton embroidery floss in colors listed in key, right

SUPPLIES

Needle

2¼×54-inch piece of fusible interfacing

Sewing thread to match linen

3¼ yards of jumbo yellow rickrack

2-inch-diameter decorative shank button

INSTRUCTIONS

Tape or zigzag edges of linen. Find center of chart, *below,* and of linen; begin stitching there. Use two plies of floss to work cross-stitches over two threads of fabric. Work straight stitches and backstitches using one ply.

Trim stitched linen strip to measure 2¼×50½ inches, centering design. Following manufacturer's directions, fuse interfacing to wrong side of linen. Trim each end diagonally to a point. Use linen as pattern to cut checked fabric for lining.

Sew rickrack around perimeter, with seam ¼ inch from edge. With right sides facing, sew lining to linen, leaving an opening for turning. Clip the corners; turn right side out. Slip-stitch opening closed.

Wrap band around hat with ends at back. Crisscross ends; tack to secure. Sew button to cover tacking stitches at cross.

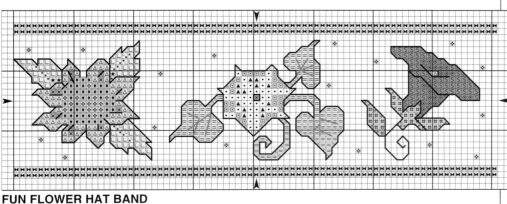

FUN FLOWER HAT BAND

A Good Marriage

Celebrate the beauty of marriage with a heartwarming sentiment you can lovingly stitch yourself. The border of **A Good Marriage Sampler** becomes a dainty floral mat when stitched over two threads of black Brittney fabric. The interior of this elegant piece is stitched on antique ivory cashel linen. We've created a wedding-day version of this memory-making piece on *page 134*. For more lovely projects, turn the page. Instructions and charts for all projects begin on *page 135*.

Presented to a bride and groom close to your heart, this cheerful **Ring Bearer's Pillow** will add even more memorable wedding-day moments. Stitched on cashel linen and accented with seed beads, the delicate flowers create an eye-catching border to surround the honored rings of gold.

Perfect to catch the bride's tears of joy is our **Butterfly Handkerchief**. The dainty motif stitches up easily on a new or antique purchased hanky. Strikingly stitched on black Jobelan fabric, anyone would be proud to display our glorious **Floral Hand Mirror** and **Bride's Treasure Box**.

Create a wedding keepsake that will be treasured for a lifetime by stitching this personalized inset for our **A Good Marriage Sampler** border. Stitched in a forget-me-not shade of blue, the alphabet and numerals stitch up quickly on cashel linen to commemorate the happy couple's special date.

134

A Good Marriage Sampler

As shown on page 131, the finished sampler measures 14½×10⅜ inches.

MATERIALS
For border design and one inset

FABRICS
15×13-inch piece of 28-count antique ivory cashel linen

22×20-inch piece of 28-count black Brittney fabric

FLOSS
Cotton embroidery floss in colors listed in key, right and below or page 138

SUPPLIES
Needle; embroidery hoop

INSTRUCTIONS
Tape or zigzag the edges of Brittney and linen fabrics to prevent fraying. Find the center of the desired inset

Continued on page 138

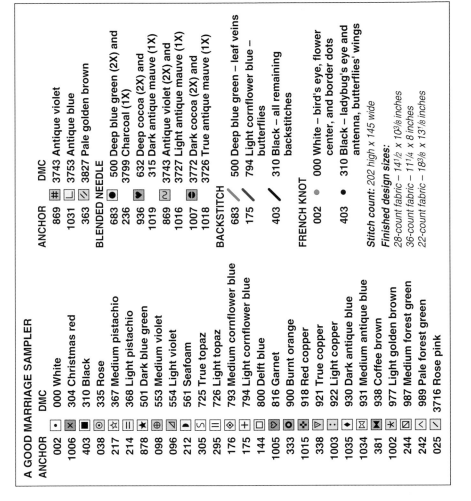

A GOOD MARRIAGE SAMPLER

ANCHOR		DMC	
002	•	000	White
1006	✕	304	Christmas red
403	■	310	Black
038	◉	335	Rose
217	☆	367	Medium pistachio
214	‖	368	Light pistachio
878	★	501	Dark blue green
098	⊕	553	Medium violet
096	◣	554	Light violet
212	▲	561	Seafoam
305	◺	725	True topaz
295	≡	726	Light topaz
176	◈	793	Medium cornflower blue
175	+	794	Light cornflower blue
144	□	800	Delft blue
1005	◙	816	Garnet
333	○	900	Burnt orange
1015	◆	918	Red copper
338	▷	921	True copper
1003	⋰	922	Light copper
1035	◆	930	Dark antique blue
1034	⊠	931	Medium antique blue
381	▦	938	Coffee brown
1002	★	977	Light golden brown
244	◿	987	Medium forest green
242	◁	989	Pale forest green
025	⁄	3716	Rose pink

ANCHOR		DMC	
869	#	3743	Antique violet
1031	⊔	3753	Antique blue
363	◢	3827	Pale golden brown

BLENDED NEEDLE

683	●	500	Deep blue green (2X) and
236		3799	Charcoal (1X)
936	▶	632	Deep cocoa (2X) and
1019		315	Dark antique mauve (1X)
869		3743	Antique violet (2X) and
1016	?	3727	Light antique mauve (1X)
1007		3772	Dark cocoa (2X) and
1018	◑	3726	True antique mauve (1X)

BACKSTITCH

683	╱	500	Deep blue green – leaf veins
175	╱	794	Light cornflower blue – butterflies
403	╲	310	Black – all remaining backstitches

FRENCH KNOT

002	●	000	White – bird's eye, flower center, and border dots
403	●	310	Black – ladybug's eye and antenna, butterflies' wings

Stitch count: 202 high x 145 wide
Finished design sizes:
28-count fabric – 14½ x 10⅜ inches
36-count fabric – 11¼ x 8 inches
22-count fabric – 18⅜ x 13⅛ inches

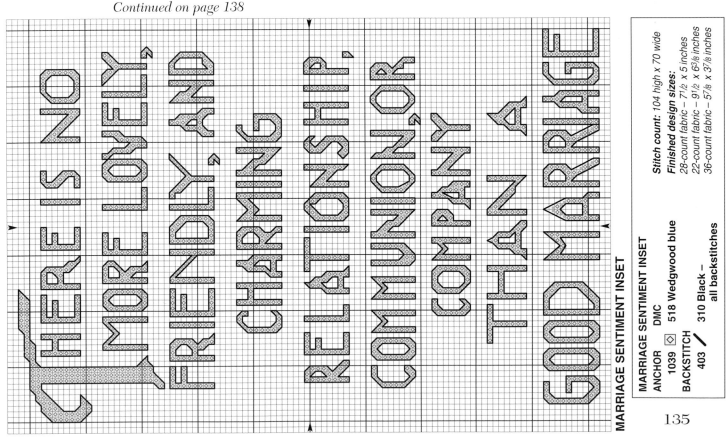

MARRIAGE SENTIMENT INSET

ANCHOR		DMC	
1039	◇	518	Wedgwood blue

BACKSTITCH

403	╲	310	Black – all backstitches

Stitch count: 104 high x 70 wide
Finished design sizes:
28-count fabric – 7½ x 5 inches
22-count fabric – 9½ x 6⅜ inches
36-count fabric – 5⅞ x 3⅞ inches

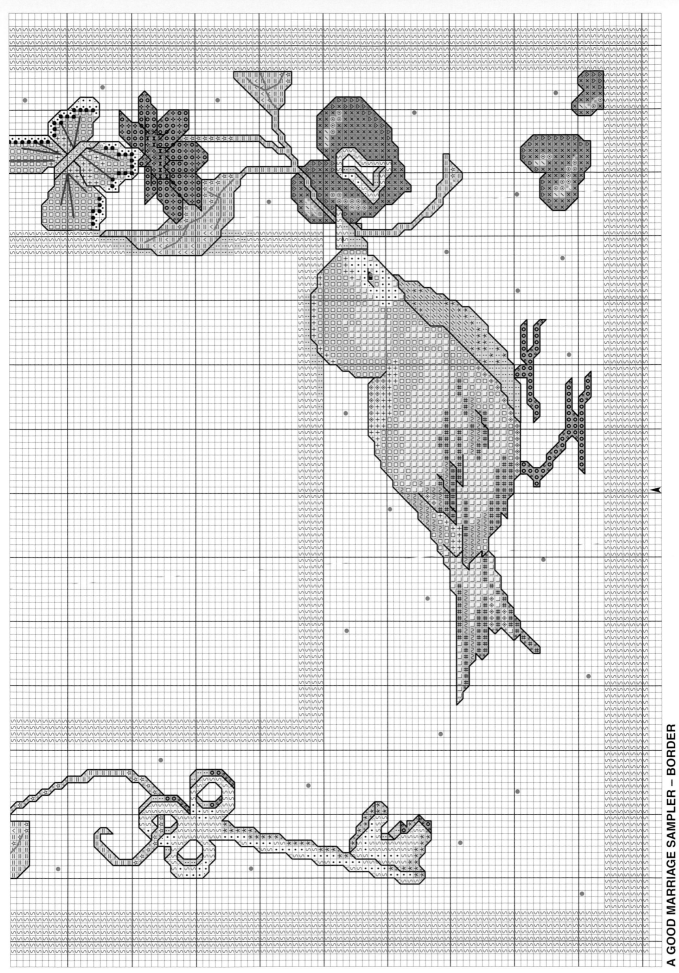

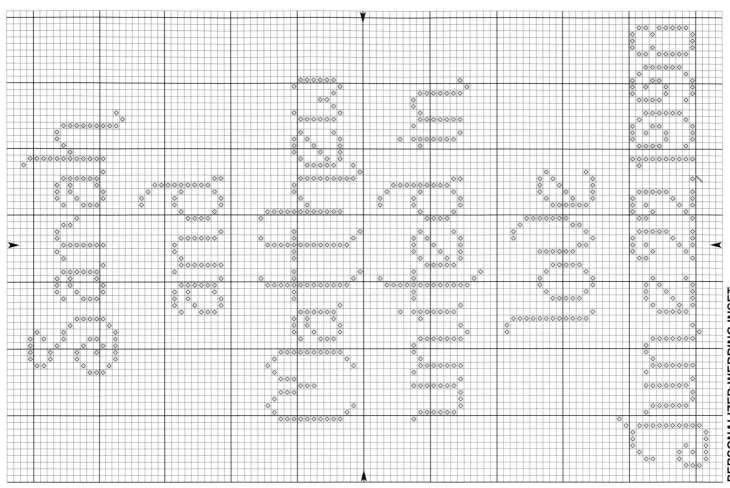

chart, *page 135* or *above*, and the center of the linen fabric; begin stitching there. Use two plies of floss to work the cross-stitches over two threads of fabric. Work backstitches using two plies of floss. Set aside.

Find the center of the border chart, *pages 136–137,* and of the Brittney fabric; begin stitching from there. Use the same number of plies of floss as used for the inset design, stitching over two threads of fabric. Work the blended needle stitches as indicated in the key, *page 135.* Use two plies to work the French knots.

Press both stitched pieces from the back. To finish the border stitchery, have a professional framer mount the stitchery to a rectangular mat suitable for the inset design. Frame the pieces as desired.

Ring Bearer's Pillow

As shown on page 132, finished pillow, including ruffle, measures 13½ inches square.

MATERIALS
FABRICS
20×20-inch piece of 28-count white cashel linen

1 yard of 45-inch-wide yellow linen
FLOSS
Cotton embroidery floss in colors listed in key on page 140
SUPPLIES
Needle; embroidery hoop

Seed beads in color listed in key

5-yard package of 4-mm-wide yellow silk ribbon

PERSONALIZED WEDDING INSET		
ANCHOR	DMC	
1039	◇	518 Wedgwood blue
BACKSTITCH		
1039	╱	518 Wedgwood blue – date

Stitch count: 104 high x 67 wide
Finished design sizes:
28-count fabric – 7½ x 47/8 inches
22-count fabric – 9½ x 6 inches
36-count fabric – 57/8 x 3¾ inches

Tapestry needle

10¼×10¼-inch piece of fleece

10¼×10¼-inch piece of fusible interfacing

1 yard of narrow gold metallic piping

2 yards of 1½-inch-wide white flat cotton lace

Polyester fiberfill

2 yards of ⅜-inch-wide peach satin ribbon

138

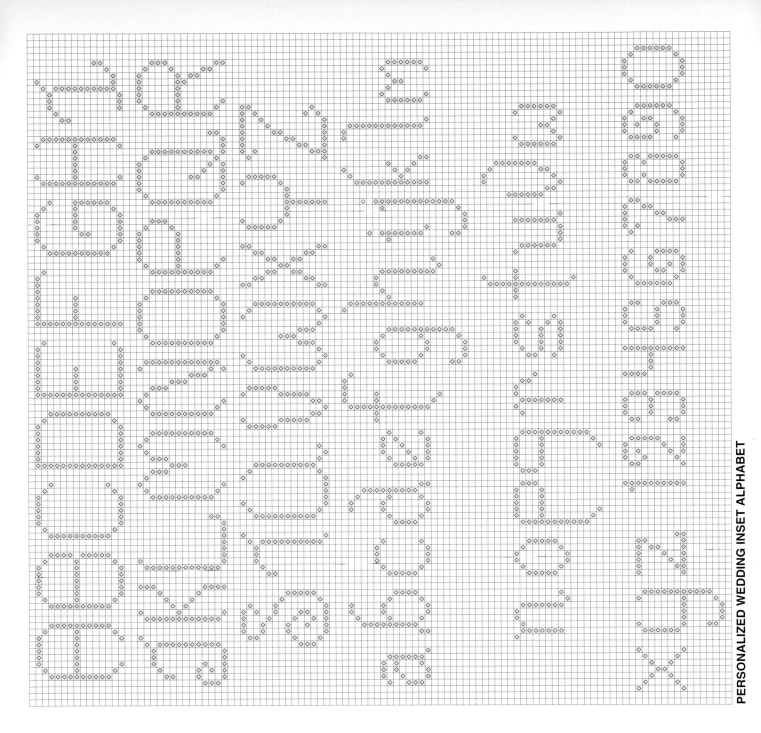

INSTRUCTIONS

Tape or zigzag the edges of the white cashel linen to prevent fraying. Find the center of the chart, *page 140*, and the center of the fabric; begin stitching there. Use two plies of floss to work cross-stitches over two threads of linen fabric. Work blended needle stitches as indicated in the key, *page 140*. Work the French knots and backstitches using one ply of floss.

Press finished stitchery from back.

Thread tapestry needle with yellow silk ribbon. Following chart, weave ribbon over and under two threads in a square around the stitched design.

Sew beads to orange cross-stitches at center of each flower using one strand of orange floss.

Cut stitched pillow front to 10¼×10¼ inches, centering design. Baste fleece to back of pillow front,

½ inch from edges. Sew piping to right side of pillow front along basting line, lapping ends.

For ruffle, cut 6-inch-wide bias strips from yellow fabric for a total of 85 inches. Join the short ends as necessary to make a circle. Press the strip in half lengthwise with the wrong sides facing. Sew lace to one side of the ruffle as shown in the photo, *page 132*.

Continued on page 141

RING BEARER'S PILLOW

RING BEARER'S PILLOW

ANCHOR		DMC
002	•	000 White
1006	✕	304 Christmas red
403	■	310 Black
038	⊙	335 Rose
217	☆	367 Medium pistachio
214	=	368 Light pistachio
878	★	501 Dark blue green
098	⊕	553 Medium violet
096	◿	554 Light violet
212	▶	561 Seafoam
295	‖	726 Light topaz
175	+	794 Light cornflower blue
144	▢	800 Delft blue
1005	♡	816 Garnet
333	◉	900 Burnt orange
338	▽	921 True copper

ANCHOR		DMC
1003	⠒	922 Light copper
1034	⊠	931 Medium antique blue
1002	★	977 Light golden brown
244	◨	987 Medium forest green
242	∧	989 Pale forest green
260	▲	3364 Loden
363	⧄	3827 Pale golden brown

BLENDED NEEDLE

683	●	500 Deep blue green (1X) and
236		3799 Charcoal (1X)
936	♥	632 Deep cocoa (2X) and
1019		315 Dark antique mauve (1X)
1018	◓	3726 True antique mauve (1X) and
1007		3772 Dark cocoa (1X)

BACKSTITCH

214	╱	368 Light pistachio – tendrils

BACKSTITCH

683	╱	500 Deep blue green – leaf veins
175	╱	794 Light cornflower blue – butterfly
403	╱	310 Black – all remaining backstitches

FRENCH KNOT

403	●	310 Black – butterfly

BEADS

●	00423 Mill Hill Tangerine seed beads

RIBBON WEAVING

╱	Pale yellow 4-mm silk ribbon

Stitch count: 110 high x 110 wide

Finished design sizes:
28-count fabric – 7⅞ x 7⅞ inches
36-count fabric – 6⅛ x 6⅛ inches
22-count fabric – 10 x 10 inches

Sew a gathering thread through both layers of ruffle ½ inch from raw edges. Pin ruffle to pillow top; adjust gathers evenly. Baste ruffle in place along piping seam.

Use pillow front as pattern to cut back from yellow fabric. Following manufacturer's instructions, fuse interfacing to wrong side of pillow back. Sew pillow front to back, right sides facing, using ½-inch seam allowance. Leave an opening for turning. Trim seams and corners, turn pillow right side out; stuff with fiberfill. Slip-stitch opening closed.

Cut peach ribbon in half. Holding lengths together, tie ribbon in bow with four long streamers. Tack ribbon to center of pillow.

Floral Hand Mirror

As shown on page 133, finished mirror measures 8×4¼ inches.

MATERIALS
FABRIC
7×7-inch piece of 28-count black Jobelan fabric
FLOSS
Cotton embroidery floss in colors listed in key, right
SUPPLIES
Needle; embroidery hoop
Seed beads in color listed in key
Small Hand Mirror by Sudberry House, or similar hand mirror with mounting board and a 3½-inch-diameter opening for inserting cross-stitch
White fabric marker
Black thread
12 inches of ⅜-inch-wide light blue flat braid
4×4-inch piece of batting
Fabric glue; crafts glue

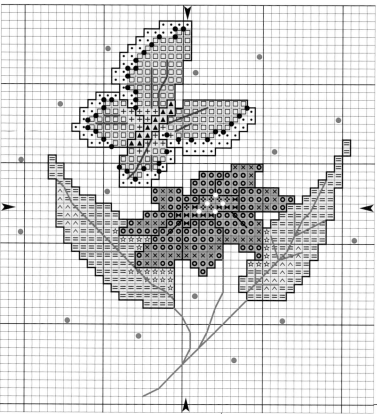

FLORAL HAND MIRROR

INSTRUCTIONS

Tape or zigzag edges of Jobelan fabric. Find the center of the chart, *above,* and of fabric; begin stitching there. Use three plies of floss to work cross-stitches over two threads of fabric. Work the straight stitches, French knots, and backstitches using two plies of floss. Attach beads using two plies of matching floss. Press finished stitchery from back.

Centering mounting board over design, draw a circle around stitchery, ¼ inch larger all around than mounting board. Use doubled thread to run gathering stitch around marked circle. Leave a ¾-inch tail and knot thread.

Cut batting slightly smaller than the mounting board; center on the top of the board.

Steam back of stitchery to soften. Pull opposite corners to straighten

FLORAL HAND MIRROR

ANCHOR		DMC	
002	·	000	White
1006	☒	304	Christmas red
217	☆	367	Medium pistachio
214	⊟	368	Light pistachio
175	⊞	794	Light cornflower blue
144	⊡	800	Delft blue
333	◉	900	Burnt orange
1015	✣	918	Red copper
381	◪	938	Coffee brown
242	⌃	989	Pale forest green
260	▲	3364	Loden

BACKSTITCH

683	╱	500	Deep blue green – leaf veins
175	╱	794	Light cornflower blue – butterfly
403	╱	310	Black – all remaining backstitches

STRAIGHT STITCH

214	╱	368	Light pistachio – stems

FRENCH KNOT

002	○	000	White – flower center
403	●	310	Black – butterfly's wings

BEADS

	●	03015	Mill Hill Snow white antique seed beads

Stitch count: 47 high x 43 wide
Finished design sizes:
28-count fabric – 3⅜ x 3⅛ inches
36-count fabric – 2⅝ x 2⅜ inches
22-count fabric – 4¼ x 4 inches

stitchery as necessary. While the fabric is still damp, position the batting-covered board on the back of stitchery and pull the thread tight, gathering to fit.

Trim excess fabric to within ¼ inch of stitching. Allow stitchery to dry completely on mounting board.

Glue braid around perimeter of covered board; allow glue to dry.

Glue board into recess in mirror. Place weight on top until glue dries.

Butterfly Handkerchief

As shown on page 133, butterfly motif measures 1¾×1¾ inches.

MATERIALS
FABRICS
Antique or new white linen handkerchief with lace trim and hemstitched border

3×3-inch piece of 14-count waste canvas

FLOSS
Cotton embroidery floss in colors listed in key, above right

SUPPLIES
Needle

Beading needle

Petite glass beads as listed in key

1¼ yards of 4-mm medium blue silk embroidery ribbon

INSTRUCTIONS
Baste waste canvas diagonally across one corner of handkerchief. Find the center of the chart, *above right*. Measure in about 2 inches from corner of handkerchief with waste canvas; begin stitching there. Use two plies of floss to work cross-stitches. Work the French knots and backstitches using one ply of floss.

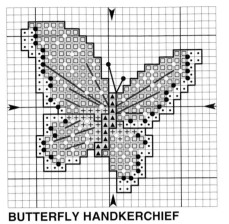

BUTTERFLY HANDKERCHIEF

Attach beads using one ply of blue floss. Press finished stitchery from the back.

Thread tapestry needle with ribbon. Weave ribbon through hemstitched border; overlap ends for one inch at starting point. Trim away excess ribbon.

Bride's Treasure Box

As shown on page 133, finished box measures 8½×8½×2¾ inches.

MATERIALS
FABRIC
14×14-inch piece of 28-count black Jobelan fabric

FLOSS
Cotton embroidery floss in colors listed in key on page 143

SUPPLIES
Needle; embroidery hoop

Seed beads in color listed in key

Carol's Fancywork Box by Sudberry House, or similar 8½×8½-inch square box with 7½×7½-inch opening for inserting stitchery

7¾×7¾-inch piece of batting

1 yard of ⅜-inch-wide flat black braid

Fabric glue; black thread

Tape

BUTTERFLY HANDKERCHIEF			
ANCHOR		DMC	
002	•	000	White
175	+	794	Light cornflower blue
144	□	800	Delft blue
260	▲	3364	Loden
BACKSTITCH			
175	/	794	Light cornflower blue – wings
403	/	310	Black – all remaining backstitches
FRENCH KNOT			
403	•	310	Black – wings
BEADS			
	○	40161	Mill Hill Crystal petite beads

Stitch count: 24 high x 25 wide

Finished design sizes:
14-count fabric – 1¾ x 1¾ inches
18-count fabric – 1⅜ x 1⅜ inches
11-count fabric – 2⅛ x 2¼ inches

INSTRUCTIONS
Tape or zigzag edges of Jobelan fabric to prevent fraying. Find the center of the chart, *page 143,* and the center of the fabric; begin stitching there. Use three plies of floss to work cross-stitches over two threads of fabric. Work blended needle stitches as indicated in the key. Work the French knots and backstitches using two plies of floss. Attach beads using two plies of matching floss. Press finished stitchery from back.

Pin stitchery onto ironing board and steam block to perfect square. Allow to dry thoroughly.

Bend back frame points from inside lid of box; press out mounting board. Center batting atop mounting board. Fit stitchery, centered, over batting. Turn edges to back side. Using thread, lace edges from side to side. Tape top and bottom edges, securing corners as necessary.

Glue braid around edge of mounted stitchery; allow glue to dry. Press covered mounting board into lid. Bend back frame points to secure.

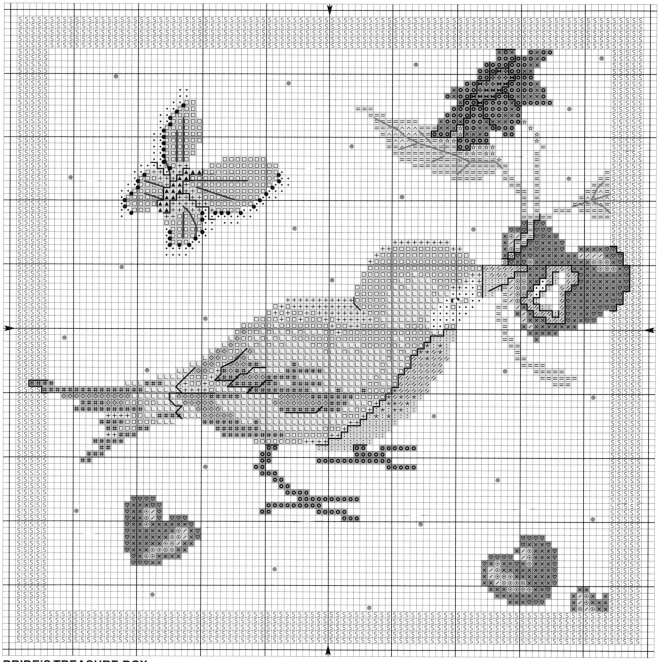

BRIDE'S TREASURE BOX

BRIDE'S TREASURE BOX

ANCHOR		DMC	
002	⊡	000	White
1006	☒	304	Christmas red
403	■	310	Black
038	⊙	335	Rose
217	☆	367	Medium pistachio
214	═	368	Light pistachio
305	S	725	Topaz
175	+	794	Cornflower blue
144	☐	800	Delft blue
1005	♥	816	Garnet
333	◖	900	Burnt orange
1015	✤	918	Red copper
1003	⣿	922	Copper

ANCHOR		DMC	
381	▣	938	Coffee brown
1002	★	977	Light golden brown
242	∧	989	Forest green
260	▲	3364	Loden
025	⁄	3716	Rose pink
869	⌗	3743	Antique violet
1031	∟	3753	Antique blue
363	⊘	3827	Pale golden brown

BLENDED NEEDLE

869	△	3743	Antique violet (2X) and
1016		3727	Antique mauve (1X)

BACKSTITCH

683	╱	500	Blue green – leaf veins
175	╱	794	Cornflower blue – butterfly

ANCHOR		DMC	
BACKSTITCH			
403	╱	310	Black – all remaining backstitches
FRENCH KNOTS			
002	○	000	White – bird's eye
403	●	310	Black – butterfly's wings
BEADS			
	●	03015	Mill Hill Snow white antique seed beads

Stitch count: 98 high x 98 wide

Finished design sizes:
28-count fabric – 7 x 7 inches
36-count fabric – 5½ x 5½ inches
22-count fabric – 9 x 9 inches

"Breit" Ideas
for Spring

Felicitations

Pick your favorite small motif from this adorable collection and stitch it on a bib for a sweet little one.

The goose doorstop design would also make a wonderful decorative pillow for any room with country flair.

Stitch these nursery rhyme characters on separate pieces of perforated plastic, back with colorful felts, and hang from ribbons for an extra-special mobile for a baby.

Omit the personalization on the sampler to create an heirloom that will be treasured for generations.

The Happy Gardener

To make an extraordinary bookmark for a gardening friend, stitch all or part of the left or right panel of the sampler design on perforated plastic.

Use waste canvas to stitch the breathtaking apron skirt design at the bottom of a denim skirt or jumper. If stitching it on a jumper, you also can use the small floral design to decorate the bodice. Most of the tiny motifs, such as the potted plants and watering can, would add a wonderful touch to pockets and shirt collars.

Any of the banding designs would also work well on towels, tote bags, eyeglass cases, basket trims—just about anything!

Try stitching and framing each of the three gardening designs separately for an interesting look.

A Good Marriage

Stitch the outside portion of the sampler design to frame the newlywed's favorite wedding photograph.

Use the sampler alphabet to personalize a wedding album cover, bed linens, or towels for the happy couple.

Create a decorative pillow that can be enjoyed every day of the year by stitching your favorite saying in the center of the ring bearer's pillow design.

Cross-stitch our bluebird of happiness as a paperweight or greeting card, or on a cosmetic or jewelry bag.

Summer

Sun, blooms, and summer tea parties make bright opportunities for stitching pleasures. The warmth of the season brings smiles and special friends to share the sunshine. You'll find tea cozies and cake mats, tote bags and party trays–all ready to stitch for summer fun.

Stitch into Summer!

Time for Tea

Even an afternoon cup of tea will become a time of celebration when served from this bright and merry **Teatime Serving Tray.** The make-you-feel-good floss colors are brilliant against the crisp white 28-count Jobelan fabric background. We've chosen a red-painted wooden serving tray and mat that compliment this fun cross-stitch design. Turn the page for more cheerful projects for your home. Instructions and charts for all projects begin on page 151.

These colorful **Teapot Coasters** are as practical as they are pretty. Stitched on 18-count white Aida fabric, this set of six will add a touch of whimsy to your next card club gathering or stitching get-together.

Beckon guests inside with this playful **Teapot Welcome Sampler.** Perfect for an entry or kitchen wall, this hospitable framed piece stitches up with ease on 16-count white Aida cloth.

Brighten your summer window with can't-wait-to-stitch **Cheery Cherry Tiebacks**. Stitched on Aida stitchband, finishing is a breeze. Stitch our **Cherry Time Teapot Cozy** on 28-count Jubilee fabric and trim with colorful checked piping.

The **Teapot Table Runner**, edged with a flowing ruffle, perks up a kitchen counter or buffet top.

Teatime Serving Tray

As shown on page 146, tray is 12³⁄₈×16⁵⁄₈ inches.

MATERIALS

FABRIC

15×18-inch piece of 28-count white Jobelan fabric

FLOSS

Cotton embroidery floss in colors listed in key, right

SUPPLIES

Needle

Embroidery hoop

Purchased serving tray kit suitable for inserting cross-stitch with glass top and a mat, if desired

13×17-inch piece of fleece

Tape

INSTRUCTIONS

Tape or zigzag edges of the Jobelan fabric to prevent fraying. Find the center of the chart, *pages 152–153,* and the center of the fabric; begin stitching there. Use two plies of floss to work cross-stitches over two threads of fabric. Work blended needle stitches, straight stitches, satin stitches, French knots, and backstitches as indicated in the key. Press the finished stitchery from the back.

   Unassemble the tray following the manufacturer's instructions. Clean the glass.

   Cut the fleece to the size of the mounting board in the tray kit. Repeat for stitchery, centering design. Layer fleece and stitched design on the mounting board; secure along edge using tape. Follow the manufacturer's instructions to reassemble the tray.

TEATIME SERVING TRAY

ANCHOR		DMC	
002	•	000	White
352	▼	300	Deep mahogany
148	◢	311	Navy
218	◆	319	Dark pistachio
118	◑	340	Medium periwinkle
013	◎	349	Dark coral
010	+	351	Light coral
009	▷	352	Pale coral
351	◈	400	Dark mahogany
267	◩	470	Avocado
162	◪	517	Dark wedgwood blue
1038	∨	519	Dark sky blue
891	✶	676	Light old gold
923	◰	699	Dark Christmas green
227	✕	701	True Christmas green
238	△	703	Chartreuse
326	◓	720	Dark bittersweet
295	╱	726	Topaz
281	▨	732	Olive
303	S	742	Light tangerine
175	◇	794	Light cornflower blue
013	♥	817	Deep coral
269	★	936	Medium pine green
298	▽	972	Canary
360	⋈	3031	Deep mocha
268	✻	3345	Hunter green
120	└	3747	Pale periwinkle
169	=	3760	Medium wedgwood blue
1015	◤	3777	Deep terra-cotta
1013	◿	3778	True terra-cotta
059	◗	3804	Dark cyclamen
062	♡	3806	Light cyclamen
386	▯	3823	Pale yellow
9575	▢	3824	Melon
890	◈	3829	Deep old gold

BLENDED NEEDLE

1049 1046	‖	301 435	Medium mahogany (1X) and Light chestnut (1X)
891 300	D	676 745	Light old gold (1X) and Light yellow (1X)
324 314	☆	721 741	Medium bittersweet (1X) and Medium tangerine (1X)

ANCHOR		DMC	
BACKSTITCH			
002	╱	000	White – candies highlight on cupcake (2X), cherry highlights around lid (1X)
010	╱	351	Light coral – flowers at top of teapot (2X)
162	╱	517	Dark wedgwood blue – lid trim (1X)
303	╱	742	Light tangerine – trim at base of teapot (2X)
862	╱	934	Deep pine green – cherry leaf vein (1X)
062	╱	3806	Light cyclamen – cupcake stripe (1X)
403	╱	310	Black – all remaining backstitches (1X)
STRAIGHT STITCH			
002	╱	000	White – cupcake ridge pattern (2X)
403	╱	310	Black – lines on cupcake paper (1X)
1038	╱	519	Dark sky blue – wrapped candy detail (1X)
169	╱	3760	Medium wedgwood blue – cupcake ridge pattern (2X)
SATIN STITCH			
267	╱	470	Avocado – cupcake trim (2X)
FRENCH KNOTS			
403	•	310	Black – flower centers at base of teapot and cherries at lid of teapot (1X)
013	•	349	Dark coral – table cloth (1X)
162	•	517	Dark wedgwood blue – handle and spout (1X); teapot and lid (2X)
281	•	732	Olive – base of teapot (1X)
303	•	742	Light tangerine – flower centers (1X)

Stitch count: 116 high x 168 wide

Finished design sizes:
28-count fabric – 8¼ x 12 inches
36-count fabric – 6½ x 9³⁄₈ inches
22-count fabric – 10½ x 15¼ inches

Teapot Coasters

As shown on page 148, coasters are 4 inches in diameter.

MATERIALS *for one coaster*

FABRIC

8×8-inch piece of 18-count white Aida cloth

FLOSS

Cotton embroidery floss in colors listed in key on page 154

SUPPLIES

Needle

Embroidery hoop

4-inch-diameter craft wood circle, ¼-inch thick

White acrylic paint

Paintbrush

4-inch-diameter circle of fleece

4-inch-diameter circle of cork, ¹⁄₁₆-inch thick

Tacky fabric glue

½ yard of ¼-inch-wide black flat braid

Fabric protector spray

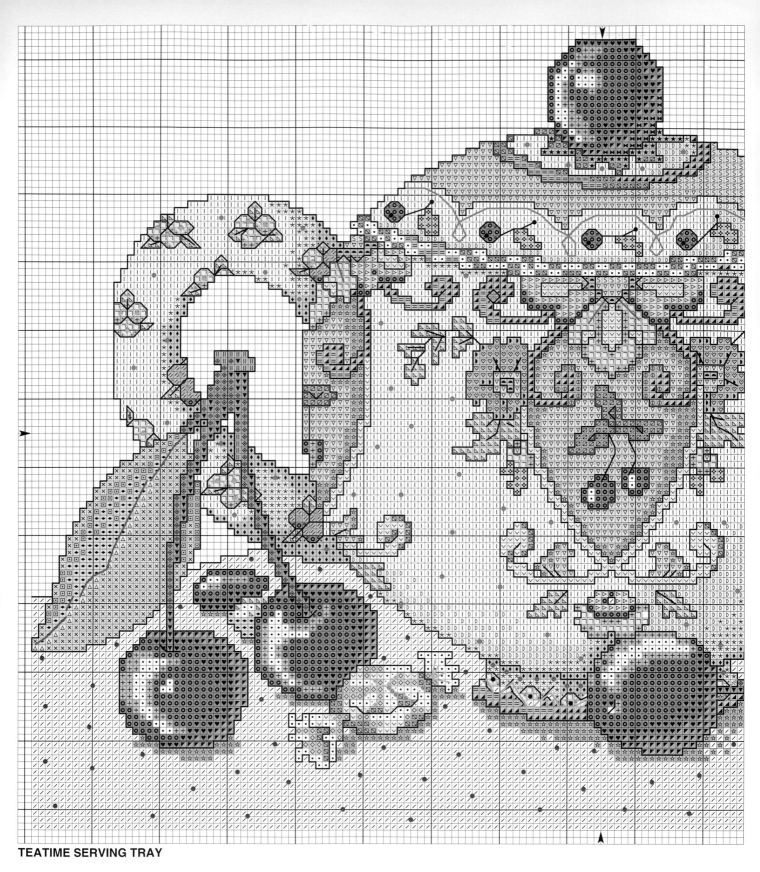

TEATIME SERVING TRAY

INSTRUCTIONS

Tape or zigzag the edges of the
Aida cloth to prevent fraying. Find
the center of desired chart, *pages
154–156,* and the center of the

Aida cloth; begin stitching there.
Use two plies of floss to work the
cross-stitches. Work the blended
needle stitches as indicated in the
key, *page 154.* Use one ply of floss

to work the backstitches. Press the
finished stitchery from the back.

Paint the wood circle white; allow
the paint to dry. Glue the fleece
circle to the top. Trim the stitchery

Teapot Welcome Sampler

As shown on page 149, the finished sampler measures 8×10 inches.

MATERIALS

FABRIC

16×18-inch piece of 16-count white Aida cloth

FLOSS

Cotton embroidery floss in colors listed in key on page 157

SUPPLIES

Needle

Embroidery hoop

INSTRUCTIONS

Tape or zigzag the edges of the fabric to prevent fraying. Find the center of the chart, *pages 156–157,* and of fabric; begin stitching there. Use two plies of floss to work the cross-stitches. Work the backstitches as indicated in key.

Press finished stitchery from the back. Mat and frame as desired.

Cherry Time Teapot Cozy

As shown on page 150, teapot cozy measures 8×10¾ inches.

MATERIALS

FABRICS

14×16-inch piece of 28-count white Jubilee fabric

½ yard of red-check fabric

12×24-inch-piece of white batiste lining

FLOSS

Cotton embroidery floss in colors listed in key on page 159

Continued on page 155

to a 4½-inch-diameter circle with the design centered. Position the stitchery atop the fleece; glue to the wood around the edge. Glue the cork circle to the bottom of the wood circle. Glue the black braid around the edge, covering the edges of fabric. Allow the glue to dry. Spray the top of the coaster with fabric protector spray.

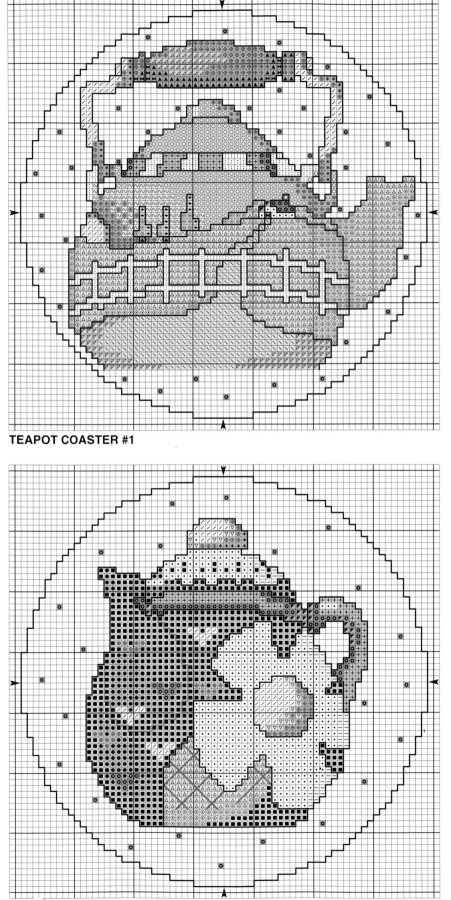

TEAPOT COASTER #1

TEAPOT COASTER #2

TEAPOT COASTERS		
ANCHOR		**DMC**
002	⊡	000 White
403	■	310 Black
218	◈	319 Dark pistachio
118	⏀	340 Medium periwinkle
013	◉	349 Dark coral
010	＋	351 Light coral
310	⊞	434 Medium chestnut
238	△	703 Chartreuse
324	✳	721 Medium bittersweet
295	∕	726 Topaz
361	▢	738 Light tan
314	⊕	741 Medium tangerine
275	⋮	746 Off white
259	∧	772 Loden
176	⊖	793 Medium cornflower blue
175	◇	794 Light cornflower blue
359	▲	801 Coffee brown
257	⊙	905 Parrot green
298	▽	972 Canary
433	⊛	996 Electric blue
360	⋈	3031 Deep mocha
886	⟍	3047 Yellow beige
1031	−	3753 Antique blue
928	○	3761 Medium sky blue
1015	◪	3777 Deep terra-cotta
899	◿	3782 Light mocha
236	●	3799 Charcoal
363	◹	3827 Golden brown
BLENDED NEEDLE		
928	∿	3761 Medium sky blue (1X) and
1043		369 Pale pistachio (1X)
BACKSTITCH		
002	∕	000 White – spout on coaster 2
218	∕	319 Dark pistachio – leaf veins on coasters 2, 4, 5, and 6
1031	∕	3753 Antique blue – detail on coaster 4
403	╱	310 Black – all remaining backstitches

Stitch count: 68 high x 68 wide
Finished design sizes:
18-count fabric – 3³/₄ x 3³/₄ inches
14-count fabric – 4⁷/₈ x 4⁷/₈ inches
11-count fabric – 6¹/₈ x 6¹/₈ inches

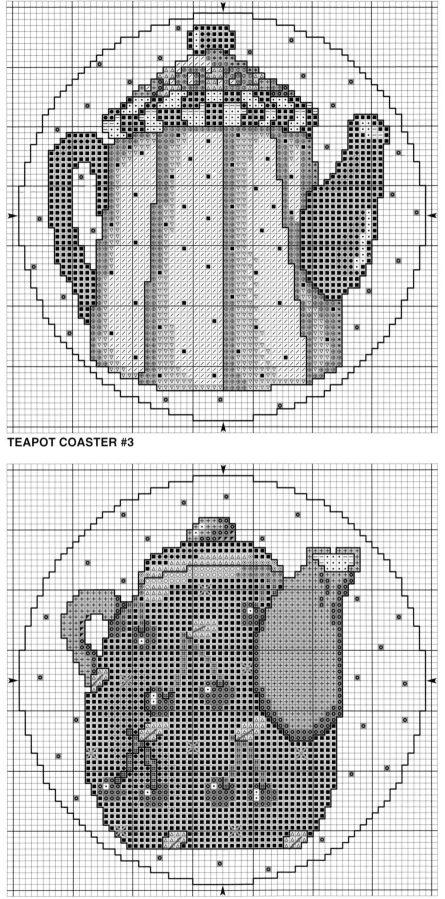

TEAPOT COASTER #3

TEAPOT COASTER #4

SUPPLIES
Needle; embroidery hoop
Tissue paper; fabric marking pen
½ yard of fleece
2 yards of narrow piping cord
White sewing thread

INSTRUCTIONS

Tape or zigzag the edges of Jubilee fabric to prevent fraying. Find the center of chart, *pages 158–159,* and center of the fabric; begin stitching there. Use two plies of floss to work cross-stitches. Work backstitches using one ply. Press finished stitchery from the back.

Cut an 11×14-inch rectangle from red-check fabric. Layer fleece behind stitchery and check rectangles; baste. Machine-quilt check rectangle as desired for cozy back.

Enlarge and trace pattern, *page 158,* onto tissue paper; cut out. Center tissue paper pattern over stitching on cozy front. Draw around pattern; cut out. In addition, use pattern to cut out cozy back from quilted rectangle and two lining pieces from batiste.

Sew all seams with right sides facing using ½-inch seam allowances. After stitching, trim seams and clip curves.

Cut enough 1½-inch-wide bias strips from check fabric to total 75 inches. Cut 6 inches off strip and 6 inches from piping cord length; set aside. Center piping cord lengthwise on wrong side of long fabric strip. Fold fabric around cording, bringing raw edges together. Use zipper foot to sew through both layers of fabric close to cording. Sew piping to curved edge of cozy front. Set remaining piping aside.

Fold the 6-inch fabric strip in half lengthwise with right sides facing. Sew long edges together; trim seam. Using turning loop and method for enclosing

Continued on page 158

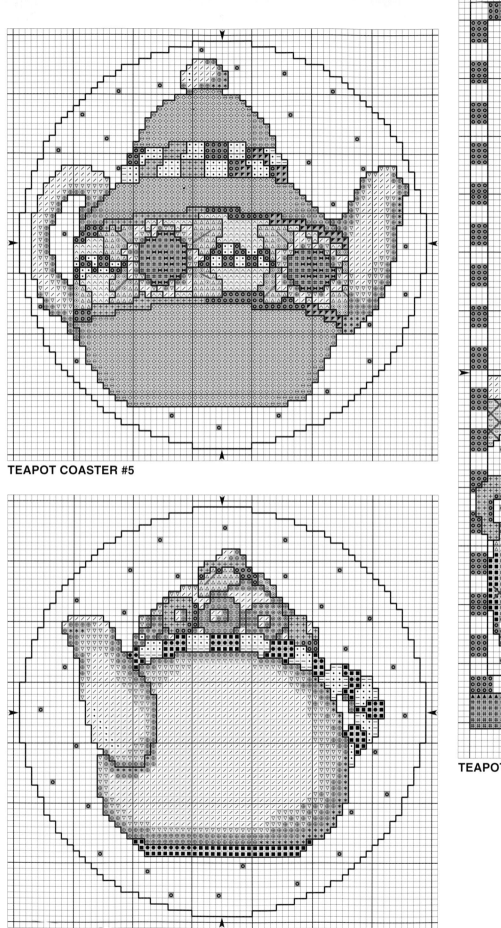

TEAPOT COASTER #5

TEAPOT COASTER #6

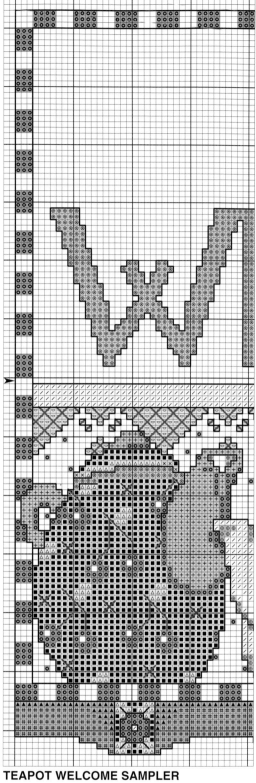

TEAPOT WELCOME SAMPLER

156

TEAPOT WELCOME SAMPLER

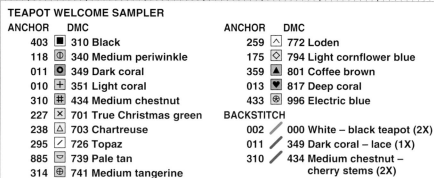

ANCHOR		DMC	
403	■	310	Black
118	⊕	340	Medium periwinkle
011	⊙	349	Dark coral
010	+	351	Light coral
310	#	434	Medium chestnut
227	×	701	True Christmas green
238	△	703	Chartreuse
295	╱	726	Topaz
885	▽	739	Pale tan
314	⊕	741	Medium tangerine

ANCHOR		DMC	
259	△	772	Loden
175	◇	794	Light cornflower blue
359	▲	801	Coffee brown
013	♥	817	Deep coral
433	⊛	996	Electric blue

BACKSTITCH

002	╱	000	White – black teapot (2X)
011	╱	349	Dark coral – lace (1X)
310	╱	434	Medium chestnut – cherry stems (2X)

ANCHOR		DMC	
433	╱	996	Electric blue – detail on teapot (2X)
403	╱	310	Black – all remaining backstitches (1X)

Stitch count: 127 high x 161 wide

Finished design sizes:
16-count fabric – 8 x 10 inches
14-count fabric – 9 x 11½ inches
11-count fabric – 11½ x 14⅝ inches

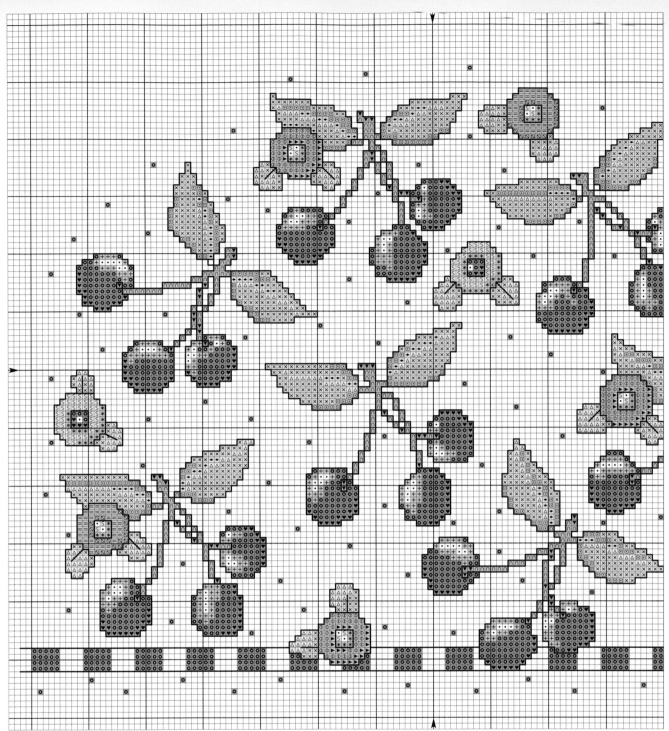

CHERRY TIME TEAPOT COZY

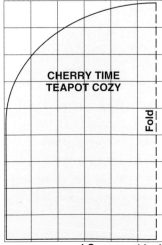

CHERRY TIME TEAPOT COZY

Fold

1 Square = 1 Inch

158

cord, cover 6-inch piece of piping cord. Bringing ends together at raw edge, sew loop to top of cozy back.

Sew cozy front to back along curved edge. Repeat for lining, leaving an opening; turn right side out. Stitch piping around bottom edge. Sew lining to cozy around bottom. Turn right side out through lining opening; sew opening closed. Press lining to inside and tack to seams, ½ inch from bottom.

Cheery Cherry Tiebacks

As shown on page 150, tiebacks measure 3¾×12 inches.

MATERIALS *for one pair*
FABRICS

Two 10×27-inch pieces of 16-count white Aida stitchband with red trim

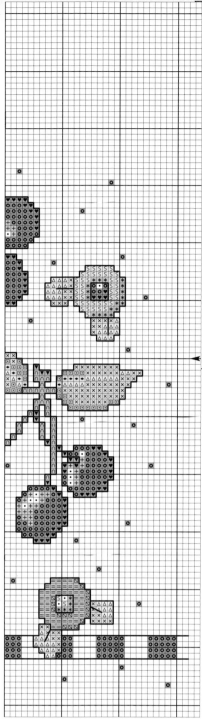

CHERRY TIME TEAPOT COZY

ANCHOR		DMC	
002	·	000	White
352	▼	300	Deep mahogany
1049	∩	301	Medium mahogany
218	◆	319	Dark pistachio
118	◑	340	Medium periwinkle
011	◉	349	Dark coral
010	+	351	Light coral
162	◩	517	Dark wedgwood blue
923	▣	699	Dark Christmas green
227	✕	701	True Christmas green
238	△	703	Chartreuse
324	✳	721	Medium bittersweet
303	S	742	Light tangerine
013	♥	817	Deep coral
1030	▶	3746	Dark periwinkle
169	=	3760	Medium wedgwood blue

BACKSTITCH

403	╱	310 Black – all backstitches

Stitch count: 110 high x 144 wide

Finished design sizes:
28-count fabric – 7⅞ x 10¼ inches
36-count fabric – 6⅛ x 8 inches
22-count fabric – 10 x 13 inches

CHEERY CHERRY TIEBACKS

ANCHOR		DMC	
002	·	000	White
352	▼	300	Deep mahogany
218	◆	319	Dark pistachio
013	◉	349	Dark coral
010	+	351	Light coral
227	✕	701	True Christmas green
238	△	703	Chartreuse
1015	◪	3777	Deep terra-cotta

BLENDED NEEDLE

1049	‖	301 Medium mahogany (1X) and
1046		435 Light chestnut (1X)

BACKSTITCH

352	╱	300 Deep mahogany – all backstitches

Stitch count: 48 high x 70 wide

Finished design sizes:
16-count fabric – 3 x 4⅜ inches
14-count fabric – 3½ x 5 inches
18-count fabric – 2⅝ x 3⅞ inches

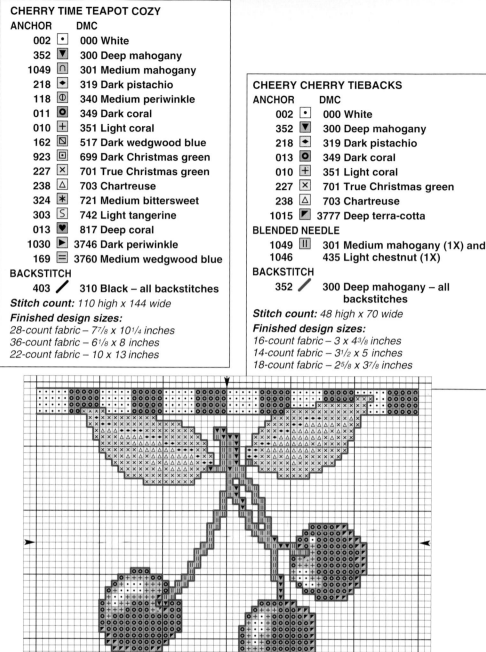

CHEERY CHERRY TIEBACKS

Two 2¾×25-inch strips of
   white batiste
FLOSS
Cotton embroidery floss in colors
   listed in key, above right
SUPPLIES
Needle
Embroidery hoop
Two 2¾×25-inch strips of fleece
White sewing thread
Two ¾-inch-diameter curtain rings

INSTRUCTIONS

Find center of chart, *above*, and of stitchband; begin stitching there. Use two plies of floss to work cross-stitches. Work blended needle stitches as indicated in key. Use one ply to work backstitches. Stitch the repeat design one time on each side of first motif. Press finished stitchery from back.

For each tieback, layer batiste and fleece; baste together. Using serger or edge-finishing stitch on machine, sew layers together around edges.

With fleece facing back of band, stitch the fleece-backed batiste strip to the cross-stitched band close to the edges. Serge or otherwise finish the raw edges at the ends. Sew the ends together, forming a circle. Press the seam open; topstitch each side of the seam to secure the seam allowances.

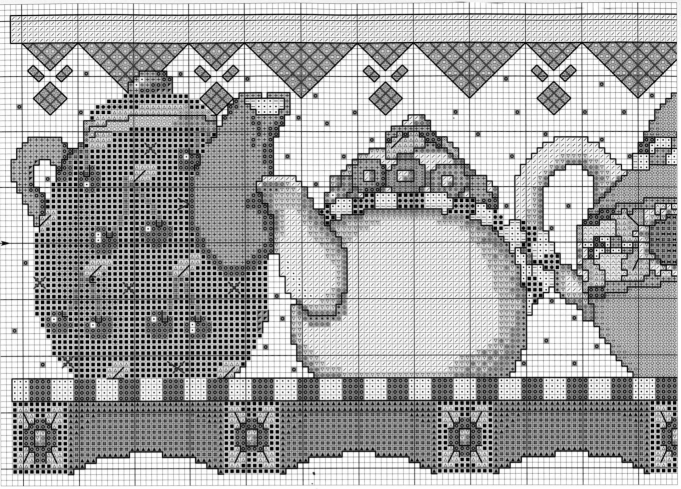

TEAPOT TABLE RUNNER

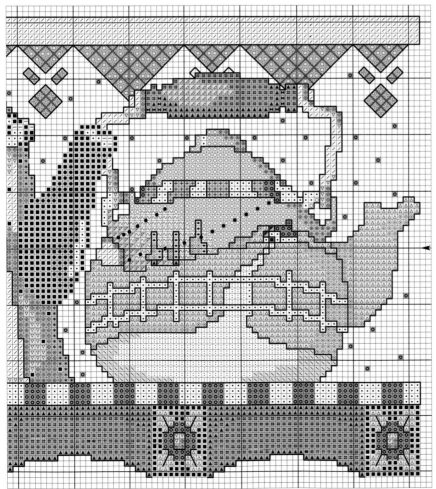

Arrange tieback with seam at back; handsew ring to top inside edge. Sew to opposite end on each tieback.

Teapot Table Runner

As shown on page 150, table runner is 10¼×26¼ inches.

MATERIALS

FABRICS
16×32-inch piece of 28-count white Cashel linen; 1 yard of 45-inch-wide bright yellow print fabric

½ yard of 45-inch-wide white batiste

THREADS
Cotton embroidery floss in colors listed in key, page 161; white sewing thread

SUPPLIES
Needle; embroidery hoop

2 yards of red piping or narrow sew-in cord

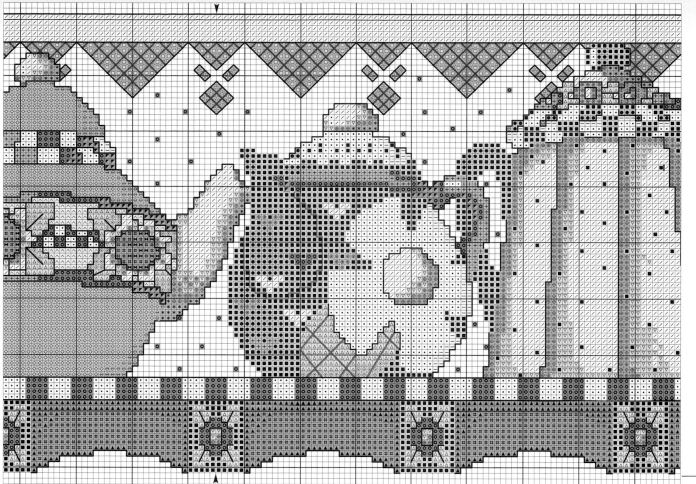

INSTRUCTIONS

Tape or zigzag edges of fabric. Find center of chart, *above*, and of fabric; begin stitching there. Use two plies of floss to work cross-stitches over two threads of fabric. Work blended needle stitches as indicated in key. Use one ply to work French knots and backstitches. Press stitchery from back.

Baste batiste to back of fabric, stitching 1¼ inches beyond design edges all around. Sew piping to front along basting line. Trim fabric ½ inch beyond piping seam.

For ruffle, cut 3-inch-wide bias strips from yellow print to total 130 inches. Sew short ends together to make a circle. Press strip in half lengthwise with wrong sides facing. Sew a gathering thread through both layers close to raw edges. Pin ruffle to front of table runner; adjust gathers evenly. Baste in place using ½-inch seam allowance.

Use table runner front as pattern to cut batiste back piece. Sew back to front with right sides facing; leave opening for turning. Trim seams and clip corners. Turn table runner right side out and sew opening closed.

TEAPOT TABLE RUNNER

ANCHOR		DMC
002	⊡	000 White
403	■	310 Black
218	◆	319 Dark pistachio
118	◖	340 Medium periwinkle
013	◎	349 Dark coral
010	+	351 Light coral
310	#	434 Medium chestnut
238	△	703 Chartreuse
324	✳	721 Medium bittersweet
295	╱	726 Topaz
361	▢	738 Light tan
314	⊕	741 Medium tangerine
275	⫶	746 Off white
259	⋀	772 Loden
176	⊖	793 Medium cornflower blue
175	◈	794 Light cornflower blue
359	▲	801 Coffee brown
257	⊙	905 Parrot green
298	▽	972 Canary
433	⊛	996 Electric blue
360	⋈	3031 Deep mocha
886	◺	3047 Yellow beige
1031	⊟	3753 Antique blue
928	◍	3761 Medium sky blue

ANCHOR		DMC
1015	◤	3777 Deep terra-cotta
899	◿	3782 Light mocha
236	●	3799 Charcoal
363	◸	3827 Golden brown

BLENDED NEEDLE

928	∿	3761 Medium sky blue (1X) and
1043		369 Pale pistachio (1X)

BACKSTITCH

002	╱	000 White – black teapot spout
218	╱	319 Dark pistachio – leaf veins
013	╱	349 Dark coral – lace
928	╱	3761 Medium sky blue – detail on black teapot
403	╱	310 Black – all remaining backstitches

FRENCH KNOT

403	●	310 Black – sky on green teapot

Stitch count: 82 high x 314 wide
Finished design sizes:
28-count fabric – 5⅞ x 22½ inches
36-count fabric – 4½ x 17½ inches
22-count fabric – 7½ x 28½ inches

It's Good to be Queen

Imagine the thrill of being queen–even for a day! Our **It's Good to be Queen Sampler** touts the pleasures of this magical feeling with finely stitched details. Every time you look at this humorous Mary Engelbreit piece you'll discover something new. The fun-loving sampler is stitched over two threads of 28-count tan Jobelan and accented with ribbons, beads, bells, and metallic threads. Turn the page for more queenly projects. Instructions and charts for all projects begin on *page 166.*

This fancily finished **Crown Pillow** is certain to bring smiles no matter where it makes its home. Stitched over two threads of 25-count lavender Lugana fabric, this lively design could be completed in a weekend.

With sparkling gem accents, our striking black **Royal Checkbook Cover** is fit for (and can be personalized for) any queen. The **Queen Paperweight** makes a wonderful little pick-me-up. The queen herself is stitched on 18-count Damask Aida cloth and is inserted into an acrylic paperweight. Trimmed with gold cord, this desk accessory keeps all royal documents in place.

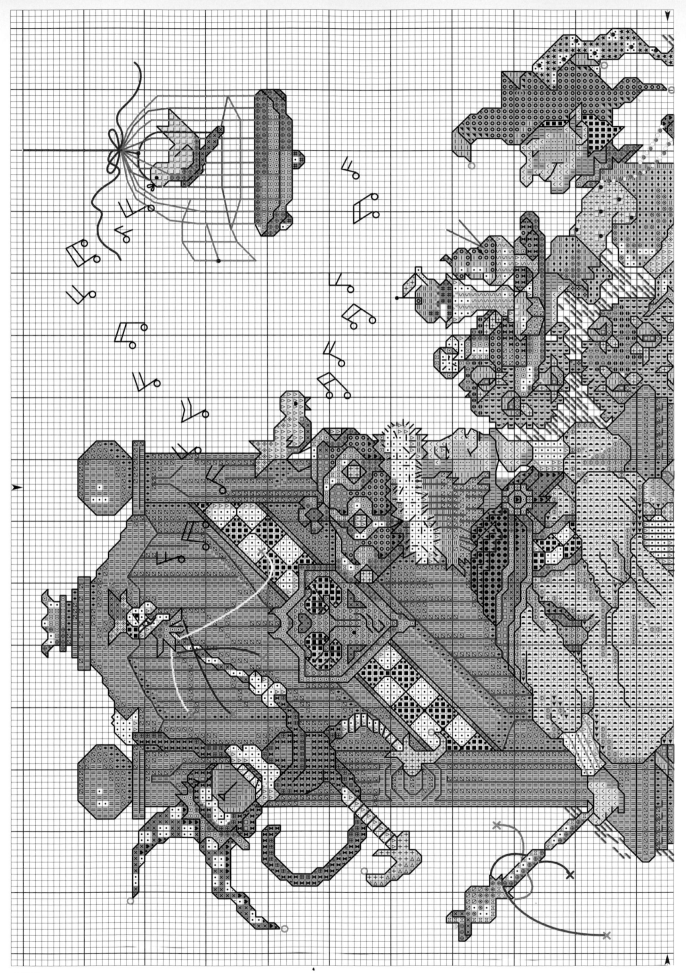

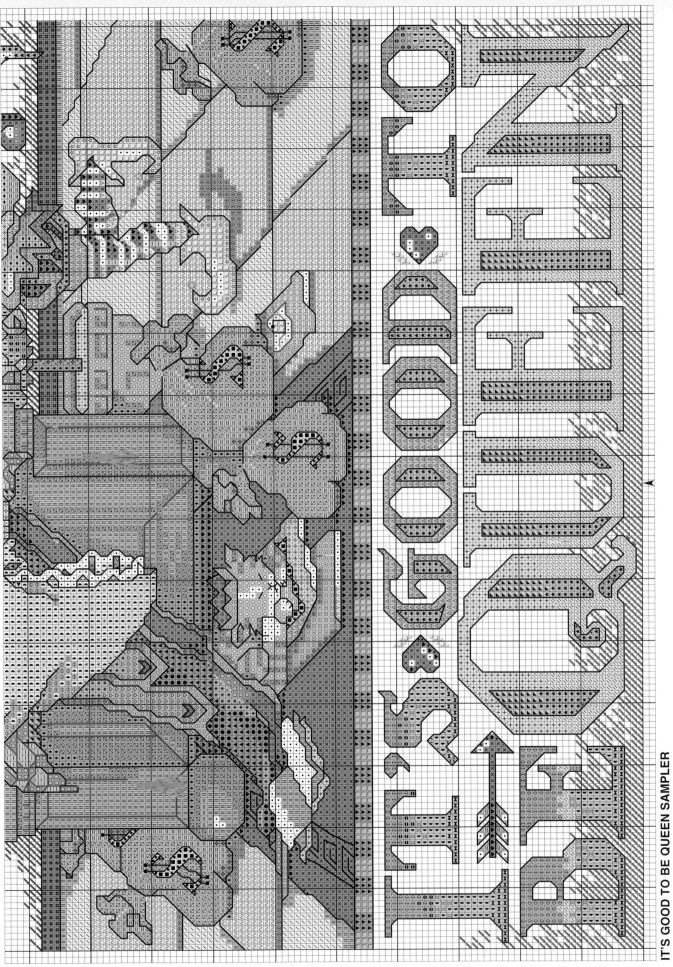

Queen Sampler

As shown on page 162, the finished sampler measures 14¾×10¾ inches.

MATERIALS

FABRIC
20×16-inch piece of 28-count tan Jobelan fabric

THREADS
Cotton embroidery floss in colors listed in key, left

Metallic thread in color listed in key

SUPPLIES
Needle; embroidery hoop

Beads and ribbons as listed in key

16¾×12¾-inch mat with 14¾×10¾-inch opening; crafts glue

Two yards of 1-inch-wide purple grosgrain ribbon; 4⅛ yards of ¼-inch-wide lavender grosgrain ribbon

INSTRUCTIONS

Tape or zigzag edges of fabric. Find the center of chart, *pages 166–167*, and of fabric; begin stitching there. Use two plies of floss to work cross-stitches and half cross-stitches over two threads of fabric. Work the blended needle stitches using one ply of each color. Use two plies to work the straight stitches, satin stitches, lazy daisy stitches, and French knots unless otherwise indicated in key. Work the backstitches using one ply. Press finished stitchery from back.

To create ribbon-striped mat, glue purple ribbon to top of mat, trimming lengths as necessary. Cut lavender ribbon into ninety-eight 1½-inch-long pieces. Glue atop purple ribbon, leaving ¼ inch between ribbons. Using photo, *page 162,* as a guide, glue lavender ribbons around mat. Let glue dry. Frame as desired.

IT'S GOOD TO BE QUEEN SAMPLER

ANCHOR	DMC	Color
002	000	White
110	208	Dark lavender
108	210	Light lavender
1026	225	Pale shell pink
1006	304	Christmas red
042	309	Light rose
403	310	Black
400	317	Pewter
100	327	Antique violet
038	335	Medium rose
013	349	Coral
217	367	Pistachio
914	407	Medium cocoa
358	433	Dark chestnut
1046	435	Light chestnut
362	437	Tan
231	453	Light shell gray
253	472	Avocado
1038	519	Sky blue
860	522	Olive drab
933	543	Pale beige brown
102	550	Deep violet
096	554	Light violet
936	632	Deep cocoa
324	721	Bittersweet
314	741	Medium tangerine
1012	754	Peach
1022	760	True salmon
1021	761	Light salmon
128	775	Baby blue
178	791	Deep cornflower blue
177	792	Dark cornflower blue

ANCHOR	DMC	Color
175	794	Light cornflower blue
161	813	Powder blue
043	815	Garnet
360	839	Dark beige brown
378	841	True beige brown
052	899	Light rose
850	926	Medium gray blue
862	934	Deep pine green
861	935	Dark pine green
268	937	True pine green
4146	950	Light rose beige
1001	976	Medium golden brown
242	989	Forest green
883	3064	Light cocoa
896	3721	Dark shell pink
779	3768	Dark gray blue
1007	3772	Dark cocoa
177	3807	True cornflower blue
1048	3826	Dark golden brown

BLENDED NEEDLE

ANCHOR	DMC	Color
1038	519	Sky blue (1X) and
399	318	Steel (1X)
102	550	Deep violet (1X) and
178	791	Deep cornflower blue (1X)
096	554	Light violet (1X) and
303	742	Light tangerine (1X) and
305	725	Topaz (1X)
379	840	Medium beige brown (1X) and
233	451	Dark shell gray (1X)
861	935	Deep pine green (1X) and
779	3768	Dark gray blue (1X)

HALF CROSS-STITCH (stitch in direction of symbol)

ANCHOR	DMC	Color
1046	435	Light chestnut
1048	3776	Mahogany

ANCHOR DMC BACKSTITCH

ANCHOR	DMC	Color
1006	304	Christmas red – stripes on Queen's sock, hearts on Queen's cape, monkey's socks, toy jester slippers
038	335	Medium rose – detail on Queen's slippers
358	433	Dark chestnut – hair, eyebrow, throne, flower pot
1038	519	Sky blue – stripes on Queen's sleeves
324	721	Bittersweet – book
303	742	Light tangerine – toy jester's hat
242	989	Forest green – book under money sack
403	310	Black – all remaining backstitches

STRAIGHT STITCH

ANCHOR	DMC	Color
1006	304	Christmas red – money sacks (6X)
403	310	Black – crown detail
096	554	Light violet – shield detail (2X)
324	721	Medium bittersweet – birdcage
314	741	Medium tangerine – birdcage
002	000	White (1X) and
1006	304	Christmas red (1X) – straws

SATIN STITCH

ANCHOR	DMC	Color
1006	304	Christmas red – Queen's mouth

COUCHING

ANCHOR	DMC	Color
1006	304	Christmas red – perch bar (3X)

LAZY DAISY

ANCHOR	DMC	Color
403	310	Black – beak of bird in cage

FRENCH KNOTS

ANCHOR	DMC	Color
1006	304	Christmas red – perch bar, birdcage door, jester's hat, jester's shirt

---

ANCHOR DMC FRENCH KNOTS

ANCHOR	DMC	Color
403	310	Black – bird's eye, toy jester's eye, shield, money sacks, cherry on sundae
305	725	Topaz – Queen's staff

MILL HILL BEADS

Code	Color
02059	Yellow seed bead – jester's necklace
02063	Red seed bead – jester's necklace
05081	Black frost pebble bead – musical notes
05557	Old gold pebble bead – hats and shoes

ATTACHMENTS

- Blue ⅛-inch satin ribbon – toy jester, Queen's staff
- Yellow ⅛-inch satin ribbon – toy jester
- Pink ⅛-inch satin ribbon – Queen's staff
- Rose ⅛-inch satin ribbon – birdcage, Queen's staff
- Star charm – Queen's staff
- Heart charm – Queen's staff
- Jingle bells – toy jester, jester

Stitch count: 210 high x 151 wide
Finished design sizes:
28-count fabric – 15 x 10¾ inches
36-count fabric – 11⅝ x 8⅜ inches
22-count fabric – 19 x 13¾ inches

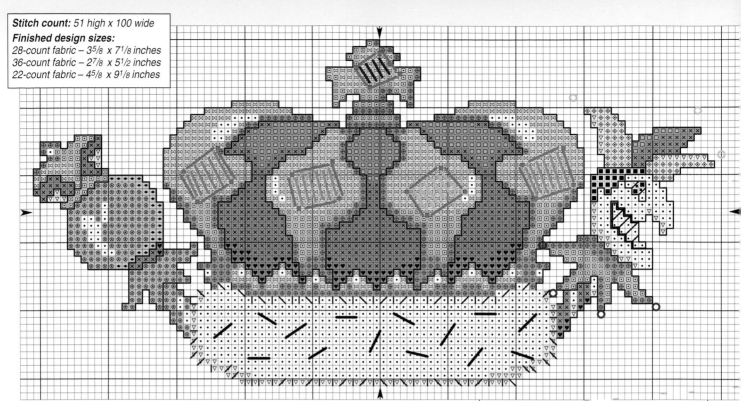

CROWN PILLOW

Crown Pillow

As shown on page 164, the finished pillow measures 11×11¾ inches.

MATERIALS

FABRICS

14×16-inch piece of 25-count lavender
  Lugana fabric

½ yard of 45-inch-wide purple satin

¼ yard of 45-inch-wide red taffeta

FLOSS

Cotton embroidery floss in colors listed
  in key, right

SUPPLIES

Needle

Embroidery hoop

Mill Hill beads as listed in the key

Five ½-inch star buttons

10-inch piece of ⅛-inch-wide lavender
  satin ribbon

10-inch piece of ⅛-inch-wide light blue
  satin ribbon

5-inch piece of ⅛-inch-wide red satin
  ribbon

5-inch piece of ⅛-inch-wide light yellow
  satin ribbon

One ½-inch heart button

3 small gold bells

11¾×12¼-inch piece of fleece

2 yards of gold metallic piping

Eight 2-inch-long gold metallic tassels

12×12-inch pillow form

INSTRUCTIONS

Tape or zigzag the edges of fabric
to prevent fraying. Find the center
of the chart, *above,* and the center of
Lugana fabric; begin stitching there.
Use three plies of floss to work the
cross-stitches over two threads of
fabric. Work blended needle stitches
as indicated in the key. Use two plies
to work straight stitches and backstitches. Attach beads and buttons
using one ply of matching floss.

Use the photograph on *page 164*
as a guide to tack ribbons in place
using one ply of matching floss. Sew
on buttons and bells at the lower
ends of ribbons as desired. Press
finished stitchery from back.

Cut thirty-eight 1½×1½-inch
squares each from purple and red
fabrics. Measurements include

CROWN PILLOW

ANCHOR		DMC	
002	•	000	White
1006	✕	304	Christmas red
403	■	310	Black
038	□	335	Medium rose
324	⊕	721	Bittersweet
314	⊡	741	Medium tangerine
128	▽	775	Baby blue
161	◈	813	Powder blue
043	♥	815	Garnet
1001	⊛	976	Medium golden brown
1048	◆	3826	Dark golden brown

BLENDED NEEDLE

303	⊠	742	Light tangerine (2X) and
305		725	Topaz (1X)

BACKSTITCH

1006	╱	304	Christmas red – jester's mouth
403	╱	310	Black – all remaining backstitches

STRAIGHT STITCH

403	╱	310	Black – fur on crown

MILL HILL BEADS

•	00557	Gold seed bead
○	05025	Ruby pebble bead
╱	72014	Black small bugle bead
╱	72052	Red velvet small bugle bead
╱	82011	Victorian gold medium bugle bead
╱	82045	Willow medium bugle bead
╱	82053	Nutmeg medium bugle bead
╱	82054	Aqua ice medium bugle bead

ATTACHMENTS

○	688	Yellow ½-inch star buttons

169

¼-inch seam allowances. Sew seams with right sides of fabric facing unless otherwise indicated.

For top and bottom borders, sew the squares together in checkerboard fashion, making two horizontal rows of 12 squares each. For each side border, sew the squares in the same manner, making two vertical rows of seven squares each.

Trim Lugana fabric so design is centered horizontally in rectangle measuring 7¾ inches long and 8½ inches wide, with top stitches of design 1¾ inches down from top edge of fabric.

Sew side border to each side of the design rectangle. Press the seams toward the borders. Sew the top and bottom borders to the design; press the seams.

Baste fleece to the back of the pillow top. Stitch piping around perimeter. Use the pillow top as a pattern to cut the pillow back from the purple fabric. Sew the pillow front to the back. While stitching, sew in the hanging loops of two tassels at each corner and leave opening along one side to insert the pillow form. Turn the pillow right side out, insert the pillow form, and sew the opening closed.

Royal Checkbook Cover

As shown on page 165, the finished checkbook cover measures 7⅛×7¼ inches.

MATERIALS
FABRICS
11×11-inch piece of 14-count black Aida cloth
¼ yard of 45-inch-wide purple cotton lining fabric
FLOSS
Cotton embroidery floss in colors listed in key, right
SUPPLIES
Graph paper
Needle
Embroidery hoop
8×8-inch piece of fleece
Black sewing thread
1 yard of narrow black sew-in braid
Six ⅝×⅜-inch oval acrylic jewels in desired colors
Fabric glue

INSTRUCTIONS
Use alphabet chart, *page 171,* to chart initials for center crest.

Tape or zigzag the edges of the Aida cloth to prevent fraying. Find the center of the chart, *below.* Measure 2¾ inches up from the bottom center of the Aida cloth; begin stitching there. Use three plies of floss to work the cross-stitches. Work the backstitches using two plies of floss. Press the finished stitchery from the back.

Trim the Aida cloth so the stitched design is centered along the bottom half of the rectangle measuring 7⅜ inches long and 7½ inches wide, with bottom stitches of the design ¾ inch above bottom edge of fabric. Baste fleece to the back; trim edges to match.

ROYAL CHECKBOOK COVER			
ANCHOR		DMC	
002	•	000 White	
1006	☒	304 Christmas red	
403	■	310 Black	
099	▶	552 Dark violet	
098	D	553 Medium violet	
256	◁	704 Chartreuse	
305	▽	725 Topaz	
303	▦	742 Light tangerine	
433	⊠	996 Electric blue	
BACKSTITCH			
403	╱	310 Black – all backstitches	

Stitch count: 35 high x 90 wide
Finished design sizes:
14-count fabric – 2½ x 6½ inches
11-count fabric – 3⅛ x 8⅛ inches
18-count fabric – 2 x 5 inches

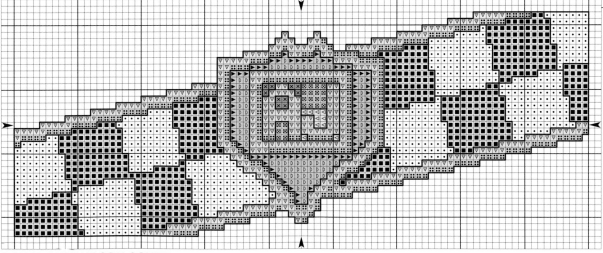

ROYAL CHECKBOOK COVER

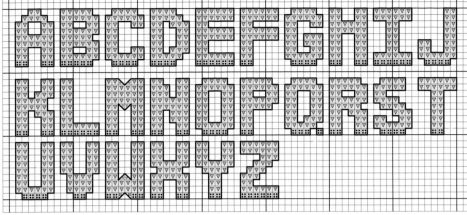

ROYAL CHECKBOOK COVER ALPHABET

Sew braid around perimeter of checkbook cover rectangle using ¼-inch seam allowance.

Cut two 2¾×7½-inch end flaps and one lining rectangle 7 inches long and 7½ inches wide. Measurements include ¼-inch seam allowances where necessary. Sew seams with right sides of fabric facing, unless otherwise indicated.

Press under ¼ inch twice along one long edge of each end flap; stitch to hem. Sew end flaps to top and bottom of cover, matching raw edges and sewing along braid seam line. Next, sew lining piece on top, stitching along side edges only. Trim corners.

Turn cover right side out through lining. Turn end flaps to right side. Glue jewels to design using photograph, *page 165*, as a guide.

Queen Paperweight

As shown on page 165, the finished paperweight measures 4×2⅝×¾ inches.

MATERIALS
FABRIC
8×6-inch piece of 18-count black Damask Aida cloth

FLOSS
Cotton embroidery floss in colors listed in key, below right

SUPPLIES
Needle

Embroidery hoop

Purchased acrylic paperweight kit suitable for mounting 3¾×2¼-inch cross-stitch

½ yard of gold metallic rattail cord

Crafts glue

Red or gold heart charm, or other desired charm

INSTRUCTIONS

Tape or zigzag the edges of Aida cloth to prevent fraying. Find the center of the chart, *above right*, and the center of the Aida cloth; begin stitching there. Use two plies of floss to work cross-stitches. Work the backstitches using one ply of floss. Press the finished stitchery from the back.

Mount the cross-stitch design into the paperweight following the instructions from the manufacturer.

Glue the gold metallic rattail cord around the top lip of the acrylic paperweight, beginning in the lower right corner. Glue desired charm to the corner, covering the ends of the rattail cord.

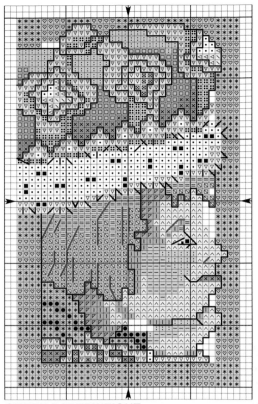

QUEEN PAPERWEIGHT

QUEEN PAPERWEIGHT		
ANCHOR		DMC
002	·	000 White
110	✳	208 Dark lavender
1006	☒	304 Christmas red
403	■	310 Black
038	☐	335 Medium rose
1046	⊟	435 Light chestnut
362	◲	437 Tan
102	●	550 Deep violet
096	♡	554 Light violet
226	◪	702 Christmas green
256	◁	704 Chartreuse
305	▽	725 Topaz
303	⊞	742 Light tangerine
1012	⋀	754 Peach
1022	⋮	760 True salmon
1021	⊟	761 Light salmon
128	▽	775 Baby blue
433	☒	996 Electric blue
883	❙	3064 Light cocoa
1008	◪	3773 Medium rose beige
BACKSTITCH		
358	╱	433 Dark chestnut – hair and eyebrow
403	╱	310 Black – all remaining backstitches

Stitch count: 60 high x 36 wide
Finished design sizes:
18-count fabric – 3⅜ x 2 inches
20-count fabric – 3 x 1⅞ inches
14-count fabric – 4¼ x 2½ inches

Bloom
Where You're Planted

This sweet Mary Engelbreit design sends a heartfelt message to be remembered always. Sure to be loved by anyone who sees them, the intricate stitches of our **Bloom Where You're Planted Sampler** are worked over two threads of 28-count light yellow Meran fabric. The border motif becomes a dimensional garden itself, with the addition of tiny crystal flowers. For more beautiful floral projects, turn the page. Instructions and charts for all projects begin on *page 177.*

Ladies of all ages will be proud to keep their mirror and hanky in this petite **Sunshine Satchel**. The delicate floral flap, laying gently against the sunny yellow fabric bottom, is cross-stitched over two threads of 36-count antique white Edinborough linen.

Any centerpiece will get extra-special attention when placed upon this delightful **Summertime Cake Mat**. Stitched on 25-count Jobelan fabric, the design is repeated for each corner and finished by weaving narrow ribbon into the border and fringing the edges.

This clever **Floral Tote Bag** is roomy enough for a few shopping treasures or your latest stitching project. The vibrant design is stitched on subtle green water lily Jobelan fabric.

Our **Special Occasion Plant Pokes** each stitch up in an evening to add a personal touch to any gift. And finishing is a snap using bits of suede and polka-dot-painted balsa wood.

BLOOM SAMPLER

ANCHOR		DMC	
002	⊡	000	White
109	⌓	209	Lavender
897	⋈	221	Shell pink
403	■	310	Black
011	◎	349	Dark coral
010	○	351	Light coral
401	▶	413	Dark pewter
374	▦	420	Medium hazel
1045	◿	436	Dark tan
362	S	437	Medium tan
232	⋈	452	Shell gray
267	▣	469	Avocado
280	◢	581	Moss green
168	◺	597	Turquoise
305	☆	725	True topaz
281	▤	732	Olive
303	▽	742	Light tangerine
1022	▷	760	True salmon
1021	▯	761	Light salmon
176	◈	793	Medium cornflower blue
161	∧	813	Powder blue
013	✳	817	Deep coral
380	◨	838	Deep beige brown
1033	∼	932	True antique blue
862	◆	934	Pine green
881	∨	945	Dark ivory
4146	◁	950	Rose beige
1010	⋮	951	Medium ivory
314	△	970	Pumpkin
263	✕	3362	Loden
1032	└	3752	Light antique blue
1031	−	3753	Pale antique blue
373	▢	3828	True hazel

BLENDED NEEDLE

977	◢	334	Baby blue (1X) and
1034		931	Medium antique blue (1X)
891	◳	676	Old gold (1X) and
874		3822	Straw (1X)
176	▦	793	Medium cornflower blue (1X) and
401		413	Dark pewter (1X)
875	▽	3817	Celadon green (1X) and
1042		503	True blue green (1X)

BACKSTITCH

002	╱	000	White – bird's eyes
400	╱	317	True pewter – window frame
373	╱	3828	True hazel – vine leaf shadow
403	╱	310	Black – all remaining backstitches

STRAIGHT STITCH

280	╱	581	Moss green – vine on letters between beads
176	╱	793	Medium cornflower blue – blue flower detail

FRENCH KNOT

403	●	310	Black – eyes

MILL HILL BEADS

	○	02058	White seed beads

Stitch count: 232 high x 173 wide

Finished design sizes:
28-count fabric – 16½ x 12⅜ inches
36-count fabric – 12⅞ x 9⅝ inches
22-count fabric – 21 x 15¾ inches

Bloom Sampler

As shown on page 172, the finished sampler measures 16⅜×12¼ inches.

MATERIALS

FABRIC

24×20-inch piece of 28-count light yellow Meran fabric

FLOSS

Cotton embroidery floss in colors listed in key, left

SUPPLIES

Needle; embroidery hoop

Beads as listed in key

INSTRUCTIONS

Tape or zigzag the edges of fabric to prevent fraying. Find the center of the chart, *pages 178–179*, and the center of the fabric; begin stitching there. Use two plies of floss to work cross-stitches over two threads of fabric. Work the blended needle stitches using one ply of each floss color. Use one ply to work the French knots, straight stitches, and backstitches. Attach beads using one ply of matching floss.

Press finished stitchery from the back. Mat and frame as desired.

Sunshine Satchel

As shown on page 174, the finished satchel measures 7¼×7 inches.

MATERIALS

FABRICS

8×11-inch piece of 36-count antique white Edinborough linen

¼ yard of 45-inch-wide yellow fabric

¼ yard of 45-inch-wide white batiste lining

FLOSS

Cotton embroidery floss in colors listed in key on page 180

SUPPLIES

Needle; embroidery hoop

1 yard of narrow piping cord

¼ yard of 45-inch-wide fleece

Fabric marking pencil

Yellow rayon twist sewing thread

1 yard of ½-inch-wide flat cotton lace

1 yard of ⅛-inch-diameter gold and white satin cord

Glass Treasures sew-on charms: 6 flowers, 4 leaves, and 1 ladybug, in desired colors

6 gold metallic petite seed beads

Beading needle

INSTRUCTIONS

Tape or zigzag the edges of fabric to prevent fraying. Find the center of the chart, *page 180*, and the center of the fabric; begin stitching there. Use two plies of floss to work cross-stitches over two threads of fabric. Work French knots and backstitches using one ply. Press finished stitchery from the back.

Cut an 8×15-inch rectangle from the yellow fabric for satchel front and back. Cut same size from fleece. For lining, cut batiste rectangle 8×19 inches. Measurements include ½-inch seam allowances. Sew all seams with right sides of fabric facing unless otherwise indicated. After stitching, trim seams and clip corners.

Mark a ¾-inch diagonal grid on right side of yellow fabric rectangle. Layer fleece behind fabric and machine-quilt along lines using rayon twist thread.

Cut cross-stitch design in rectangle ¾ inch beyond design. Cut fleece to same size. Layer fleece behind stitchery; baste layers together

Continued on page 180

BLOOM SAMPLER

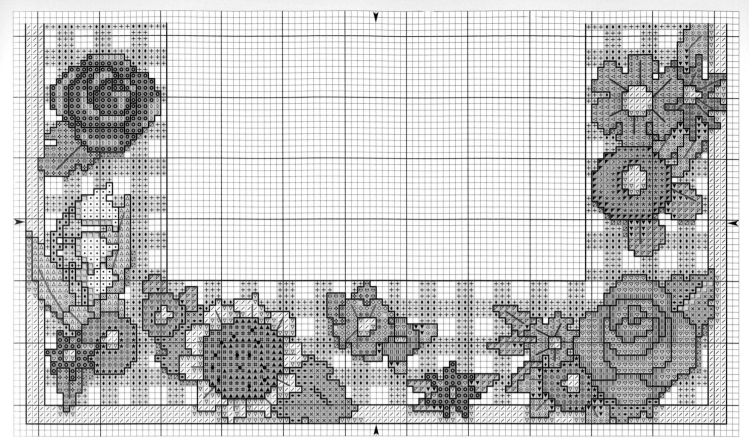

SUNSHINE SATCHEL

½ inch from edges. Sew the cross-stitch flap to one end of the quilted fabric. Sew lace around the sides and the end of the flap.

Fold yellow part of rectangle in half with flap folding over onto the front; mark the bottom fold of the purse. To make the piping, cut 1½-inch-wide bias strips to total 1 yard. Sew the short ends together to make one long strip. Center the piping cord lengthwise on the wrong side of the strip. Fold the fabric around the cording, bringing the raw edges together. Use a zipper foot to sew through both layers of the fabric close to the cording. Sew the piping along the sides and the top edge of the satchel front. *Note:* The flap is attached to the satchel back.

Sew side seams. Using the same configuration with the lining fabric, sew the side seams of the lining. Sew the lining flap to cross-stitched flap; turn flap to right side. Tuck lining into satchel. Hand-stitch one end of

satin cord to each side of satchel between outer fabric and lining at top corners. Blindstitch lining to base of piping along top edge.

Sew the glass charms to the satchel flap as desired, using glass seed beads to secure the charms in place.

SUNSHINE SATCHEL

ANCHOR		DMC	
002	·	000	White
215	⌐	320	True pistachio
059	◉	326	Deep rose
119	✴	333	Deep periwinkle
038	‖	335	Medium rose
118	▷	340	Medium periwinkle
217	⊿	367	Medium pistachio
683	✽	500	Deep blue green
098	⊕	553	Medium violet
096	◁	554	Light violet
228	◆	700	Medium Christmas green
226	⊙	702	Light Christmas green
256	△	704	Chartreuse
324	⊕	721	Medium bittersweet
295	／	726	Light topaz
303	▽	742	Light tangerine
1021	⌐	761	Light salmon
178	◪	791	Deep cornflower blue
360	▲	839	Dark beige brown
027	♡	894	Carnation
333	★	900	Burnt orange
204	＋	913	Nile green
089	▶	917	Plum
862	◆	934	Pine green
054	D	956	Geranium

ANCHOR		DMC	
246	▼	986	Dark forest green
189	⊖	991	Dark aquamarine
187	▽	992	Medium aquamarine
410	⊛	995	Dark electric blue
433	◇	996	Medium electric blue
263	✕	3362	Loden
087	▽	3607	Fuchsia
5975	#	3830	True terra-cotta

BACKSTITCH

ANCHOR		DMC	
683	／	500	Deep blue green – leaf veins
333	／	900	Burnt orange – orange flower, sunflower
089	／	917	Plum – flowers
246	／	986	Dark forest green – leaf veins
410	／	995	Dark electric blue – blue flower
403	／	310	Black – all remaining backstitches

FRENCH KNOT

ANCHOR		DMC	
403	●	310	Black – sunflower

Stitch count: 65 high x 114 wide

Finished design sizes:
32-count fabric – 4 x 7⅛ inches
28-count fabric – 4⅝ x 8⅛ inches
36-count fabric – 3⅝ x 6⅜ inches

Summertime Cake Mat

As shown on page 175, finished cake mat measures 17½×17½ inches.

MATERIALS

FABRIC
22×22-inch piece of 25-count antique ivory Jobelan fabric

FLOSS
Cotton embroidery floss in colors listed in key, below right

SUPPLIES
Needle; embroidery hoop

5-yard package of 7-mm-wide yellow silk ribbon

Tapestry needle

INSTRUCTIONS

Tape or zigzag the edges of the Jobelan fabric to prevent fraying. Find the center of the chart, *upper right*, and the center of the Jobelan fabric; begin stitching there. Use three plies of floss to work the cross-stitches over two threads of fabric. Work the French knots and backstitches using two plies of floss. Press finished stitchery from back.

Remove one thread from the Jobelan fabric 1 inch beyond the stitched design on all sides.

Thread needle with yellow silk ribbon and weave the ribbon through the pulled thread spaces, working over and under every two threads. Refer to the photograph, *page 175*, as a guide. Trim the fabric 1½ inches past the ribbon on all sides.

Pull the threads from all of the edges to make ½-inch-long fringe.

SUMMERTIME CAKE MAT

SUMMERTIME CAKE MAT

ANCHOR	DMC		ANCHOR	DMC
002	000 White		189	991 Dark aquamarine
215	320 True pistachio		187	992 Medium aquamarine
059	326 Deep rose		410	995 Dark electric blue
119	333 Deep periwinkle		433	996 Medium electric blue
118	340 Medium periwinkle		263	3362 Loden
098	553 Medium violet		5975	3830 True terra-cotta
096	554 Light violet		**BACKSTITCH**	
228	700 Medium Christmas green		683	500 Deep blue green – leaf veins
226	702 Light Christmas green		333	900 Burnt orange – sunflower
256	704 Chartreuse		246	986 Dark forest green – leaf veins
324	721 Medium bittersweet		410	995 Dark electric blue – flower petals
295	726 Light topaz		403	310 Black – all remaining backstitches
314	741 Medium tangerine			
303	742 Light tangerine		**FRENCH KNOT**	
1021	761 Light salmon		403	310 Black – sunflower
360	839 Dark beige brown			
333	900 Burnt orange			
204	913 Nile green			
862	934 Pine green			
054	956 Geranium			
246	986 Dark forest green			

Stitch count: 165 high x 165 wide

Finished design sizes:

26-count fabric – 12⅝ x 12⅝ inches

28-count fabric – 11⅞ x 11⅞ inches

36-count fabric – 9⅛ x 9⅛ inches

Floral Tote Bag

As shown on page 176, finished tote measures 12½×17¾×4 inches.

MATERIALS

FABRICS

8×20-inch piece of 25-count water lily Jobelan fabric

Fabric yardages are for 45-inch-wide fabrics:

1 yard of yellow-and-white checked fabric

1 yard of white batiste lining fabric

¼ yard of green print fabric

FLOSS

Cotton embroidery floss in colors listed in key, right

SUPPLIES

Needle; embroidery hoop; 1 yard of fleece

Fabric marking pencil

Yellow rayon twist sewing thread

2 yards of piping cord

INSTRUCTIONS

Tape or zigzag edges of Jobelan fabric. Find the center of chart, *right,* and of fabric; begin stitching there. Use two plies of floss to work cross-stitches. Work backstitches using one ply.

Cut a 19×30½-inch rectangle each from yellow check, batiste, and fleece. Cut a 5×19-inch rectangle each from fleece and batiste. In addition, cut two 3×19-inch strips from yellow check and two 2×19-inch strips from fleece for handles. Measurements include ½-inch seam allowances. Sew seams with right sides facing unless otherwise indicated.

Layer fleece behind yellow check; baste layers together. Using fabric pencil, mark a 1-inch diagonal grid on right side of yellow check fabric. Machine-quilt along lines using rayon twist thread.

Cut stitchery to measure 5×19 inches with design centered. Layer fleece behind design; baste. Set aside.

To make piping, cut 1½-inch-wide bias strips from green print to total 75 inches.

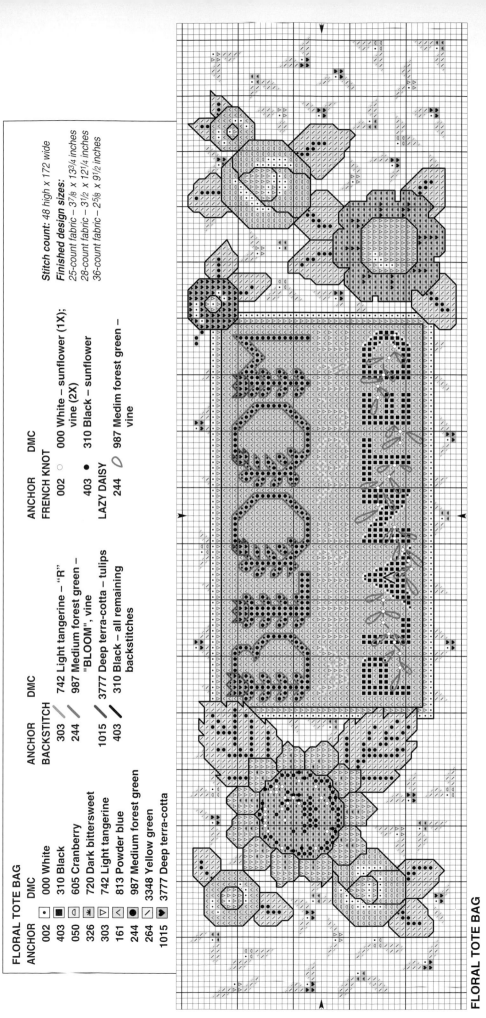

Stitch count: 48 high x 172 wide

Finished design sizes:
25-count fabric – 3⅞ x 13¾ inches
28-count fabric – 3½ x 12¼ inches
36-count fabric – 2⅝ x 9½ inches

FLORAL TOTE BAG		
ANCHOR	DMC	
002	000	White – sunflower (1X); vine (2X)
403	310	Black – sunflower

LAZY DAISY

244	987	Medim forest green – vine

FLORAL TOTE BAG		
ANCHOR	DMC	
		BACKSTITCH
303	742	Light tangerine – "R"
244	987	Medium forest green – "BLOOM", vine
1015	3777	Deep terra-cotta – tulips
403	310	Black – all remaining backstitches

FLORAL TOTE BAG		
ANCHOR	DMC	
002	000	White
403	310	Black
050	605	Cranberry
326	720	Dark bittersweet
303	742	Light tangerine
161	813	Powder blue
244	987	Medium forest green
264	3348	Yellow green
1015	3777	Deep terra-cotta

Sew short ends together to make long strip. Center piping cord lengthwise on wrong side of strip. Fold fabric around cording, bringing raw edges together. Use zipper foot to sew through both layers of fabric close to the cording.

Sew piping to bottom edge of cross-stitch rectangle, matching raw edges. Sew 5×19-inch batiste lining piece to piped edge. Turn lining to back of cross-stitch; baste raw edges together. Baste top and sides of cross-stitch to one end of check rectangle, wrong side of cross-stitch facing right side of check rectangle. (This end becomes top front of bag.)

Press each handle fabric strip in half lengthwise, wrong sides facing. Slip fleece strip inside, next to fold. Turn raw edges in ½ inch toward center; topstitch edges together, enclosing fleece. Tie half knot in center of each handle. Sew each end of one handle to bag top 4½ inches in from corner. Repeat to attach remaining handle to opposite end.

Fold bag rectangle in half; sew side seams. Turn bag to right side and sew piping around top edges. Turn bag back to wrong side. To make boxed bottom on bag, fold each bottom corner so side seam lies along bottom fold. Sew a perpendicular seam crossing side seam 2 inches in from the bottom corner point.

For lining, sew side seams and make boxed corners as for bag. Sew lining to bag around top edge; leave opening for turning. Turn bag right side out; sew the opening closed.

Plant Pokes

As shown on page 176, each plant poke measures 18 inches tall.

MATERIALS *for one plant poke*
FABRICS
3×4-inch piece of 14-count perforated plastic

Two 3×5-inch pieces of felted imitation suede fabric in desired colors

FLOSS
Cotton embroidery floss in colors listed in key, below right

SUPPLIES
Needle; embroidery hoop

½×¼×18-inch strip of balsa wood

Crafts glue; pinking shears

Acrylic paint in two colors as desired

Paintbrush; acrylic spray varnish

Two 1-yard lengths of ⅛- or ¼-inch-wide ribbon in desired colors

INSTRUCTIONS
Find the center of desired chart, *below,* and the center of the plastic; begin stitching there. Use two plies of floss to work cross-stitches. Work the backstitches using one ply of floss.

Trim plastic one square beyond stitching. Center plastic on one piece of imitation suede fabric; glue. Cut fabric ¼ inch beyond plastic using pinking shears. Next, glue to second piece of imitation suede fabric. Cut fabric ¼ inch beyond first fabric using pinking shears.

Paint balsa wood one color; dot with second color using end of brush. When dry, spray with varnish.

Glue fabric-backed cross-stitch design to wood stake near top. Tie ribbons in bow around stake at base of design.

> **Stitch count:** 30 high x 44 wide
> **Finished design sizes:**
> 14-count fabric – 2⅛ x 3⅛ inches
> 10-count fabric – 3 x 4⅜ inches
> 7-count fabric – 4¼ x 6¼ inches

PLANT POKES ALPHABET

PLANT POKES		
ANCHOR	**DMC**	
059	◎	326 Deep rose
683	❖	500 Deep blue green
098	⏀	553 Medium violet
096	◁	554 Light violet
226	⊙	702 Light Christmas green
256	△	704 Chartreuse
926	‖	712 Cream
295	╱	726 Light topaz
303	▽	742 Light tangerine
360	▲	839 Dark beige brown
089	▸	917 Plum
1003	▷	922 Copper
862	◆	934 Pine green
054	▯	956 Geranium
187	⊿	992 Medium aquamarine
410	⊛	995 Dark electric blue
433	◇	996 Medium electric blue
263	✕	3362 Loden
5975	⊞	3830 True terra-cotta
BACKSTITCH		
683	╱	500 Deep blue green – leaf veins
333	╱	900 Burnt orange – sunflower
403	╱	310 Black – all remaining backstitches
FRENCH KNOT		
403	●	310 Black – comma

"Breit" Ideas
for Summer

Time for Tea

To coordinate your entire kitchen using the teapot and cherry theme, use the designs as inspirations to cut your own stencils. Then you can add painted motifs on everything from your recipe box to your walls!

Stitched on afghan fabric, the teapot and cherry designs would brighten up a sun porch or family room.

For a special gift, stitch one of the bright and cheery coaster designs and finish it as a jar topper—what a great addition to your homemade jellies, jams, and sauces!

The floral motifs from the top of the "Welcome" sampler would add a touch of summer to a colorful t-shirt when stitched using waste canvas.

It's Good to be Queen

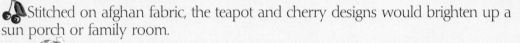

Use the crest and initial design from the checkbook cover to personalize a hand mirror, tote bag, bookmark, or robe pocket.

Stitch the motto, "It's Good to be Queen," for a lighthearted (and much appreciated) gift to a co-worker.

To make special gift tags or enclosure cards, stitch one of the small motifs from the sampler on perforated paper, such as one of the little birds or a single mini flower.

Stitch the paperweight design over one thread of 28-count fabric for an eye-catching pendant or brooch.

Bloom Where You're Planted

To cross-stitch a tablecloth using either the frame or cake mat designs, simply repeat the checkerboard design between the floral corner motifs until the desired size is reached.

The plant pokes add a meaningful touch to a floral bouquet, food basket, cake, or centerpiece for any special occasion.

For a quicker-to-stitch sampler, eliminate the border and stitch only the sweet gardener scene from the center of the design.

For cute-as-a-button hair accessories, stitch some of the floral motifs from the tote bag design on perforated plastic and attach a barrette back.

Four Seasons Memory Frame

A special photograph gets the attention it deserves when displayed in our colorful **Four Seasons Memory Frame.** Capturing year-round pleasures, this creative Mary Engelbreit design can also be seen on the cover of this book. The seasonal motifs are stitched over two threads of 30-count cracked wheat Murano fabric. The textured background was created using a sprinkling of dark tan French knots.

Four Seasons Frame

As shown above, the stitched mat measures 11½×10¼ inches with a 5½×7-inch opening.

MATERIALS
FABRIC
17×18-inch piece of 30-count cracked wheat Murano fabric

FLOSS
Cotton embroidery floss in colors listed in key on page 186
SUPPLIES
Needle; embroidery hoop
Desired mats and frame

INSTRUCTIONS
Tape or zigzag the edges of fabric to prevent fraying. Find the center of chart, *pages 186–187,* and of fabric; begin stitching from there. Use two plies of floss to work cross-stitches

and half cross-stitches over two threads of fabric. Work the blended needle stitches, backstitches, straight stitches, blended straight stitches, satin stitches, lazy daisy stitches, and French knots as indicated in the key. Fill in background with French knots, as desired, using DMC 436.

Press stitchery from back. Have a professional framer create a mat using the stitchery; leave center opening the desired size and shape. Add additional mats, if desired, and frame.

FOUR SEASONS PHOTO FRAME

ANCHOR		DMC	
002	·	000	White
403	■	310	Black
218	▲	319	Dark pistachio
9046	✕	321	Christmas red
038	☐	335	Rose
214	−	368	Light pistachio
374	◎	420	Medium hazel
373	‖	422	Light hazel
098	☆	553	Medium violet
096	○	554	Light violet
832	◮	612	Medium drab brown
886	S	677	Old gold
226	+	702	Light Christmas green
238	◇	703	True chartreuse
361	⊟	738	Light tan
885	L	739	Pale tan
158	∧	747	Sky blue
1005	♥	816	Garnet
027	I	894	Carnation
333	●	900	Burnt orange
1003	✶	922	Light copper
274	:	928	Gray blue
075	⊕	962	Medium rose pink
073	∼	963	Pale rose pink
888	#	3045	Yellow beige
292	⊘	3078	Lemon
059	★	3350	Dusty rose
025	♡	3716	Light rose pink
869	⊓	3743	Antique violet
167	▽	3766	Peacock blue
876	⊠	3816	Celadon green
386	▱	3823	Yellow
306	⊡	3820	Straw

BLENDED NEEDLE

227	◆	701	True Christmas green (1X) and
246		986	Forest green (1X)
256	△	704	Light chartreuse (1X) and
278		3819	Moss green (1X)
305	◐	725	True topaz (1X) and
1002		977	Light golden brown (1X)
944	✳	869	Dark hazel (1X) and
906		829	Bronze (1X)
340	▣	920	Medium copper (1X) and
1001		976	Medium golden brown (1X)
338	⊠	921	True copper (1X) and
1002		977	Light golden brown (1X)
1003	▷	922	Light copper (1X) and
1002		977	Light golden brown (1X)
297	⬚	973	Canary (1X) and
295		726	Light topaz (1X)
1050	▼	3781	Mocha (1X) and
905		3021	Brown gray (1X)

HALF CROSS-STITCH
(stitch in direction of symbol)

| 1045 | / | 436 | Dark tan – background |

ANCHOR		DMC	

BACKSTITCH

002	/	000	White – holly berries, flower on watering can (1X)
218	/	319	Dark pistachio – autumn leaf veins, watering can leaf veins (1X)
1046	/	435	Chestnut – mitten detail (1X)
683	/	500	Blue green – scarf detail (1X)
098	/	553	Medium violet – scarf detail (1X)
889	/	610	Deep drab brown – acorn caps (1X)
238	/	703	True chartreuse – watering can detail (1X)
305	/	725	True topaz – scarf detail (1X)
338	/	921	True copper – autumn leaf veins (1X)
236	/	3799	Charcoal – outline of pine needles (1X)
403	/	310	Black – all remaining stitches (1X)

STRAIGHT STITCH

| 403 | / | 310 | Black – bird's eye (1X) |
| 059 | / | 3350 | Dusty rose – flower center (1X) |

BLENDED STRAIGHT STITCH

295	/	726	Light topaz (3X) and
1002		977	Light golden brown (2X) – scarf fringe
779	/	3809	Dark turquoise (2X) and
851		3808	Deep turquoise (1X) – pine needles

SATIN STITCH

| 9046 | / | 321 | Christmas red – scarf fringe knots (2X) |

LAZY DAISY

| 238 | ⬭ | 703 | True chartreuse – watering can detail (1X) |

FRENCH KNOTS

002	●	000	White – yellow flower by birdhouse (2X)
403	●	310	Black – watering can, bird's eye (1X)
9046	●	321	Christmas red – mitten detail (1X); scarf detail (2X)
238	●	703	True Chartreuse – watering can detail (1X)
246	●	986	Forest green – mitten detail (1X)

Stitch count: 172 high x 154 wide

Finished design sizes:
30-count fabric – 11½ x 10¼ inches
28-count fabric – 12¼ x 11 inches
36-count fabric – 9½ x 8½ inches

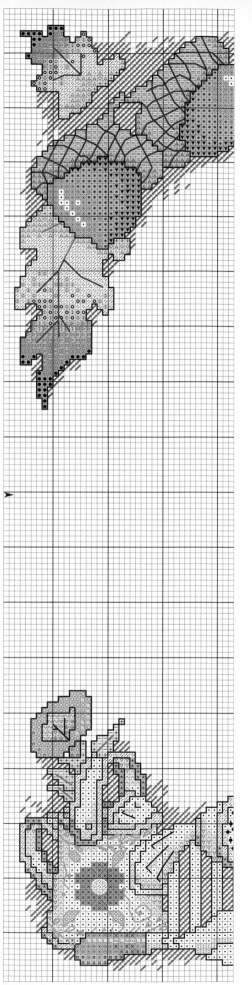

FOUR SEASONS PHOTO FRAME

Cross-Stitch Basics

GETTING STARTED

Cut the floss into 15- to 18-inch lengths and separate all six plies. Recombine the plies as indicated in the project instructions and thread into a blunt-tipped needle. Rely on project instructions to find out where to begin stitching.

BASIC CROSS-STITCH

Make one cross-stitch for each symbol on the chart. For horizontal rows, stitch the first diagonal of each stitch in the row. Work back across the row, completing each stitch. On most linen and even-weave fabrics, stitches are usually worked over two threads as shown in the diagrams, *below*. Each stitch fills one square on Aida cloth.

Cross-stitches also can be worked in the reverse direction; just remember to embroider the stitches uniformly. That is, always work so that the top half of the stitch is worked in the same direction.

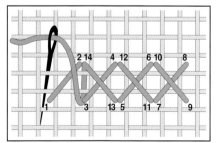

Basic Cross-Stitch in Rows

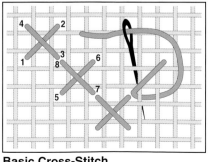

Basic Cross-Stitch Worked Individually

HOW TO SECURE THREAD AT BEGINNING

The most common way to secure the beginning tail of a piece of thread is to hold it under the first four or five stitches.

Or, you can use a waste knot. Thread needle and knot end of thread. Insert needle from right side of fabric, about 4 inches away from placement of first stitch. Bring needle up through fabric and work first series of stitches. When stitching is finished, turn piece to right side and clip the knot. Rethread needle with excess floss and push needle through to the wrong side of stitchery.

When you work with two, four, or six plies of floss, use a loop knot. Cut half as many plies of thread, but make each one twice as long. Recombine plies, fold the strand in half, and thread all the ends into the needle. Work the first diagonal of the first stitch, then slip the needle through the loop formed by folding the thread.

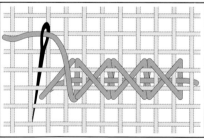

How to Secure Thread at Beginning

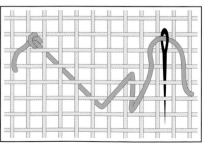

Waste Knot

HOW TO SECURE THREAD AT END

To finish, slip threaded needle under previously stitched threads on wrong side of fabric for four or five stitches, weaving thread back and forth a few times. Clip thread.

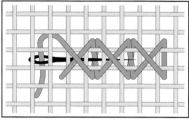

How to Secure Thread at End

HALF STITCHES

A half cross-stitch is simply a single diagonal or half of a cross-stitch. Half cross-stitches usually are listed under a separate heading in the color key and are indicated on the chart by a diagonal colored line in the desired direction.

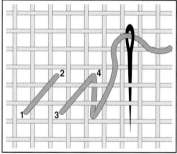

Half Cross-Stitch

QUARTER AND THREE-QUARTER STITCHES

Quarter and three-quarter cross-stitches are used to obtain rounded shapes in a design. On linen and even-weave fabrics, a quarter stitch extends from the corner to the center intersection of threads. To make quarter stitches on Aida cloth, you'll have to estimate the center of the square. Three-quarter stitches combine a quarter stitch with a half

FABRIC/NEEDLE/FLOSS		
FABRIC	TAPESTRY NEEDLE SIZE	NUMBERS OF PLIES
11-COUNT	24	THREE
14-COUNT	24-26	TWO OR THREE
18-COUNT	26	TWO
22-COUNT	26	ONE

cross-stitch. Both of these stitches may slant in any direction.

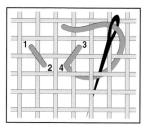

Quarter Cross-Stitch

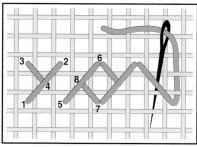

Three-Quarter Cross-Stitch

CROSS-STITCHES
WITH BEADS

When beads are attached using a cross stitch, work half cross-stitches, and then attach the beads on the return stitch.

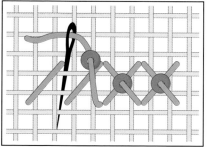

Cross-Stitch with Bead

BACKSTITCHES

Backstitches are added to define and outline the shapes in a design. For most cross-stitch projects, backstitches require only one ply of floss. On the color key, (2X) indicates two plies of floss, (3X) indicates three plies, etc.

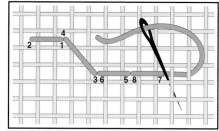

Backstitch

FRENCH KNOTS

Bring threaded needle through fabric and wrap floss around the needle as illustrated. Tighten the twists and insert needle back through the same place in the fabric. The floss will slide through the wrapped thread to make the knot.

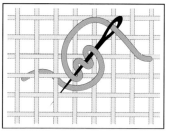

French Knot

WHIPSTITCHES

A whipstitch is an overcast stitch that often is used to finish edges on projects that use perforated plastic. The stitches are pulled tightly for a neatly finished edge. Whipstitches also can be used to join two fabrics together.

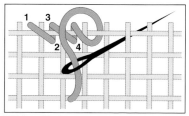

Whipstitch

FEATHERSTITCHES

This decorative stitch produces a featherlike shape as long or as short as desired. Bring threaded needle to front at top of feather. Insert needle back into fabric approximately four threads away, leaving stitch loose. Bring needle to front again, slightly lower than center of first stitch; catch thread from first stitch. Repeat in an alternating motion until desired length is achieved. End feather by stitching a straight-stitched quill.

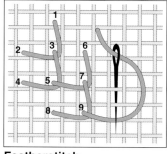

Featherstitch

LAZY DAISY STITCHES

To make this petal-shaped stitch, bring the needle to the front. Using a sewing-style stitch, insert the needle back through the same hole and out again two or more threads away, catching the loop under the needle. Gently pull to shape the loop. Push the needle back through the fabric on the other side of the loop to tack the loop in place.

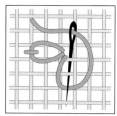

Lazy Daisy Stitch

Cross-Stitch Basics

MATERIALS FOR CROSS-STITCH

Counted cross-stitch has become a popular form of stitchery. Many stitchers like to work cross-stitch designs on different fabrics and use different threads than are specified in the projects. The following information will help you understand the projects in this book so you can adapt them to your own needs.

CROSS-STITCH FABRICS

Counted cross-stitch can be worked on any fabric that will enable you to make consistently sized, even stitches.

Aida cloth is the most popular of all cross-stitch fabrics. Threads are woven in groups separated by tiny spaces. This creates a pattern of squares across the surface of the fabric and enables a beginning stitcher to easily identify where cross-stitches should be placed. Aida cloth is measured by squares per inch; 14-count Aida cloth has 14 squares per inch.

Aida cloth comes in many varieties. 100-percent cotton Aida cloth is available in thread counts 6, 8, 11, 14, 16, and 18. 14-count cotton Aida cloth is available in more than 60 colors. For beginners, white Aida cloth is available with a removable grid of prebasted threads.

Linen is considered to be the standard of excellence for experienced stitchers. The threads used to weave linen vary in thickness, giving linen fabrics a slightly irregular surface. When you purchase linen, remember that the thread count is measured by threads per inch, but most designs are worked over two threads, so 28-count linen will yield 14 stitches per inch. Linens are made in counts from 14 (seven stitches per inch) to 40.

Even-weave fabric also is worked over two threads. The popularity of cross-stitch has created a market for specialty fabrics for counted cross-stitch. They are referred to as even-weave fabrics because they are woven from threads with a consistent diameter, even though some of these fabrics are woven to create a homespun look. Most even-weave fabrics are counted like linen, by threads per inch, and worked over two threads.

Hardanger fabric can be used for very fine counted cross-stitch. The traditional fabric for the Norwegian embroidery of the same name has an over-two, under-two weave that produces 22 small squares per inch.

Needlepoint canvas is frequently used for cross-stitching, especially on clothing and other fabrics that are not suitable alone. Waste canvas is designed to unravel when dampened. It ranges in count from 6½ to 20 stitches per inch. Cross-stitches also can be worked directly on mono-needlepoint canvas. This is available in colors, and when the background is left unstitched, it can create an interesting effect.

Sweaters and other knits often are worked in duplicate stitch from cross-stitch charts. Knit stitches are not square; they are wider than they are tall. A duplicate-stitched design will appear broader and shorter.

Gingham or other simple plaid fabrics can be used, but gingham "squares" are not perfectly square, so a stitched design will seem slightly taller and narrower than the chart.

Burlap fabric can easily be counted and stitched over as you would stitch a traditional counted-thread fabric.

TYPES OF NEEDLES

Blunt-pointed needles are best for working on most cross-stitch fabrics because they slide through holes and between threads without splitting or snagging the fibers. A large-eyed needle accommodates the bulk of embroidery threads. Many companies sell such needles labeled "cross-stitch," but they are identical to tapestry needles, blunt-tipped and large-eyed. The chart on *page 189* will guide you to the right size needle for most common fabrics. One exception to the blunt-tipped needle rule is waste canvas; use sharp embroidery needles to poke through that fabric.

Working with seed beads requires a very fine needle to slide through the holes. A #8 quilting needle, which is short with a tiny eye, and a long beading needle with its longer eye are readily available. Some shops carry short beading needles with a long eye.

THREADS FOR STITCHING

Most types of thread available for embroidery can be used for counted cross-stitch projects.

Six-ply cotton embroidery floss is available in the widest range of colors, including variegated ones. Six-ply floss is made to be separated easily into single or multiple plies for stitching. Instructions with each project in this book tell you how many plies to use. A greater number of plies will result in an embroidered piece that is rich or heavy; fewer plies will create a lightweight or fragile texture.

Rayon or silk floss is similar in weight to cotton floss, but the stitches have a greater sheen. Either thread can be exchanged with cotton floss, one ply for one ply, but because they have a "slicker" texture, they are slightly more difficult to use.

Pearl cotton is available in four sizes: #3, #5, #8, and #12 (#3 is thick; #12 is thin). It has an obvious twist and a high sheen.

Flower thread is a 100-percent cotton, matte-finish thread. A single strand of flower thread can be substituted for two plies of cotton embroidery floss.

Overdyed threads are being introduced on the market every day. Most of them have an irregularly variegated, one-of-a-kind appearance. Cotton floss, silk floss, flower thread, and pearl cotton weight threads are available in this form. All of them produce a soft shaded appearance without changing thread colors.

Specialty threads can add a distinctive look to cross-stitch. They range in weight from hair-fine blending filament, usually used with floss, to ⅛-inch-wide ribbon. They include numerous metallic threads, richly colored and textured threads, and fun-to-stitch, glow-in-the-dark threads.

Wool yarn, usually used for needlepoint or crewel embroidery, can be used for cross-stitch. Use one or two plies of three-ply Persian yarn. Select even-weave fabrics with fewer threads per inch when working cross-stitches in wool yarn.

Ribbon in silk, rayon, and polyester becomes an interesting texture for cross-stitching, especially in combination with flower-shaped stitches. Look for straight-grain and bias-cut ribbons in solid and variegated colors and in widths from 1⁄16 to 1½ inches.

CROSS-STITCH TIPS
PREPARING FABRIC

The edges of cross-stitch fabric take a lot of abrasion while a project is being stitched. There are many ways to keep fabric from fraying while you stitch.

The easiest and most widely available method is to bind the edges with masking tape. Because tape leaves a residue that's almost impossible to remove, it should be trimmed away after stitching is completed. All projects in this book that include tape in the instructions were planned with a large margin around the stitched fabric so the tape can be cut away.

There are some projects where you should avoid using masking tape. If a project does not allow for ample margins to trim away the tape, use one of these techniques: If you have a sewing machine readily available, zigzag stitching, serging, and narrow hemming are all neat and effective methods. Hand-overcasting also works well, but it is more time consuming.

Garments, table linens, towels, and other projects that will be washed on a regular basis when finished should be washed before stitching to avoid shrinkage later. Wash the fabric in the same manner you will wash the finished project.

PREPARING FLOSS

Most cotton embroidery floss is colorfast and won't fade. A few bright colors, notably reds and greens, contain excess dye that could bleed onto fabrics if dampened. To remove the excess dye before stitching, gently slip off paper bands from floss and rinse each color in cool water until it runs clear. Then place floss on white paper towels to dry. If there is any color on the towels when the floss is dry, repeat the process. When dry, slip the paper bands back on the floss.

CENTERING THE DESIGN

Most of the projects in this book instruct you to begin stitching at the center of the chart and fabric. To find the center of the chart, follow the horizontal and vertical arrows on the chart to the point where they intersect.

To find the center of the fabric, fold it in half horizontally; baste along the fold. Then fold the fabric in half vertically; baste along the fold. The point where the basting intersects is the center. Some stitchers like to add some additional lines of basting every 10 or 20 rows as a stitching guide.

CLEANING YOUR WORK

You may want to wash needlecraft pieces before mounting and framing them because the natural oils from your hands eventually will discolor the stitchery. Wash stitchery by hand in cool water using mild detergent. Rinse until the water is clear.

Do not wring or squeeze the needlecraft piece to get the water out. Hold the piece over the sink until dripping slows, then place flat on a clean terry-cloth towel, and roll tightly. Unroll and lay flat to dry.

PRESSING YOUR WORK

Using a warm iron, carefully press the fabric from the back before framing or finishing it. If the piece has lots of surface texture stitches, place it on a terry-cloth towel or other padded surface to press.

FRAMING YOUR DESIGN

For most purposes, omit glass when framing your cross-stitch. Moisture can build up between it and the stitchery, and sunlight is intensified by the glass. Both can cause damage to the fabric. If you must use glass, be sure to mat the piece so the stitchery does not touch the glass.

Index/Sources

INDEX OF PHOTOGRAPHY

Scott Little: Pages 41, 59, 73, 74, 75, 118, 119, 120, 162, 165, 172

Hopkins Associates: Pages 10, 12, 13, 14, 25, 26, 27, 28, 29, 39, 40, 42, 43, 56, 58, 60, 61, 76, 86, 88, 89, 101, 102, 103, 104, 116, 131, 132, 133, 134, 146, 148, 149, 150, 164, 174, 175, 176, 185

Santa: Harold Marine, Ankeny, IA.

SOURCES

Chapter 2 — Pumpkins, page 27: Pumpkin Masters, P.O. Box 61456, Denver, CO 80206; website: www.pumpkinmasters.com.

Chapter 3 — Kitty Towel Trim, page 42: Huck towel— Charles Craft, P.O. Box 1049, Laurinburg, NC 28353, 800/277-0980.

Chapter 9 — Floral Hand Mirror and Bride's Treasure Box, page 133: Wood mirror and box—Sudberry House, Box 895, Old Lyme, CT 06371.

Chapter 10 — Teatime Serving Tray, page 146: Tray— Sudberry House.

Chapter 11 — Queen Paperweight, page 165: Acrylic paperweight—Ramco Arts, Inc., 5209-C Davis Blvd., Ft. Worth, TX 76180, 817/281-3733.

Fabrics — Charles Craft; Wichelt Imports, Inc., R.R. 1, Stoddard, WI 54658; Zweigart, 2 Riverview Dr., Somerset, NJ 08873-1139, 908/271-1949

Threads — Anchor, Consumer Service Dept., P.O. Box 27067, Greenville, SC 29616; DMC, Port Kearney Building 10, South Kearney, NJ 07032-0650; Kreinik Manufacturing, 800/537-2166.

Framing — Dot's Frame Shop, 4223 Fleur Drive, Des Moines, IA 50321.